Advertising and Popular Culture

FOUNDATIONS OF POPULAR CULTURE

Series Editor: GARTH S. JOWETT
University of Houston

The study of popular culture has now become a widely accepted part of the modern academic curriculum. This increasing interest has spawned a great deal of important research in recent years, and the field of "cultural studies" in its many forms is now one of the most dynamic and exciting in modern academia. Each volume in the **Foundations of Popular Culture Series** will introduce a specific issue fundamental to the study of popular culture, and the authors have been given the charge to write with clarity and precision and to examine the subject systematically. The editorial objective is to provide an important series of "building block" volumes that can stand by themselves or be used in combination to provide a thorough and accessible grounding in the field of cultural studies.

1. **The Production of Culture: Media and the Urban Arts**
   by **Diana Crane**

2. **Popular Culture Genres: Theories and Texts**
   by **Arthur Asa Berger**

3. **Rock Formation: Music, Technology, and Mass Communication**
   by **Steve Jones**

4. **Cultural Criticism: A Primer of Key Concepts**
   by **Arthur Asa Berger**

5. **Advertising and Popular Culture**
   by **Jib Fowles**

Advertising and Popular Culture

Jib Fowles

Foundations of Popular Culture

5

SAGE Publications
International Educational and Professional Publisher
Thousand Oaks   London   New Delhi

For information address:

SAGE Publications, Inc.
2455 Teller Road
Thousand Oaks, California 91320
E-mail: order@sagepub.com

SAGE Publications Ltd.
6 Bonhill Street
London EC2A 4PU
United Kingdom

SAGE Publications India Pvt. Ltd.
M-32 Market
Greater Kailash I
New Delhi 110 048 India

Printed in the United States of America

Library of Congress Cataloging-in-Publication Data

Fowles, Jib.
   Advertising and popular culture / Jib Fowles.
      p. cm. — (Foundations of popular culture ; vol. 5)
   Includes bibliographical references and index.
      ISBN 0-8039-5482-4 (cloth: acid-free paper). —ISBN
   0-8039-5483-2 (pbk.: acid-free paper)
      1. Advertising—Social aspects—United States. 2. Popular
   culture—United States. I. Title. II. Series.
   HF5805.F69 1996
   659.1′042′0973—dc20   95-41754

This book is printed on acid-free paper.

96 97 98 99 10 9 8 7 6 5 4 3 2

Sage Production Editor: Astrid Virding

There is no way out of the game of culture.

—Pierre Bourdieu

When you're on TV in a sitcom, there's a loose reality that lends itself to doing commercials, which are also on TV. As long as you're on TV pretending to be something you're not anyway, why not do it for a commercial?

—Jerry Seinfeld

Theories of consumption which assume a puppet consumer, prey to the advertiser's wiles, or consumers jealously competing for no sane motive, or lemming consumers rushing to disaster, are frivolous, even dangerous.

—Mary Douglas

Figure 0.1. Misbehavior in advertising. (Used with permission of Request Jeans®.)

Contents

Series Editor's Introduction   xi

Preface   xiii

Acknowledgments   xvii

1. Energizers   1

   Popular Culture and Advertising Contrasted   9
   Commonalities   17
   Definitions: Symbol, Meaning, Culture, Audience, Viewer   20

2. Origins   26

   An Expanding Need for Goods   28
   The Production/Consumption Economy   30
   The Rise of Modern Advertising   34
   Popular Culture Joins Advertising   42
   Communicating to the Consumer   48

3. Flagrant Criticisms   52

   The Critique of Popular Culture   53
   The Critique of Advertising   60
   Analyzing the Critiques   66

4. The Dynamics Behind the Advertisement 77

The Client Versus the Agency   78
Research Versus the Creative   79
The Product Versus the Appeal   80
Words Versus Images   83
The Contested Frame   87
Intertextual Strains   90
The Advertisement Versus the Consumer   93
The One Versus the Many   94
Proselytizing   96

5. The Dynamics of Popular Culture 103

Why Is Popular Culture Popular?   104
Situation Comedies   112
Stars   116
Popular Music   119

6. Exchanges 123

Stars as Endorsers   126
Music in Advertising   131
"Is It on Straight?": Humor in Advertising   136
Cycles of Attractiveness   139
Advertising Overtakes Popular Culture?   143

7. The Surface of the Advertisement,
   Composed and Consumed 148

The Dominant Theme in Advertising Imagery   149
Social Values and Advertising   157
How Consumers Exploit Advertising   161

8. Deciphering Advertisements 167

Deciphering Guidelines   171
Jordache Deciphered   174
Diet Sprite Deciphered   179
Go Forth   183

9. Mixed Receptions   184

    Receiving *Roseanne*   185
    Meanings From the Mix   193

10. The Project of the Self   197

    Gender in the Media   199
    Using Gender Portrayals   215
    The Symbol Domains and Self-Identity   225

11. In Perspective   228

    Untouched by Advertising and Popular Culture   232
    The Future of Advertising Imagery   235
    The Future of Popular Culture   241
    The True Meaning of Christmas   244

Bibliography   252

Author Index   266

Subject Index   270

About the Author   278

List of Product Ads

0.1 Request Jeans®   vi
1.1 Energizer Bunny®   2
1.2 Bud Light   12
1.3 Swatch®   15
2.1 Kodak   36
2.2 Nujol   45
3.1 Coca-Cola   69
3.2 Seagram's Gin   74
4.1 Perry Ellis   82
4.2 Savvy   85
4.3 Canadian Mist   88
4.4 Anne Klein   89
4.5 Heineken   92
4.6 Fila   95
4.7 Tabasco®   99
4.8 Jensen   100
6.1 Vuarnet   128
6.2 Kenwood   130
6.3 Yahama   134
6.4 Noxzema   141
7.1 Logitech   150
7.2 Kotex   154
7.3 Code Bleu Jeans   155

7.4 Bestform   158
8.1 Jordache   175
8.2 Diet Sprite   180
10.1 Palmetto's   200
10.2 Evian   202
10.3 Evian   203
10.4 Sears   204
10.5 Fisher-Price   206
10.6 Caboodles   207
10.7 Jerzees   209
10.8 Lilyette   210
10.9 One-a-Day   212
10.10 Florsheim   213
10.11 Newport Harbor®   214
10.12 Toyota   216
10.13 Brut   218
10.14 Jansport®   219
11.1 Jack Daniel's   230
11.2 AT&T   231
11.3 Waterford   237
11.4 Absolut   245
11.5 Salvation Army   248
11.6 Mazda   249

Series Editor's Introduction

Advertising is one of the most ubiquitous manifestations of modern popular culture, and yet it has seldom been examined as a form of popular culture in its own right. In the past, advertising has been evaluated as an aid to the marketing and selling of goods; as a form of economic, social, and cultural utility; and as a source of many of the most serious ills that beset our modern consumerist society. Yet the important interrelationship between advertising and everyday cultural practices has, in fact, received very little attention despite the fact that they are totally interwoven.

In this pathbreaking study, Jib Fowles has torn down the barriers that had tended to isolate advertising from other cultural practices. Through his masterful survey of the critical literature and penetrating insights, he lays open the nature of the symbolic relationship between advertising and popular culture. Fowles is uniquely equipped to undertake this study, having worked in the advertising industry as well as having previously written an important book on the "star" phenomenon in modern society. This background provides him with a solid platform on which to build his analysis of the role of advertising in modern popular culture.

In this book, Fowles examines the various critiques of advertising that have emerged over the years, but he is particularly interested in the latest "critical" methods used to analyze the "meanings" of advertisements. His survey of these often complex methodologies provides the reader with a clear understanding of the strengths and weaknesses of these various approaches. Fowles also provides his own schema for the analysis of the content of advertising, and this clear but comprehensive set of evaluative categories should prove extremely useful to the reader.

As Fowles has pointed out, "If the future may know us through our advertising and popular culture, it is curious that we ourselves have little articulated knowledge of the workings of these allied symbol domains." With the publication of this important study, Fowles has gone a very long way to solving the problem he so eloquently stated.

—GARTH S. JOWETT
Series Editor

Preface

Advertising and popular culture are the two grand domains of public art in these times. Ostensibly their aims diverge: Advertising messages always have ulterior motives, whereas popular culture (such as prime-time television shows) is usually designed for little more than immediate and pleasurable gratification. Yet they share much in common: Both are the careful products of sizable "culture industries"; both traffic heavily in images; they borrow themes, sounds, and personalities from one another; and they frequently appear in the presence of each other. Together they dominate today's environment of symbols, overriding more traditional forms of expression. Like the twin strands of DNA which determine biological constitution, so the twin strands of advertising and popular culture knit together contemporary expressive culture. Pretensions aside, no one is exempt from their force; their sights and sounds flow broadly through everyone's mind. The time that Americans surrender to them dwarfs time spent on any other activity save work and sleep. Instances of advertising and popular culture that survive will provide those in the future with more penetrating insights into the current national psyche than will all the worn-down skyscrapers, all the irradicable highway cuts, all the fossilized industrial debris.

If the future may know us through our advertising and popular culture, it is curious that we ourselves have little articulated knowledge of the workings of these allied symbol domains. There are several formidable reasons for this failing. The first is that those who are trained to investigate social phenomena of this magnitude—largely, those in the academic community—often regard these two symbol domains with condescension if not disdain. When the sharpest minds turn to these topics, they can bring to bear an excoriating attitude that demands its own display and that ultimately subverts comprehension of the nominal subjects. Much of this aversion is a comment on the social loci of those who voice it rather than on anything intrinsic to advertising and popular culture.

Second, even if those who devalue advertising and popular culture were to suffer changes of heart and attempt with good will to sort through these domains, the briefest of attempts would reveal that the content that initially looks so slight is in truth highly intricate and extremely resistant to analysis. Moreover, for the content to be dissected successfully, it cannot be considered independently but must be understood within a multitude of contexts; the complexities double and redouble. Finally, none of this stands still for the investigator; rather, it whirls on in time, seemingly capriciously and certainly elusively.

Advertising and Popular Culture attempts to make some headway toward the goal of understanding these complex domains and their roles in contemporary existence. The effort is undertaken with intentions of a dispassionate exploration. To sketch the nature of each of these towering symbol domains is the first order of business. Quickly the question arises about the kinds of interrelationships in which the two are engaged. What are the larger forces at work when rock and roll hits are drawn from the realm of popular culture and used in automobile commercials, when a brewery decrees that its costly commercial seconds comprise the "Coors Light Channel," when Cher, a queen from the realm of popular culture, commandeers an infomercial half hour, touting her own product line?

Historically, both symbol domains have achieved their present stature relatively recently, within the past century or so. What social forces have called them into prominence, and what social functions do they perform? Of foremost concern throughout this book is the spectatorship of the two domains. What do members of the audience bring with their voluntary participation, and what do they take away?

One cannot venture out on a mission like this without a stock of intellectual supplies. In selecting that equipment I have taken instruction from James Carey. After deploring the limitations within American communication studies of the long-dominant "effects" tradition (which took as its task the determination of audience "effects" supposedly inflicted by the media), Carey (1989) recommended turning instead to more discerning European scholarship (p. 20). Accordingly, this book is informed by two schools of thought: French semiotics and British cultural studies.[1] Semiotics (proposed by linguist Ferdinand de Saussure[2] and realized in the work of anthropologist Claude Lévi-Strauss and cultural critic Roland Barthes) provides an intellectual aperture on human existence through its focus on the communication of meanings. That which may be perceived as meaningful is formed from a wide variety of signs—linguistic, pictorial, and otherwise. Semiotics in its purest form is concerned with the symbols that enter into the encoding or construction of communicated content. Cultural studies (as developed by Raymond Williams, Stuart Hall, and John Fiske, among many others) is less concerned with the encoding process and more concerned with the decoding done by individuals at the receiving end. In particular, cultural studies explores how meanings, such as those drawn from popular culture offerings, are interpreted and used in everyday life.

Beyond an objective examination of the two leading contemporary symbol domains, this book intends to endorse consumers (who are, after all, exactly like you and me, no better and no worse, only replicated numerously beyond our spheres of empathy) and to validate the individual consumer's personal interpretations both of advertising messages and of advertising's companion and matrix, popular culture. These interpretive activities, done by one and all, are not to be slighted, and are to be understood as important and purposive. The idea that spectators discriminatingly use popular culture for personal purposes and satisfactions has recently gained standing within the fields of British cultural studies and its American cousin, popular culture studies. The parallel concept, that additionally consumers make discerning use of advertising imagery, is generally disregarded. It is to the ascendancy of this new version of the purposefulness of the consumer that this book aims at making a contribution. Instead of the frequently heard claim that advertising exploits consumers, it is the contention here that just the reverse is the case, that consumers exploit advertising.

Emphasis cannot be placed on advertising and popular culture equally. As the book's title implies, advertising has primacy and receives fuller consideration. Popular culture, the larger and more varied of the two symbol domains, must be given comparatively more cursory treatment.

Notes

1. Although the present work is informed by these two schools of thought, it is not a doctrinaire reflection of them. In particular, the political, or Marxist, orientation of these European schools is largely muted here (perhaps in keeping with the American experience). The intent of this book is primarily to advance understanding of advertising and popular culture, not to further the political ideologies often implicit in semiotics and cultural studies.

2. Unknown to Saussure, his call for "a science that studies the life of signs," or "semiology," had been anticipated by American philosopher Charles Sanders Peirce (1839-1914), who described at some length a "formal doctrine of signs," which he labeled "semiotic." As profound as Peirce's analysis was, his scholarly impact was less so, as he published few papers in his lifetime. In weighing the merits of either Saussure or Peirce as the founder of the field, Wendy Leeds-Hurwitz (1993) states that "I would recommend Saussure as the less obscure and more readily applicable to actual behavior. Saussure's scant comments have been expanded by his many followers, so there is no dearth of material available for inspiration" (p. 6). Nevertheless, it is curious that a variant of Peirce's name for the field has overtaken Saussure's.

Acknowledgments

Advertising and Popular Culture is my sixth book and may be the right occasion to pause and express appreciation to those who, in the course of my life, have been especially inspiring and generous.

My father, Lloyd Wright Fowles, was the head of a secondary school history department and a writer of local histories. His fascination with the sweep of history led in turn to my own. In one of the multitude of memories I retain of him, I am a small boy, trudging in fresh furrows behind him; he is following a tractor and plow, looking for uncovered arrowheads. When he finds one, repose and reflection cross his face. I reach for the piece of worked stone, and he puts it in my hand.

At Wesleyan University, Pulitzer prize-winning historian and novelist Paul Horgan was my teacher and mentor. Paul taught me to love words and tried to teach me to write with care. Through him, through his humanitarian vision, I learned to look for the deeper drama in human affairs.

Cultural critic Neil Postman was my dissertation adviser at New York University, my guide at the start of my academic career, and remains a friend to this day. His good spirits, commitment to ideas, and care in crafting language were instructive to a young professor. Although few of his ideas were to become incorporated in my own, it was through disagreement with him that I was able to formulate my positions. Definition is often oppositional, as will be seen in the pages ahead.

In the University of Houston system, popular culture scholar Garth Jowett has been a friend for many years. His breadth of knowledge I always find engaging and informative. This book results from his suggestion.

What these men share in common, it strikes me, is an indefatigable curiosity and a commitment to the written word. However much I am in their debt, I need to emphasize that all of them would, to one degree or another, take issue with the notions advanced in *Advertising and Popular Culture*. Of course I must accept total responsibility for the point of view expressed here regarding advertising, popular culture, consumption, and the individual's participation in these symbol systems.

The University of Houston-Clear Lake was extremely supportive during the preparation of this manuscript. In 1993 the university funded my attendance at a seminar on cultural studies at MIT. For the following school year I was allowed to teach half-time while drafting the manuscript, and during the summer of 1994 I received additional salary support. My division, the School of Human Sciences and Humanities, supported my attendance at the annual meetings of the Popular Culture Association in 1994 and 1995, where I delivered papers based on the content here.

I am thankful for my researchers, each of whom demonstrated perseverance and ingenuity well beyond the call of duty—Jan Phillips, John Ryan, James Webb, Melissa Neely, Wendy LeGrand, and Edwina Lewis. Chapter 8 could not have been written without the transcript of a *Roseanne* episode and its commercials which was meticulously produced by Marilea Ferguson.

Finally, nothing would have been possible without the love and support of my immediate family—my wife Joy, my daughter Celeste, and my son Nathaniel. I labored on this book, and they stood by me.

1

Energizers

At the White House one day in 1992, then President George Bush impulsively took charge of a visiting group of schoolchildren and led them on his own lengthy and voluble tour of the interior. When the children finally exited, reporters immediately gathered around them and quizzed the youngsters about their special tour and its singular guide. "He kept going and going and going," responded 11-year-old Lonnie Thomas, and then finding himself in the middle of an advertising slogan, he finished brightly with a pithy metaphor that conveyed exactly what his experience with a hyperactive president had been—"just like an Energizer bunny" (Rosenthal, 1992, p. 14).

The Energizer bunny—are there any people left who do not carry in their minds a picture of the pink rabbit, marching everlastingly to the beat of its own bass drum? Through a mammoth and successful advertising campaign that began in 1989, the Eveready Battery Company and its advertising agencies (originally DDB Needham; subsequently Chiat/Day) have apparently managed to insert an indelible image of the creature into the consciousness of nearly every sentient American.[1] To this effort Eveready allocates roughly $30 million annually for television commercial time, supplemented by print ads and other promotions. Sensing a general awareness of the symbol, young Lonnie could be assured that

1

Figure 1.1. The Energizer bunny®. (Courtesy of the Eveready Battery Company, Inc.)

his characterization would be readily communicated not only to those correspondents immediately visible to him but, through them, to millions of distant newspaper readers reached through the press services.

Some concerned with the roles of advertising and popular culture in modern-day life might be troubled with the implications of Lonnie Thomas's particular choice to describe his president. With no loftier intentions than to sell batteries in volume, Eveready Battery Company has seemingly managed to alter the vocabulary of symbols—and not in a minor way. The advertiser has created and displayed and advanced a symbol that has perhaps shoved aside other symbols and metaphors, ones that in all likelihood did not have such commercial origins. This might seem to confirm an impoverishment of culture, a flattening of symbolic range. Symbols are nothing less than the means by which people find meaning in the world; the use of symbols is what distinguishes humans from the rest of the animal kingdom. To reduce symbols to business-serving items could conceivably be a perilous maneuver. In his critical *Captains of Consciousness*, Stuart Ewen (1976) may have been speaking for many thoughtful people when he decried "the eradication of indigenous cultural expression and the elevation of the consumer marketplace to the realm of an encompassing 'truth'" (p. 67). Similarly, Herbert Schiller (1989) lamented, "The corporate 'voice' now constitutes the national symbolic environment" (p. 44).

But let's reflect on the Energizer bunny and its emergence as a viable symbol in both commerce and society at large. The creative team at DDB Needham did not fabricate this image totally out of the blue, producing a completely unique one devoid of anterior allusions.[2] Julie Liesse, an *Advertising Age* reporter who has covered the Energizer campaign from its inception, said in an interview that the bunny was suggested by the mechanical toys featured in advertising for Duracell, the rival consumer battery (Ryan, 1994). Toys powered by Duracell batteries had been depicted as outlasting "ordinary" batteries, racing on while the weaker toys faltered; Energizer executives wanted it known that their battery was not an "ordinary" one and could keep up with Duracell. In selecting a toy rabbit to promote their client's claims, however, the DDB Needham creative team was doing more than lampooning a competitor's campaign. Of all the conceivable toys that might have served their purposes, they chose one that came with an extensive—and for this duty, largely useful—set of associations. Agency personnel were unlikely to have pondered their choice analytically, but they might have recognized intuitively that the rabbit, a culturally familiar figure, could symbolize several qualities pertinent to their marketing agenda.

What a rabbit "means" has long since been divorced from the real, breathing animal that hops through the underbrush. Only a hunter or a naturalist—and not all of those—is going to reflect on the species *Leporidae* when the subject of rabbits comes up. For modern humans in particular, living metropolitan lives, encounters with real rabbits are rare, but even when people had greater proximity to nature, the rabbit-as-symbol still weighed heavily in their conception of things. The symbolizing rabbit has always dwelled in a thicket of intertextual references.

In many traditional cultures—among them, several Native American and West African peoples—the rabbit appears as a trickster, a frolicsome role echoed in the new advertising symbol. For millennia the rabbit served as a pagan emblem of fertility, before picking up greater overlays of meaning as it was knit into the iconography of Christianity. The symbol itself is reborn majestically each springtime for the celebration of Easter, when millions of bunny figures go on display. This rich mythological strain offered lavish pickings for the symbol-makers desiring to invoke new meanings. Here was a powerful and ready-made symbol for potency, renewal, endurance—just the sort of meanings the advertiser wished to touch on.

In the contemporary world, when a greater proportion of children than ever before in history has access to an amplitude of toys, stuffed rabbits are a common plaything; there are likely to be several in every child's menagerie. Young people grow up snuggling their toy bunnies, which are tirelessly appreciated since they suffer none of the failings of live animals. Children read, or are read, stories and books that amplify the adorability of the rabbit. Most especially, Peter Rabbit in his blue jacket carries on in the million minds of the read-to and the readers. Peter brings to the rabbit symbol a disregard for rules and a survivor's instinct which would apply to the new image. If Brer Rabbit is read in a particular family, then the association of the rabbit with wiliness and endurance will be strengthened. All the fondness for all these childhood rabbits, all the meanings already imparted by people to the figure of the bunny, were drawn on by the creators of the Energizer bunny.

But it is through widely mediated popular culture that citizens of the 20th century are most likely to form their understandings of the rabbit-as-symbol. Movies, television, comic books, and magazines surround modern humans, driving favorites among constructed bunnies their way. Some popular culture creations as the Playboy bunny and Roger Rabbit were too randy to be exploited directly for the new symbol, but even they made distant contributions to the vitality of the Energizer mascot. Perhaps the most widely appreciated of mediated rabbits is Bugs Bunny, now woven into the lives of four generations of Americans. Bugs contributes much to the rabbit-as-symbol: In his dealings with Elmer Fudd he exhibits not only persistence, vis-à-vis the carrot patch, but more fundamentally, the capability of interacting purposefully with humans (or more exactly in the case of Fudd, a humanoid). A most important attribute of Bugs Bunny, to be borrowed by the creators of the Energizer bunny, is that of *play*. Bugs is both a playful and a mischievous fellow (defined in opposition to Elmer), but he also exists in a universe of play as a cartoon figure. The enterprise of cartooning has established a broad territory for play, and in this Bugs and his pals reside. Thus a well-established aura of playfulness was available to be transferred onto the Energizer bunny.

Drawing on symbols already extant in popular culture, the creators of the Energizer rabbit were then able to construct their own particular image. In an act which French anthropologist Claude Lévi-Strauss (1966) called *bricolage* (from the French word for the workman who assembles things from odds and ends; see p. 33), the creative team working on this account unreflectingly but deliberately built up the singular Energizer bunny. Their starting point was the rabbit as a friendly emblem of spontaneity, of rejuvenation, of perseverance. The rabbit, in essence, represents the quality of being thoroughly alive. This general symbol they had to refashion into one clearly their own, signifying one specific product. First, they colored their rabbit a shocking pink—a flamboyant color that made their creature all the more sportive and endearing. Then, in the way that elements of a symbol may clash and the symbol take on added charge, they equipped the rabbit with a pounding drum. The figure became both cute and abrasive, like some children's toys. The drum itself resonates along the corridors of symbolism—the military drum, the parade drum, the advertising "drummer," all functioning to attract attention. The intrusiveness of the drum was no doubt intended by the symbol makers to cut through the drone of television programming. Letting its drum do its talking for it, the rabbit was not to possess human speech and so remained firmly within the domain of toys. Also, by being mute the Energizer bunny minimized the chances that the new symbol might take on too large a personality in its own right and overwhelm the product.

Descriptive details of the bunny have changed slightly over the years, the greatest change being the complement of pool thongs and dark glasses. These further particularized the bunny, making him "cool" in addition to his other qualities. "Coolness" is an attractive feature to the younger portion of the target market (like Lonnie Thomas) and situates the bunny within the world of leisure and play, where in fact most of the purchased batteries are employed. This is the world of least drudgery and most liberation, the sphere of pleasant activities and associations with which Eveready wants to be identified.

The fact that the bunny is a mechanical one is an attribute inherited from the Duracell competition, but its retention constitutes another distinguishing feature (especially since Duracell has since abandoned the theme of mechanical toys). Because the bunny is mechanical and requires an energy source, there is some purpose for the product that is being sold; the creative team needed to link the product as closely as possible with the new figure. As is the goal for all advertising, they wanted the symbol's meanings to transfer onto the product. The mechanicalness of the rabbit gives the batteries something to do, but it comes loaded with allusions of its own. It suggests repeatability and endurance as well as other inferences that double back on the denotations of play and a toy to connote work and the machines axiomatic to the workplace. Underneath all the playfulness, there is serious business going on. Finally, should there be the slightest chance that viewers might confuse this rabbit with any other rabbit or not get the new meaning the advertiser was striving to create, the drum was emblazoned with the word "Energizer."[3] The spelled-out word completed the new symbol.

But it was not enough just to fabricate this image. In the presentation of the bunny and the advertising message, the creators used yet another ingredient from popular culture, one that gave form to the content: parody. Popular culture is frequently insolent, and parody is among its chief devices. It is one way the less powerful get to wreak symbolic vengeance against the resented more powerful. Television viewers may have certain levels of resentment toward haranguing advertisers, and the creative team used this predisposition for its own ends. The Energizer campaign began by pointedly parodying Duracell commercials, but having found this stratagem successful, the agency extended the mode broadly and took on various conventional advertising styles. A representative, early Energizer commercial begins with what looks like a standard commercial for a product other than batteries—until the drum is heard and the pink rabbit marches through the "commercial," devastating it. Viewers' vague antagonism toward commercials in general is discharged by the bunny's destruction, and laughter can result. Attention toward the screen rises. Disarmed by the bunny's antics, the viewers' skepticism may recede, and they are then ripe for the truly intended advertising message. In content and manner, these commercials are clever and strategic pieces of advertising art, as full of delicious counterpoints and contradictions as popular culture itself.

Widespread acceptance of the bunny led to an infrequent occurrence in advertising, a breakthrough of the advertising symbol back into popular culture. This unexpected reemergence caught even the advertiser off guard; the vice president of marketing at the Eveready Battery Company was quoted as saying, "We didn't know the Bunny would reach the level of pop culture icon—and we know it's not wearing out by our research" ("Charged-up Foes," 1993, p. 3). His surprise is worth remarking on, for it indicates how rare such success is within the annals of advertising. This time, people set aside their resistance to a symbol's mercantile function and appropriated it for their own thoughts, using it for their own purposes.

The symbol has now added to its possible meanings: Besides signifying a particular product, it stands metaphorically for a kind of behavior, a perseverance that on occasion can be slightly loony. Entering the domain of popular culture, the Energizer bunny is now available for sale as a toy animal. When the pink rabbit begins to appear at professional baseball games between innings, as it has, then it is making inroads into another brand of popular culture (Liesse, 1992). As the campaign developed, the foothold of the bunny within accepted popular culture was emphasized when the mascot appeared in a James Bond-ish commercial and subsequently was paired with, in turn, Darth Vader, King Kong, and Wile E. Coyote.

Anything that exists in culture, that is, in the world of shared symbols and meanings, is a candidate for parody; the established can be burlesqued by the yet-to-be-established, the "ins" by the "outs." Proof that something indisputably is "in" occurs when it is spoofed. Thus, it is hardly surprising that once the Energizer bunny was widely acknowledged, it too became a candidate for parody. The parodist was to be parodied. When Coors Beer developed commercials lampooning the Energizer bunny (Teinowitz & Liesse, 1991), was Eveready Battery Company, rebels against the conventional decorum of advertising, going to stand aside, bemused, at the tactic of this upstart? Absolutely not—they took Coors to court. Eveready, the expert at parody, recognized how subversive the Coors plan was. In the chain of parody, power resides with the latest arrivals, if they are artful to any degree. They seem to have the firmest standing place, they have seized the offensive, they may well be able to invoke the feelings of being an outsider which lurk in everyone, however slightly, and the objects of their derision can seem to be tottering, a pose that Eveready did not want thrust upon itself. The company had too much invested in the symbol and the campaign to have it exhausted prematurely.

A glance at the Energizer bunny has offered preliminary indications not only about the complex and mutually energizing relationship between advertising and popular culture but also about the relationships among the two symbol domains and their creators, on the one hand, and receivers, on the other. Material—in this case, both content (the rabbit image) and form (parody)—flows in two directions between advertising and popular culture, occasionally picking up nuances in transit.

Typically, advertising draws on popular culture's repository of symbolic material (images or text or music) in an attempt to fabricate new symbols with enlivened meanings. The older symbolic material had already been accepted by people as an ingredient in their culture. All advertisers can do is recondition the public's symbols and pray that consumers will supply agreeable meanings to the new creation. Very few of these contrived symbols actually get appropriated by the public; most are deflected as meaningless and die unlamented deaths along the roadway of commerce—Bud Man (Budweiser Beer), the Noid (Domino's Pizza), the Swedish Bikini Team (Old Milwaukee Beer). That the Energizer bunny should find popular endorsement marks it as the exception, not the rule. Contrary to apprehensions, advertising does not—and cannot—dexterously mold the symbolic landscape. Its power is limited to tinkering with extant symbolic elements, cobbling together new ones, and hoping against hope that they will take. It is a further comment on advertising's limitations that, although the bunny's prominence allowed Energizer to claim a larger share of the battery market, Duracell retained the lead in sales.

Popular Culture and Advertising Contrasted

To proceed successfully, terms defined only inferentially must now be delineated with greater care. What is meant by *popular culture* and by *advertising*?

In an otherwise admirable essay, Chandra Mukerji and Michael Schudson (1991) state that "popular culture refers to the beliefs and practices, and the objects through which they are organized, that are widely shared among a population" (p. 3). In trying to make their definition inclusive, they have extended its range far past the point where utility ends. A multitude of things that meet their criteria—for example, airlines, the Roman Catholic Church, or the roofing industry—cannot be productively considered popular culture. A tighter definition comes from John Storey (1993): "Ultimately, I have argued that popular culture is what we make out of the products and practices of mass-produced culture" (p. 201). Storey has packed into this sentence references to the creators (those who "mass produce" culture), their output (the "products and practices"), and the users (the "we" who make something of the product) and, in doing so, has pointed out the direction toward a useful definition.

Popular culture is expressive content that is produced and consumed: It is light entertainment (or so it looks at first blush) that is assembled by what Marxist critics Max Horkheimer and Theodor Adorno (1944/1972) derisively but accurately labeled "the culture industries," then is delivered through the channels of the mass media, and finally is absorbed voluntarily, to be interpreted by the individual who receives it. Back to the culture industries goes a flow of information in the form of ratings or sales figures that will influence the subsequent round of offerings.

Popular culture consists of symbols; the actual act of skiing is not an example of popular culture as defined here, but a dramatic movie featuring skiing is one because it is composed of images intended to be meaningful to spectators. Popular culture often (but not always) is deployed as a narrative, often (but not always) is relayed through a performance, and often (but not always) has a visual component. Instances of popular culture are television series, Hollywood films, comic books, romantic novels, and Top 40 songs. Popular culture typically elicits pleasurable sensations upon reception; this pleasure-giving feature is a central aspect of the popular culture experience, an aspect to be underscored.

In sum, for present purposes *popular culture* is entertainment that is produced by the culture industries, composed of symbolic content, mediated widely, and consumed with pleasure. A final attribute of popular culture is that it is frequently the object of censorious disdain. As John Fiske (1989b) put it, "The combination of widespread consumption with widespread critical disapproval is a fairly certain sign that a culture commodity is popular" (p. 106). When MTV cartoon characters Beavis and Butt-head were widely reproved for supposedly misguiding young people and were then driven to a late hour in the broadcast day, their popularity was certified.

Some scholars see advertising as a subset of popular culture (Danna, 1992; McQuade & Williamson, 1989), but the argument here is that advertising, while sharing many attributes with popular culture, is a categorically different sort of symbolic content. Advertising messages, coming in the form of print advertisements or electronic commercials, are conspicuously more tendentious than instances of popular culture; their intent is to get consumers to do something that consumers might well not do without them. Their purposefulness is greeted with some degree of skepticism, so the negotiation between message and receiver is very different than it is for popular culture choices.

There are two varieties of advertisements: *simple*, where all the content pertains directly to the commodity being sold (as a classified ad), and *compound*, where, besides the commodity information, there exists noncommodity material (the symbolic elements that constitute the appeal). Compound advertising is typical of national consumer goods advertisements and is the only sort considered in this book. The task of the advertisement is to get consumers to transfer the positive associations of the noncommodity material onto the commodity, so that freedom and ruggedness equal Marlboro cigarettes, and friendship equals Bud Light (see Figure 1.2). If this transfer occurs, the logic behind it is nothing more than the juxtaposition of the two orders of content within the frame of the advertisement or commercial.[4] As Judith Williamson (1978) explained about images, "Things 'mean' to us, and we give

Figure 1.2. Compound advertising usually has as its underlying intention the transfer of the appeal associations onto the product. This advertiser could well be hoping that the depiction of friendship will kindle in the reader an affiliative sensation that would at some level come to be linked with the beverage. At a time in the nation's history when close personal ties are increasingly scarce, this appeal can be a poignant one. (Thanks to Bud Light.)

this meaning to the product, on the basis of an irrational mental leap invited by the form of the advertisement" (p. 43).

Briefly defined, *advertising* refers to paid-for messages that attempt to transfer symbols onto commodities to increase the likelihood that the commodities will be found appealing and be purchased; because of this motive, advertising may be consumed warily. Although advertising comes in nonmediated forms (e.g., billboards and direct mail), interest here is focused on advertising carried by the mass media—in particular, television, radio, and magazines.

Noting the differences between advertising and popular culture can aid in uncovering their separate characteristics. As indicated, the two symbolic domains differ most importantly, and in a way that permeates every pixel of their content, on the matter of intentionality. The creators of popular culture fabricate their offerings with no other goal than that it be found diverting and attractive by the public. There is no thought of a postponed consequence (aside from the hope that others in times to come may want to attend to the offering just as those in the present do so that the production may retain economic value). Popular culture, then, deals only in a set of first-order intentions. Advertising, however, is developed with both first-order and second-order intentions in mind. The first order is, as with popular culture, that communication occurs. This communication is unlikely to be as easy and ample as it can be with instances of popular culture because of the audience's awareness of and ambivalence about the second-order intentions integral to the message. The second-order intentions are of course, those of marketplace consumption, of purchasing the advertiser's wares. Advertising aims at changing behavior, whereas the function of popular culture (detailed in Chapter 5) is not one of change but one of maintenance. Advertising's task is by far the stiffer one.

Another distinction, which may at first appear inconsequential but which has important ramifications, is that instances of advertising are almost always briefer than instances of popular culture. A magazine advertisement is rarely more than a page or two in length, whereas a story can run on and on; a 30-second television commercial is a mere mite compared to a series episode lasting nearly 30 minutes. There are several reasons for this curtailment: Not only is consumers' tolerance of advertising limited to some extent, but media time and space are expensive, and advertisers have to work within budget constraints. The brevity of advertising necessarily results in severe impositions on the content. To oblige the first- and second-order intentions as fully as possible, an advertisement must be much more focused than an instance of popular culture. Popular culture has more latitude to ramble, to touch on auxiliary themes that may be of interest to the audience, to follow plots where they lead. Popular culture is thematically broader than advertising.

Although advertising's content is more constrained than that of popular culture, the style of presentation is likely to be more perfectly wrought, with a more highly polished aesthetic surface. There must be no imperfections or unintended rough edges on a television commercial or magazine advertisement, or they will detract from the communication the advertiser is paying dearly to achieve. When in 1993 the misspelling in Artic ice beer was called to the attention of the Adolph Coors Company, chagrined officials could only claim weakly that it had been a deliberate choice; the new product's marketing campaign was hobbled by the error. The execution of a commercial or advertisement is much more costly, calculated as dollars per unit of time or space, than the production of the surrounding content, and these allocations show up as a more highly perfected presentation. Advertising's valorization of style caused Stuart Ewen (1988) to reflect that "the power of provocative surfaces speaks to the eye's mind, overshadowing matters of quality or substance" (p. 22). The creation of communication style is one of advertising's greater successes and a leading export into the domain of popular culture.

One way to show the contrasting employment of content and style is to examine the use of women in the two domains. Models in advertising are much more likely to be flawless in appearance than actresses in popular culture productions (see Figure 1.3). Appearance is the key to success in advertising, whereas personality is the key to success in acting. Advertising's perfected style leads to an emphasis on surfaces at the expense of all else; popular culture is more complex, dealing in interior matters as well, and

A great, big watch.

P.O.P
swatch

Dayton Hudson

Figure 1.3. From *Vogue*. Do you know anyone who looks like the model? She herself may not fully recognize the person here, for she has been costumed, made up, lighted, and photographed with a special lens. Advertising professionals have converted her into an ideal of feminine beauty, an ideal which increasingly over the 20th century consumers have wanted to see. Although some observers assert that such depictions are disheartening to consumers, in one experimental study young women shown idealized portrayals of femininity came away feeling thinner and happier (Myers & Biocca, 1992). (Reproduced with permission of Swatch® U.S.)

so the dramatic content that exposes the inner self, and the performers who can personify it, come to the fore. A sign of the distinctiveness of the two realms is that women who find success at modeling often have difficulty in transferring that success to popular culture productions.

One reflection of the differences between advertising and popular culture is the tendency toward anonymity for advertising's creators and the lack of anonymity in popular culture productions. Although those involved in the creation of advertising are increasingly being acknowledged, still models, agency art directors, advertising photographers, and commercial directors are generally not known by name, yet popular culture performers and directors are always listed in the attached credits and are sometimes widely known. The advertiser for the most part does not want any individuals inserted between the product and the consumer—it must be an unimpeded relationship. Typically, nothing is named except the product itself, which ought to be, as advertising leader David Ogilvy (1983) proclaimed, the "hero of the communication" (p. 18). A popular culture production, however, gains texture and meaning from the recognition of its talented participants. These human heroes lend familiarity and weight to the production, which may gain accretions of meaning from the associations that viewers have with those names. Popular culture is more layered, advertising less so.

The contrast between advertising and popular culture can be summarized in the matter of who pays for each order of expressive content. Advertising is created and sent at the expense of advertisers, who currently pay out approximately $150 billion annually because this communication activity suits their marketing purposes. So greatly do advertisers want to get notice of their products across, that in effect they are willing to pay additionally for the production and transmission of some of the surrounding, more appreciated content, underwriting much of television programming, for example, through the costly purchase of media time. The remainder of people's popular culture diet is purchased directly when they pay for tickets, recordings, novels, VCR rentals, and all the rest—a total of $144 billion in 1992, an amount comparable to advertising expenditures (U.S. Bureau of the Census, 1994, p. 240). Thus, advertising is paid for by and so serves advertisers, whereas popular culture serves audience members. The gulf between advertising and popular culture is captured in the conventional thinking regarding their sites of production: that advertising is Madison Avenue, New York City, East Coast, whereas popular culture is Hollywood, Los Angeles, West Coast.

Commonalities

However, advertising and popular culture could hardly be mutually energizing domains if they did not share much in common. Both are the products of culture industries—giant capitalistic bastions whose activities are governed absolutely by the search for profits. The content they put forth usually issues from large, multitiered organizations, which may well be determined by their place in yet larger conglomerates. The output from these culture corporations, if it is to make economic sense, must be as regular as the output from any manufacturing concern. Those toiling within these organizations are specialists, contributing only fractional pieces to the eventual product, which can be said to originate in no single person. In light of the manufacturing process that describes both popular culture and advertising, the production effort must be undertaken in a most calculated and self-conscious way, with an eye toward extracting the most revenue possible from consumers. By description, the culture industries would not seem to be inspirational settings.

Yet both popular culture and advertising must be understood as artistic products, at least in their pretensions.[5] The more artistic they are, the more successful they are likely to be. Only when the individual viewer experiences the communication as artistic, where symbols artfully reach through cognition to the layers of feelings and do so in an ultimately pleasurable way, is that individual likely to be touched significantly by the content. To make their content as delectable as possible, both advertising and popular culture pay great attention to style. Although advertising on the whole is more stylish than popular culture, the surfaces of both are well polished, the result of much professional effort at the production stage. A high degree of artistic professionalism is a hallmark of both the advertising industry and the popular culture industries.

The contents of both domains also share much in common. The people featured in the two are often epitomes of masculinity and femininity. Certain personages appear in both: The performer who becomes well known in the realm of popular culture as an athlete, actor, or musician may reemerge in the realm of advertising as a celebrity endorser. Music in both domains is similar if not duplicative. There is generally a narrative thrust to the content, certainly for most of popular culture, but even print ads are constructed to imply a story. Often, the story involves magic: Superman flies, and so does the woman in a cleanser ad. The activities depicted in both are likely to be extraordinary, purposeful, and perfected—realizations of the wishful thoughts of audience members.

Advertising and popular culture further resemble one another in that they share the same conveyance system to their audiences; they comprise most of what the mass media disseminate.[6] Were they to be somehow eliminated from the media, these systems would lose almost all of their content and function. Thus, in their own everyday life, the two domains are wedded to each other and infrequently appear apart. Both are then jointly mediated to extremely large numbers of people; the enormity of their spectatorship is one of their signature qualities.

On the receiving end, although popular culture is more welcomed than advertising, both orders of symbolic content suffer the same general type of reception, in that only a portion of what is sent is actually absorbed. The popular culture industries are supplicants, pleadingly doing their utmost to win a following, but only a limited percentage of their productions inspire the response desired. So it is that multi-million-dollar movies can go unwatched, television series are canceled, shelves of romance novels languish unsold, new albums receive a deaf ear. Similarly, advertisers and their agencies labor to fabricate the messages they think will strike home with consumers, only to watch their product sink in the marketplace. Down goes Campbell Soup's Souper Combo, down goes Weyerhaeuser's Ultra Softs diapers, down go Anheuser-Busch's L.A. beer, General Mills' Benefit cereal, and Kimberly-Clark's Once Overs cleaning towels, down, down go Crystal Pepsi and R. J. Reynold's Premier cigarettes. (In fact, of the 22,000 new consumer products introduced in 1994, an estimated 90% failed in spite of promotional efforts; Weisz, 1994.) Both advertising and popular culture are completely subject to the fickleness, the choices, and, in the final analysis, the control of the audience.

Yet to look at the matter of success from another perspective, both domains are successful overall in that, as industries, their financial statures are undeniable. What is uncertain in the small is indisputable in the large. Enough of this symbolic material is striking home that there can be no denying the viability of the two. On average, Americans spend over 30 hours weekly partaking in their selections from the advertising/popular culture mix. Most of this material is absorbed uneventfully, but occasionally there is a cataclysmic event that lets observers sense the depth of what is going on below the surface. Mania over a particular celebrity as well as the phenomenal success of a blockbuster movie testify to the power of popular culture, just as runaway sales occasionally result from advertising. Whenever fan clubs sprout up or people organize themselves into consumption communities (as with Pepsi-Cola drinkers in opposition to Coca-Cola fanciers), then the power of these two symbolic domains is made manifest. When people increasingly outfit themselves with symbols of their popular culture teams or heroes (the Raiders, Mickey Mouse, the Power Rangers) or have the name of particular products legibly featured on their apparel (Budweiser T-shirts, Gucci glasses, Avon caps) and this becomes their leading message to the world at large, then it is clear that advertising and popular culture have become one means for nothing less than signaling personal identity.

Another similarity between advertising and popular culture is that both present an opacity when confronted by analytical efforts. They are woven so tightly into everyday life that to hold them at an objective distance and to comprehend them deeply is not easy. The scrutinizer is lulled into complacency by their familiar surfaces, and when urged to analyze an instance of advertising or popular culture often makes statements like, "There's really nothing much to this. It's all so obvious," and when led into a deconstruction of the material may protest and say, "I wonder if we're seeing things that really aren't there. You're making too much out of this." But advertising and popular culture, for all the slickness of their deceptive surfaces, are highly complex messages and deserve careful exploration, a teasing out of the deep structures through the exercise of what anthropologist Clifford Geertz (1975) called "thick description." Conclusions wait to be drawn about the symbolic constituents, the meanings intended, and the surreptitious ideological underpinnings.

Last, advertising and popular culture resemble each other in that throughout the 20th century the two have been the subject of prolonged critical invective. The very vitality of these two symbolic domains and the fact that they can in no way be considered ineffectual or trivial are confirmed by the unrelenting attack on their production and enjoyment. An analysis of this attack is the subject of Chapter 3; for the moment, it is sufficient to point out its existence and its sweeping and frontal assault on these public arts. Popular culture and advertising are so resilient that they are continuously drawing this attack into their own fold, invigorating themselves from it. A 1994 Chevrolet pickup truck commercial was noisily depicting the pounding that the pickup could take before a booming voice-over announced, "For those who think there is too much violence on TV . . . these few seconds of quiet," and silence ensued. Ever voracious, advertising and popular culture can even convert criticism into usable material.

Definitions: Symbol, Meaning, Culture, Audience, and Viewer

While most of the terms used in subsequent chapters should pose little difficulty, a few require discussion now: *symbol, meaning, culture, audience,* and *viewer.*

Used here, *symbol*[7] is the generic term for anything that refers to something else beyond itself—"broadly, a sign, object or act that stands for something other than itself, by virtue of agreement among the members of the culture that use it" (O'Sullivan, Hartley, Saunders, Montgomery, & Fiske, 1994, p. 312). Words are symbols—arbitrary items that point to sectors of semantic space. So are images, even when they look artless; they are not the thing depicted but a manipulated representation of the thing. Music too is symbolic, typically designating emotional territory. Symbols are the means by which people condense and organize all that they care to recognize. The world of symbols is rife with turmoil, as old symbols recede or metamorphose and new ones emerge from various quarters.

Symbols are what are sent, but meanings are what are received. It is at those moments when symbols are absorbed that the fascinating enterprise of *meaning* occurs. Meaning comes in the form of a response; it is in the mind of the receiver. The act of understanding or interpreting only takes place when symbols find an affinity within a person's store of symbolic references. If an incoming symbol closely matches a stored symbol, that becomes its meaning; if the incoming symbol does not resemble a stored symbol but still can be understood as composed of familiar elements, then it will be assigned a meaning location in relation to those already housed within the symbolic store (as occurred with the example of the Energizer bunny when new). In either case, for meaning to transpire, a valence must exist between the incoming symbol and a stored symbol. If the incoming symbol is so unique that there is no valence, then no meaning can be produced, at least not immediately.[8] "Apparently our mind is so avid for meaning that it will go on searching and integrating as if it were hungering for it all the time, ready to devour anything that is offered, provided it can satisfy this need once it is roused," commented Ernst Gombrich (1981, p. 24).

Raymond Williams (1983) observed that "culture is one of the two or three most complicated words in the English language" (p. 87). Here, *culture* is most easily understood as the entirety of a particular way of life: It is correct to speak of French culture or Navaho culture or youth culture. Culture is an invisible construct made visible in symbols, objects, and practices. Advertising and popular culture are two symbolizing components within modern cultures. Because symbolic vocabularies differ among national cultures, popular culture and advertising often do not travel perfectly across borders, and when they do, they may not mean there what they mean here.[9] A culture's particular set of symbols establishes patterns and limits for that culture. The meanings that predominate in the minds of most members of a culture are the meanings that define that culture. Cultures are little constrained by reality or nature; they are nearly self-contained human constructions that exist within nature, intersecting it only at points.

Discussion turns now to the difficult and flawed notion of *audience*, a word which usually refers in an undifferentiating manner to those who receive mediated content and which carries implications about the nature of their reception. This "audience" exists only as a concept, and not a very powerful one at that—John Hartley (1987) refers to audiences as "invisible fictions" (p. 125). The feebleness of the concept may be traded off by some against its convenience, for "audience" is a facile way to indicate all at once the conditions of reception as opposed to those of inception or transmission. The word is drawn from the world of theater performances; people were congregated in one spot at one time, had committed the identical act of buying a ticket, seemed to behave more or less in concert, and so might reasonably be thought of as a unity, a "thing." Even when crowd dynamics are actively in operation, however, during the intermissions and at the end people are drawn to speak to each other about the performance, checking one's interpretation and evaluation against another's because there is no uniformity in reception. The idea of an audience as a collectivity with indistinguishable responses, then, does not hold up even at the concept's point of origin and holds up even less when it is applied to in-home spectating. The so-called television "audience" consists of people whose participation occurs from myriad, dissimilar situations, no one identical to another. Each audience member is out of sight of most other spectators and so can hardly be said to exist in a collectivity; the diversity in reception is why senders must try extensively to cue desired responses through laugh tracks or commanded studio applause. In short, there is no such thing as a monolithic audience responding unvaryingly to the mass media. Insistence on the concept of the "audience" may stem from a condescending desire to diminish and render as uniformly passive the enterprise of reception.

If the concept of *audience* nearly evaporates when it is thoughtlessly applied to the mass media and in particular to the television experience, the concept of *viewer* undergoes the opposite transformation, growing more robust and more elaborate. A program and its advertising cannot truly be said to have meaning until an individual viewer supplies that meaning.[10] Although symbols exist at the extraindividual level and are formed by social agreement, those symbols are only in repose and cannot be activated as meanings until they are greeted in the mind of an individual and matched against that individual's store of meanings. Conceived of this way, the individual spectator becomes the paramount element in mediated communications. With focus on the viewer as individual, the extent and complexity of any one viewer's symbolic system becomes conspicuous. Incoming symbols will collide with that interior symbolic apparatus in a multitude of ways, depending on the nature of the viewer's symbolic store and that person's temperament and needs at the moment.

There is, on the decoding side of mediated communication, a vast range of possible responses, all of them accounted for by the variations between people and by the variations in any one person's disposition over time. People select from what is offered to suit themselves, picking voluntarily, without coercion, whatever is serviceable. Thus, the advertising/popular culture mix is hardly a monolithic force, hammering all exposed to it down to the same level. Rather, it is lavish, open, approachable. The symbolic material is greeted by the viewer as if it were a fruit orchard, some of it ripe for the taking.

Notes

1. The bunny was created by DDB Needham in fall 1988. This agency and its client began to disagree about marketing goals, and in an incident telling of the

practice of advertising, Eveready simply shifted the creation to a different agency. After all, it had paid for the new symbol and could do with the bunny as it wished (Liesse, 1991).

2. DDB Needham's creative personnel declined, through the firm's public relations director, to be interviewed for this chapter. Possibly, authorship of the Energizer bunny and the loss of the Energizer account remain delicate matters at the agency.

3. It is true that many consumers thought the bunny was advertising Duracell, the competitor. Duracell claimed that up to 40% of those who recalled the bunny campaign thought it was touting their product. From Eveready's point of view, although the confusion was a nuisance it did not obliterate the greatly increased brand awareness that their battery enjoyed as a result of the campaign (Liesse, 1990).

4. The transfer of the appeal symbols to the product is analogous to a similar transfer within the realm of popular culture, when the meaning of an entertainment is transferred to the performer of it—for example, movies about rebelliousness offer up meanings to the personality of Marlon Brando or mournful songs get infused in the public image of Willie Nelson.

5. "Artistic" is taken to mean products of the imagination fixed in a communication medium and found to be estimable by observers.

6. Even news and information, ostensibly another order of media content, can be seen as exhibiting close affinities to advertising and popular culture. News and information are unlikely to be antithetical to the advertising imperative because advertising revenues sustain them. Like popular culture, a news story is typically selected with a broad audience in mind and is formatted along a story line to make it digestible. By the time it gets to its ultimate destination, it may little resemble whatever instigated it.

7. Symbol is preferred here to "sign" because sign is so fully identified with the Saussurian tradition and with Saussure's definition of a sign as a fusion of "signifier" (the arbitrary word or image, devoid of meaning) and "signified" (what the signifier refers to–its meaning). Adopting this perspective, as intellectually fertile as it has proved to be, demands locating "meaning" within the sign itself rather than within the observer of the sign. While I in no way deny that signs have agreed-on meanings (if they did not, communication between people would be impossible), it is the contributions of the audience members that I wish to emphasize here. Thus, meaning can be said to lie not in the sign but in the observer of the sign (or here, symbol). This is not an inconsequential matter.

8. In fact, one way to understand the concept of "meaning" is to consider episodes of its opposite, the occasional moment when a real scene or a mediated scene is "meaningless." Minds will struggle fiercely to make sense out of something jumbled. By recalling the sensation when something is meaningless, the remedy to it would then describe what "meaning" amounts to.

9. For example, Madonna conjures up a different set of meanings in Japan than she does in the United States. Marshall Blonsky (1992) overheard a conversation among Japanese regarding Madonna: "When I heard 'nothingness nested inside nothingness,' I knew that Madonna had been assimilated into the pantheon of Japanese Zen Buddhism" (p. 8).

10. Even scholars writing in the Marxist tradition, where one theme has long been the manipulation of essentially hapless masses by capitalistic media and the imposition of a "false" consciousness, have come to concede the active role of the consumer in the generation of meaning. Robert Goldman (1992) admits, "Viewers' interpretive participation is absolutely necessary to the *completion* of commodity-signs. Consumers *produce value*, they don't just consume it" (p. 226), and Sut Jhally (1990) goes so far as to note, "The recognition that the activity of the audience itself plays a vital role in the use-value of messages takes us away from the ultimately fruitless notion of manipulation and conspiratorial control by advertisers" (p. 132).

2

Origins

Needless to say, not all intellectuals have been convinced that human beings are best understood as symbol-using creatures. For the luminous philosopher Karl Marx (1818-1883) and the generations of like-minded thinkers who have followed in his considerable wake, the bedrock of human existence was materialism and its economic context. Marx stated (1859/1904) that "the mode of production in material life determines the general character of the social, political, and intellectual processes of life" (p. 12). Delving into the debate of whether people are better conceived of as fundamentally symbol-using or fundamentally economic creatures, Marshall Sahlins (1976) aligned himself strongly with the first position and against the second. He rejected the Marxist notion that material goods and their production and exchange formed the basis of social life and instead insisted upon the primacy of culture, relegating goods to a secondary role as the manifestations of symbolic codes. Sahlins wrote at one point that the modern economy, "ostensibly in command, is in reality the servant" of symbolic codes (p. 170) and at another point said, "The finalities as well as the modalities of production come from the cultural side" (p. 207). Although subsistence concerns do dictate cultural responses of one sort or another, he allowed, the final form of the response belongs to a symbolic system that is complete and self-referring: "We have seen that nothing in the way of their capacity to satisfy a material (biological) requirement can explain why pants are produced for men and skirts for women, or why dogs are inedible [in American culture] but the hindquarters of the steer are supremely satisfying of the need to eat" (p. 207). When Sahlins affirmed, "In its reliance upon symbolic reason, . . . our culture is not radically different from that elaborated by the 'savage mind' " (p. 220), he was grafting contemporary existence onto the age-old legacy of symbol usage.

Despite Sahlin's (1976) dismissal of it, however, an economic orientation has much to offer in the effort to situate the symbol domains of advertising and popular culture within the context of modern life. His insistence that contemporary existence is "not radically different" from primitive life is at once both true and misleading. He cannot be faulted in his explication of the ongoing primal force, at once invisible and majestic, of culture and its symbols and its symbolizing objects; at this he has few peers. But he must be faulted for his failure to acknowledge that contemporary culture is marked by economic conditions that are so different from primitive ones that they constitute a difference not just in degree but in kind. Focusing on what we have in common with our ancestors, Sahlins lost sight of how we stand out in stark contrast.

What is novel about the contemporary human condition is the astonishing growth over the past few centuries of the economic sphere and the permeation of its activities and similes into all aspects of existence. An economic perspective provides a vista over the ever-rising floodtide of goods and services that began noticeably before Marx's day and continues through the present. It was not until massive production and consumption reared up, overshadowing the ancient traditions of agricultural economies, that mediated advertising and mediated popular culture even appeared. Advertising and popular culture have come to occupy central positions within this extravagant economic sphere, not only deriving their technologized form from it but also having something to do with keeping it cohesive and swelling. So advertising and popular culture must be approached as economic entities as well as symbolic entities. Establishing the macroeconomic context will help in locating the precise societal functions of the two newly dominant symbol domains.

An Expanding Need for Goods

In their *The World of Goods*, anthropologist Mary Douglas and economist Baron Isherwood (1979) investigated intellectual terrain similar to that of Sahlin's (1976) work, but they did so from a somewhat different perspective. What prompted them, they stated, was that economists could not successfully explain the demand for commodities. For what reasons do people want to obtain goods? A response with great explanatory power came not from the discipline of economics but from anthropology and ethnography: "It is standard ethnographic practice to assume that all material possessions carry social meanings and to concentrate a main part of cultural analysis upon their use as communicators" (p. 59). By extension, the material possessions of the modern consumer have value to that consumer in the way they communicate social meanings. Consumers when shopping are composing social messages about themselves, messages they intend to radiate to others for their study and to themselves for their own personal reflection. Familiarity with the code of objects allows people to receive in turn the messages sent by others and so to enter the social world.

Thus, in Douglas and Isherwood's view, human's participate in the consumption of goods so as to participate in the world of meanings, outside of which they would be lost. Goods are the visible, material markers of invisible, immaterial, but highly significant, culture. Moreover, culture is always in flux, and goods are one way of restraining that fluidity. Goods, then, lie at the core of human existence because they make meanings palpable and provide a means for people to situate themselves within the larger culture.[1] When Douglas and Isherwood (1979) write, "So here we are, with an interpretation of consumer behavior that lines us all up to-gether, us with our machine-made merchandise and the tribesmen with their home-bred flocks and herds and hand-hafted hoes and hand-woven baskets" (p. 96), they are sounding much like Sahlin's (1976) observation regarding the identity between the primitive and the modern.

The question that remains, one that Sahlins never confronts, is why do modern people covet, and hold, *so many more* possessions? Why are present-day people collectively involved in the enterprise of mass consumption, absorbing most of the output from mass production? For this, Douglas and Isherwood (1979) offer a tantalizing suggestion: Because people need goods to articulate meanings in their cultural world, should that cultural world for any reason enlarge, then so would the number of matters demanding new symbols and more goods (p. 78).

The world of Western culture has been on an expansionist path for some 500 years, along a multitude of dimensions. Once the technology of the ocean-going sailing vessel had been mastered, the geographical expansion of European culture across the face of the planet between the 16th and 18th centuries defeated ancient parochial sureties and compelled Europeans to engage and render sensible the near totality of the world's cultures. This geographical diffusion, visible and undeniable, parallels less visible extensions going on as well. The enterprise of science extended human consciousness into any number of realms previously partitioned off. Not only did knowledge of the unknown increase but so did knowledge of the forgotten, as past learning (Hebrew, Greek, and Latin) was recaptured and disseminated. Over time and in the large, social frameworks grew less constraining; awareness of other ways of life geographically distant was echoed in a growing awareness of ways of life socially distinct but inviting. Opportunities for social mobility became more frequent. The multifaceted opening up of European society meant that people were exposed to a vastly broader scope than their forebears had been and would likely need a greater complement of symbols and symbolizing goods to help make the expanded world meaningful.

The opportunities and burdens of this unprecedented expansion of the cultural world descended on the individual, especially when a new center of Western culture appeared on the North American continent during the 19th century and a second stage was ignited. The individuation of human life demanded that not just each household but each person had to possess an adequate measure of symbol familiarity and symbolizing goods in order to navigate the expanded cultural world. The increasing prominence of the individual occurred at the expense of some of the rigor of such traditional framing institutions as church, hierarchy, community, ethnicity, lineage, profession, family, and gender. Earlier, these institutions had assumed near complete responsibility for granting people firm definitions as well as social locations. The self-identities that were once forged by constraining and imposing social forces were now more likely to be created and nurtured by the individual;[2] to accomplish this historically novel task, to cultivate interior meanings, called for more symbolic equipment, more personal goods. Grant McCracken (1986) notes that "contemporary North American culture leaves a great deal of the individual undefined. One of the ways individuals satisfy the freedom and fulfill responsibility of self-definition is through systematic appropriation of the meaningful properties of goods" (p. 80).

These and allied developments did not evolve at a steady, predictable rate, but rather at an uneven although generally accelerating one; to withstand the rush, one might resort to additional stabilizing objects, ones whose set symbolic properties countered the fluidities of change. More items were also required for use as gifts to strengthen the interpersonal relationships that could no longer be taken for granted, that were being stretched and weakened by the social transformations under way. The upshot was a voluminously increased demand for goods, a demand that could not be met by ancient methods of hand production. By 1870, enterprise and ingenuity were at work to create the foundations of a new manufacturing system.

The Production/Consumption Economy

The modern whirring, expanding economy is, in the longer historical context, very much an anomaly. Earlier economies were, for the most part, static and invariant. With the intermittent exceptions of maritime, trading societies (from the Phoenicians circa 1000 B.C. to the English in the 18th century), most economies were based on agriculture and so were rural in nature. On the farm, people produced what others consumed and consumed what they produced. Only the smallest proportion of the populace gathered at trading centers, working at crafts or finances; at the time of the first U.S. census in 1790, less than 5% of the population lived in settlements having more than 2,500 residents (U.S. Bureau of the Census, 1975, p. 12). The other 95% lived as people always had— dispersed across rural areas, occupied at agricultural pursuits. Largely self-sufficient, they entered into very few economic transactions; most of their infrequent exchanges were through barter rather than cash.

Summarizing the premodern economy as an ideal type, there was little production outside of agriculture; life was rural and unchanging; there were few marketplace transactions, and so the market as such only existed in physical and rudimentary form; there was little cash in use, or needed.

The evolution from that condition to the present is the content of the history of the 19th and 20th centuries. Over time, production and consumption became ever more sharply delineated spheres. The production and consumption which used to be comingled on the farm separated into two discernible activities, signaled by their new and distinct loci in time and space. The day became exactingly sectioned into work and nonwork time; work took place apart from the home, in a building especially constructed to contain it. The autonomous factory, where no one lived but many worked, was virtually unknown before industrialization but quickly became the standard. The division of human life into exclusive cells of production and consumption allowed for the creation of the flows between them that were to be the lifeblood of the new creation—an economy that would prosper rather than lie everlastingly stagnant. Reflecting the stature of the new economy, the nature of the marketplace remarkably changed from a small physical locale within settlements to an abstracted institution permeating much of an existence wherein most things have price tags, if only figuratively.

Following the Civil War (1861-1865), the evolution of the modern production/consumption economy received its greatest boost when giant strides were made in the development of continuous-process production machinery (Beninger, 1986, chap. 6). Due to advances in iron making, in the machine tool industry, and in mechanical engineering, new machines that were much faster and much more capacious than any previously built were developed almost simultaneously in several different consumer goods industries. Machines that could daily turn out thousands of units of, for instance, kitchen matches, razor blades, cigarettes, or breakfast cereals were set into operation. Production at a scale never before imaginable was loosed upon the nation. Manufacturers were quick to confirm that the greater profits were to be had not in producing a limited number of goods for the relatively affluent but, once the machines and production lines were set up, in turning out a vast number of inexpensive, replaceable items that could be retailed by the millions to Americans.

The boom in factory productive capability was complemented by advances in extractive machinery—the machines that took iron ore from the ground or harvested the wheat. The product of these efforts found their way to manufacturing plants by means of a new, quick, and efficient railway system. The same railroads that brought in raw materials took away the finished goods, speeding them along lengthy routes to the wholesaler, the retailer, and finally the customer. With a whoosh what nature provided was rapidly transformed into a flow of widely distributed, finished products. Consumer demand was now being matched by the forces of production.

By 1900, as the urbanizing population reached the 40% mark, the goods that Americans used were decreasingly those fabricated through their own handiwork at home and increasingly those produced by machine elsewhere. Michael Schudson (1984) points out that near the start of the 19th century 80% of all clothing had been made in the home, whereas near the end of that century, only 10% was (p. 156). Soap, harnesses, dairy products, decorations, sheet music, nails, lard, confectionaries, rugs—the list of items homemade in 1800 and store-bought in 1900 is extensive. The market, which at the beginning of the century had been a shallow and almost incidental institution, was at its end a pulsating, all-embracing system for the allocation of products and money.

The transition from an agricultural economy to a production/ consumption one was accompanied by extensive changes in the nature of public and private lives. Compared to the Americans of 1800, the people of 1900 displayed very different behaviors toward one another and had very different self-conceptions. Factories, mills, foundries, and plants located at transportation hubs drew job seekers into urban centers. Leaving farms and hamlets to live in towns and cities, people left one way of life behind and were compelled to take up another. The mode of social control in one setting was the reverse of what prevailed in the other. In the traditional pattern, farm work may have been isolating but what leisure hours or days families had were frequently spent in the company of others—in a church service or supper, at a grange or fraternity meeting, at a quilting bee or a dance. Community and community sentiments (which could be at turns caring or derisive) figured large in the lives of rural people. They were ordinarily well integrated into rural institutions and were supported and restrained by them, at times to the point of confinement.

"As Americans fled the surveillance of the village," explains historian T. Jackson Lears (1984), "they encountered the anonymity of the city" (p. 6). For all of its employment advantages, urban life offered fewer of the usual communal connections. Life under crowded conditions invited a certain wariness in dealings with others. People often did not know, or care to know, their city neighbors. Being compelled to work closely with others all day long made privacy after hours much more attractive. The institutions that had been so prominent in rural life now began to recede, and their bracing support grew more tenuous. All this had the effect of turning the individual back upon the self. For all the proximity of others, then, urban people were more atomistic, less socially resolved. These were characteristics which the newly appearing advertisers could not help but notice.

The Rise of Modern Advertising

Most manufacturing concerns in the last quarter of the 19th century experienced vexing difficulties with distribution, despite the efficiencies of the railroads (Pease, 1958). The various tiers of wholesalers and ultimately the retailers the manufacturer had to deal with constituted an uneven patchwork system, one replete with opportunities for extortion and fraud. To conquer impediments in distribution systems, one option that manufacturers had was to integrate vertically, taking over wholesaling and even perhaps retailing. Although some exercised this option to a greater or lesser extent, it was hardly a perfect solution: It brought manufacturers into areas of business where they had no previous expertise, the startup costs were high, and the maintenance of a distribution chain carrying a few products compared poorly in efficiency and cost to other chains moving the varied products that retailers had to offer.

Another solution, less expensive and more efficient, presented itself (Pope, 1983, p. 82). If manufacturers could persuade customers to demand the product from their plant, and that product alone, this would in effect draw the product through the distribution networks and set limits on the connivance and manipulation of middlemen. For the masters of mass production, the idea of constructing messages that would bring notice of their products directly to potential customers became very attractive.[3]

Two fundamental conditions had to be met for this marketing strategy to work. In order that customers be able to ask for a product by name, that product first had to have a name, one that distinguished it from all others. At the time, manufactured items were not commonly so labeled. For most of the 19th century, most products were generic in type; a cracker was a cracker, whoever the manufacturer was. When production had been labor intensive and sluggish, manufacturers had all they could do to meet the demand by wholesalers and saw no reason to label their output. Labeling could bring more exposure and accountability than these small manufacturers cared to have. But when the new machinery turned out mountains of products, which had to be efficiently distributed, marketing became much more competitive, and the advantages of brand names to differentiate one manufacturer's output from another's quickly became obvious. These brand names were to be printed on packages containing standardized portions of the product (another way that mass-produced products could be distinguished from the earlier generic sort, which were sold in bulk) so that a customer could not get them home and onto the shelf without being repeatedly reminded of the name (see Figure 2.1).

Naming, however, would be futile if the names had no legally protected standing. Brand names and trademarks were first safeguarded when Congress passed appropriate legislation in 1870; 121 were registered that year (Strasser, 1989, p. 44). When in 1878 the American Cereal Company was able to get customers to ask for Quaker Oats instead of the generic staple of oatmeal, it was taking full advantage of the trademark act (Atwan, McQuade, & Wright, 1979, p. 186). The legalities surrounding trademarks fluctuated owing to differing judicial rulings, but when the practice received its final codification in 1905, there were some 10,000 trademarks registered—ample testimony to the success of this marketing approach.[4] Artemas Ward, a well-known editor and copywriter of the period, remarked at the turn of the century,

> It is wonderful to note the volume of package trading in food products, groceries, and patent medicines. Sugar, molasses, vinegar, flour, cheese, dried apples—a hundred and one things once regarded as stables to be sold only in bulk now come within the package field . . . . There has been a revolution in the methods of American trade within the past twenty years. (quoted in Strasser, 1989, p. 29)

The application of specific names to distinguish products had broader ramifications than marketing ones; through the act of naming, a product, something lifeless, was transformed into something lifelike, with possible meanings attached. Just as an animal is an animal until it is named and becomes a pet, so too named products were drawn into more intimate relations with individuals. It is not just soap, it's Ivory; it is not just a screwdriver, it's a Stanley; it is not just a car, it's a Ford. The naming of products

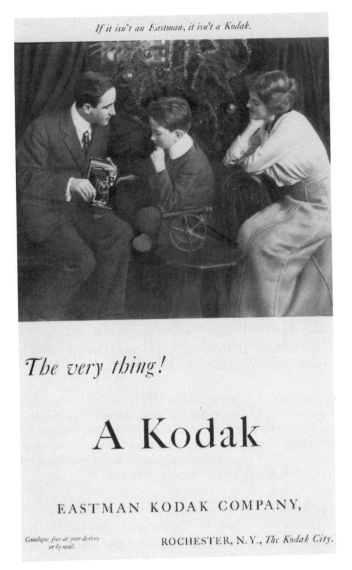

Figure 2.1. Safeguarded by law after 1870, brand names and trademarks permitted products to retain singular identities with consumers. George Eastman invented the brand name "Kodak" because he thought it would be a memorable word and he knew it could be protected. Kodak would have quickly lost market value if just anyone could have appropriated the name.

and the attachments thus created brought yet more energy to the spiral of production and consumption.

The second precondition was that there had to be a ready means to transmit notice about these brand-name products to customers, preferably right into their homes. When the promotion of brand-name goods began in the 1870s, advertisers had little choice but to use newspapers. Newspapers, however, were less than the ideal vehicle, for at that time type was set into columns separated by metal rules; to abolish rules and run a display ad two or three columns wide, as more and more national advertisers wished to do, posed grave production difficulties for newspapers, many of which had to decline the offered business. An even greater obstacle for national advertisers was newspapers' localized coverage. To campaign nationally involved dealing with the staff of each newspaper in each city and town. It was a logistical nightmare.

However, in American enterprise few dilemmas promising profits await solutions for long. Magazines and journals, having regional or national audiences, quickly learned that their true purpose in life was not to provide appropriate editorial content for their subscribers, as they had thought, but rather to construct a large and devoted readership and then sell that readership to advertisers. Aware of the efficiencies that magazines offered, the new advertisers flocked to them. In 1871, *Harper's*, the leading general interest magazine, carried only 5 pages of advertising in its November issue; the same issue 20 years later contained over 100 advertising pages (Norris, 1990, p. 26). New publications, such as *Ladies' Home Journal* (founded in 1883), joined into the hunt after the attention of the expanding middle class. The publisher of *Ladies' Home Journal*, Cyrus H. K. Curtis, once confided to an audience of manufacturers,

Do you know why we publish the *Ladies' Home Journal*? The editor thinks it is for the benefit of American women. That is an illusion, but a very proper one for him to have. But I will tell you: the real reason, the publisher's reason, is to give you people who manufacture things that American women want and buy, a chance to tell them about your products. (quoted in Norris, 1990, p. 36)

A chance to tell Americans about products, and to do so with the charm and presence of a storyteller, would seem to be what the new medium of radio was offering advertisers in the 1920s. Yet for several years, all the concerned parties—the broadcasters, the ever more muscular advertisers, the regulatory offices of the federal government, and sectors of the public—hesitated tentatively. There was a sense abroad that radio was too invasive, too beguiling to encounter the same skeptical negotiation that greeted print advertising. Thus a period of feint and thrust ensued, as advertising was tried on some stations and proscribed on others. When the networks were established in 1926 and 1927 and their search for revenues got under way, no "direct" advertising (resembling modern commercials) was permitted; "indirect" advertising, in which the sponsor's name was discreetly featured, as with the *Kodak Chorus Hour*, was the norm. But gradually indirect surrendered to direct, and undisguised sales pitches came to punctuate broadcasting. The medium's decade-long struggle with the matter of advertising resulted in the ground rules for further developments in the electronic media: that advertisers would pick up the entire bill, and that broadcasting would faithfully serve the requirements of advertisers.

The newer medium of television, as it developed in the 1940s and 1950s, represented a kind of perfection to the national advertisers of the day. None of the earlier contests over advertising's role in broadcasting had to be refought; what had been uncertain and at times contentious in the 1920s was in the 1950s considered normal. Television has been sardonically described as "just radio with pictures," and there is much truth to this in that many of the essential features of radio, including network centrality, carried over into this newer medium, but the person who uttered the phrase may not have understood what a difference pictures make. "Seeing comes before words," John Berger (1972) began his treatise on art and vision (p. 7), asserting the primacy of sight in communication. The addition of visual imagery presented advertisers with an inviting opportunity for multisensory persuasion. Radio had offered as tools the modalities of music, words, and sound effects, but the radio listener was left to conjure up the visual imagery—a condition often nostalgically admired, but not by advertisers. From the advertisers' point of view, the ultimate message might be too much the individual creation of the listener and not sufficiently that of the sender. The supplement of pictures permitted more control over communication and helped limit the range of perhaps miscreant interpretations. As well as showing personages and tableaus, because the pictures were moving they could also convey vignettes; nothing establishes resonances with people more than seeing other people in action. The range of possible symbols and intended meanings manifoldly increased.

Each medium in the historical sequence of newspapers, magazines, radio, and television found its purpose as a purer and more perfected advertising vehicle (Leiss, Kline, & Jhally, 1990, chap. 5), thereby increasing the comprehensiveness of the swelling production/consumption economy. The idea that the media were to serve "the public interest," as the issuer of federal broadcast licenses nobly decreed, must be balanced against the fact that the financial underwriters of the media were largely advertisers. Each new medium lent advertisers a greater communication repertoire— from text alone, to text plus pictures, to the immediacy of sound, to moving pictures with compelling imagery. As more and more advertisements were sent and received, *advertisements* gave away to *advertising,* in that individual ads lost much of their singularity to the surround of advertising in general. The very magnitude of advertising created a new enclosing spherical surface for the display of commercial symbols, one nearly impossible to escape.

To recapitulate, mass production necessitated mediated advertising as a marketing device so that manufacturers could smooth out their unruly distribution lines. Advertising came to be the major communications link between mass production and mass consumption: The forces of production, in the attempt to control consumption, bombarded Americans with attractive messages, and consumers en masse, by responding to some messages and not to others, informed producers about the appropriateness of message content. This order of communication became so important to the operations of a production/consumption economy that it could command sufficient revenues from businesses to subsidize mammoth mass communication systems.[5] The formation of mass communication, in particular the television system to which Americans now allocate 80% of their media time (Cutler, 1990, p. 38), is advertising's most important by-product.

Another by-product of the advertising initiative—and further indication of the centrality of advertising within the modern economy—is the development of a whole industry and a profession dedicated solely to its execution. When the production boom began in the 1870s and 1880s, there were few advertising agents. Those who plied this occupation labored not for mass producers but for the medium of newspapers; working on behalf of one or more papers, they solicited advertising, collected payments, kept a large percentage for themselves, and passed the rest on to the publication. They were brokering advertising space between newspapers and advertisers, working for the more venerable of the two because mass manufacturers and the advertising strategy were at an incipient stage. But as it became clearer that national advertisers of mass-produced goods were going to be a mighty financial force, agents began to switch allegiance, working for the advertisers instead of the media.[6] At first, they only negotiated costs for space in newspapers and magazines and handled the details of placement, but in the 1890s, responding to a perceived demand from advertisers, they began to add to their staffs people who could help in writing advertising copy and constructing layouts. By 1910, some agencies were beginning to do marketing research for their larger clients, and by 1920, major agencies had taken on a group of artists to work with the copywriters in the newly established creative departments, which labored feverishly to construct imagery and text that would communicate their clients' messages to an expanding middle class of discerning consumers.

Because manufacturers, then as now, always try to trim costs so as to increase their profits, why didn't they bring the advertising function within the firm and retain the revenues that the agencies were clearly making? That they did not is further evidence of the economic importance of the advertising strategy. For advertising to be at its best, it must be executed by someone situated between the producer and the consumer, able to comprehend both parties so as to translate the offerings of one into the needs of the other. Those manufacturers who did try to internalize the advertising effort found themselves at a disadvantage compared to others who hired independent agencies. Advertising was too important to do less than well.

The year 1920 can be considered pivotal in the momentous transition from an agricultural economy to a production/consumption one, for the national census conducted that year revealed that the majority (52%) of Americans were living in towns and cities (U.S. Bureau of the Census, 1975, p. 11). The nation had tipped from being a predominantly rural society to being a predominantly urban one; there was to be no going back. The urbanized population had little choice but to enter into marketplace transactions to obtain all that was needed to sustain themselves. Like it or not, they had become committed consumers. Increasingly, they had the wherewithal to be proficient at consumption: The work hours of the employed had been on a gradual decline for 30 years, dropping to 50 hours weekly in 1920; the proportion of women who elected to stay out of the paid workforce was on the rise, so household time available for consumption expanded; also, average nonfarm wages were climbing, up from $490 in 1900 to $1,489 in 1920 (U.S. Bureau of the Census, 1975, pp. 168).

The 1920s proved to be a period of unparalleled economic growth, accelerating the spins of production and consumption. Within this economic vortex, consumers had to struggle to feel their personal ways. The certainties of the past were to some extent gone; what loomed were anomie and the temptations of the moment. Uneasy consumers sought orientation. The strength of older institutions paled in comparison to the vigor of the market and the advertising that trumpeted it everywhere.

It was during this time that simple advertising was eclipsed by compound advertising. The centrifugal forces of the production/consumption economy pushed the advertising imperative beyond the role of notification and product effects, and into the realm of personal meanings. Textual descriptions, hyperbolic or not, gradually surrendered costly space to the pictorial communication that might penetrate deeply into minds. But to communicate successfully, advertising had to reach into the store of previously established symbolizing images, and to put them to use. One convenient repository of symbols was that of popular culture.

Popular Culture Joins Advertising

A useful concept from Marxist thought is that of *commodification*. As entrepreneurs seek out areas of human existence as yet untouched by the mechanisms of the production/consumption economy and attempt to insert products and marketplace transactions there, they are said to be commodifying what had previously been uncommodified. Currently, for example, fitness and exercise are being commodified. From a Marxist perspective, the idea of commodification carries with it the implication that anything can be subjected to the insistence of the capitalistic production/consumption economy. It is more probable, however, that successful commodification occurs only when the demand, or consumption, side of the economy presents unclaimed areas of opportunity.

One area of human life near totally commodified after 1870 is that of diversion. Before the installation of the modern economy, some diversions were purchased, such as theater tickets and horse racing admissions, but most were of a more casual nature. Forms of local entertainment arose spontaneously in the search for play rather than for profit. To distinguish them from modern popular culture, these less formal diversions are often referred to as folk culture—a noncommercial, rustic brand of amusement, involving such activities as live music, dancing, and storytelling. The arrival of the modern economy brought with it an expanded and even desperate need for diversion, indeed on a daily basis. The immediate pressures of the workday in a production/consumption economy combined with the unremitting obligations for the emotional maintenance of the self dictated heightened needs for fantastic and diversionary content. As soon as a wage-earning, urbanized population appeared and the demand for extensive entertainment became evident, some entrepreneurs began to make play their life's work. The culture industries, dispensing amusements to customers near and far, were born into the world of commerce, and diversion was henceforth commodified.

Entertainment purchased by the urbanized population early in the 20th century included spectator sports (baseball, boxing, horse racing), vaudeville performances, legitimate theater, and as the 1920s transpired, the tempo-setting craze of city life, dance music. But more and more entertainment was sought from the burgeoning communication systems, for such content was less costly for the consumer, more accessible, and often more polished and enjoyable.

To the forefront came the historically unique provision of an amplitude of photographed imagery, a bequest from the invention of photography decades earlier in the 19th century. Through the now largely forgotten mass medium of stereography (where twin photographs mounted on a card and inserted into a stereoscope holder produced a three-dimensional effect), Americans vastly increased their stores of visual symbols (Fowles, 1994). Stereograph cards and stereoscopes were present in virtually every middle-class household before 1920. Additionally, once half-tone photographic duplication was technically possible, newspapers and magazines, whose pages of text had previously been interrupted by only an occasional wood-block illustration, now carried picture after picture, transmitting to the eyes of the nation selected meaning-eliciting images. But most strikingly, after 1913 photographed images, diversionary content, and broad dissemination combined to reach their apotheosis in the new rage of moving pictures. By 1921, Americans were spending $301 million annually for movie tickets, as opposed to $81 million for traditional theater performances and $30 million for spectator sports (U.S. Bureau of the Census, 1975, p. 401). These movies were soundless, to be appreciated through the eyes only, so their visual qualities were paramount.

It was to this sudden largess of visual imagery—imagery which had quickly taken on symbol duties—that advertisers began to turn. Advertisements which in 1910 carried only a simple illustration of the product would by 1920 contain a social scene only tenuously related to the product but designed to invoke a positive association from the reader. Very rapidly, most national consumer goods advertising became this compound sort, with product information overtaken by noncommodity artwork that extended itself to the impulses and anxieties of the consumer. From the existing pictorial media was extracted the limited number of images that would serve the advertising mission. Advertisers chose recognized visual symbols of what a higher-status household looked like, of what a successful husband looked like, of what contented children looked like (see Figure 2.2).

Historian Roland Marchand (1985) calls these advertising scenes "tableaux" and says that many of them, like biblical parables that used everyday events to illustrate religious veracities, constituted secular parables for the new faith of consumerism (see Chapter 7, this volume). These pictorial parables were used in so many campaigns for such a wide range of products that they amounted to the instructive iconography of the day. The more common ones that Marchand details are:

The Parable of the First Impression: "According to such tableaux, first impressions brought immediate success or failure" (p. 208). In the newly urbanized society, human contacts were indeed more frequent and fleeting; cosmetic details were not merely cosmetic. The right soap, the right business suit, the right silverware could make all the difference. Moral: Conquer the transitoriness of urban life with a few appearance-correcting purchases.

The Parable of the Democracy of Goods: The leisured rich, which all aspire to be, demonstrably enjoy the good life, as a succession of ads depict. The average consumer too can participate in the good life by buying this moderately priced product. Moral: America is the land of equal access to goods. Simply buy.

The Parable of the Captivated Child: One mother fed her child bitter vegetables, and he grew up to be sickly and resentful. Another

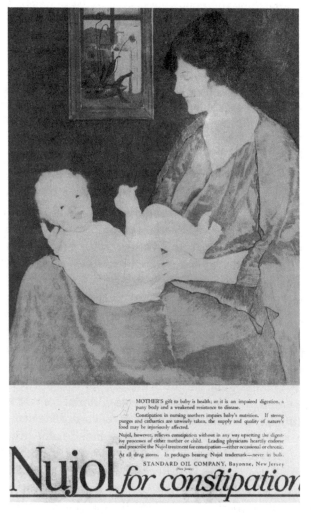

Figure 2.2. There are many ways to sell laxatives; this depiction might not be among the more likely of them. But in this early (1917) compound advertisement, the advertiser recognized that in order to establish contact and to sell this product to women, their strongly held feelings would first have to be invoked. There need be no logical tie between the pleasures of motherhood and the purposes of this patent medicine, between the appeal and the product. The acknowledgment of consumer sentiments has been a guiding principle of advertising communication from the 1910s onward.

mother fed her child nutritious, fun-to-eat food like canned soup or packaged cereal, and he grew up to be robust and loving. Moral: The successful parent pampers her child and serves brand-name foods.

The Parable of Civilization Redeemed: Individuals, turning their backs on the vigorous life of yore, have allowed themselves to grow puny and unhealthy. Smiles have faded, intestines have gone lazy, nervousness is on the rise. But help is no further away than your local store which stocks this cereal, that gum, this laxative. Moral: Civilization, which has brought the wrath of Nature down upon itself through overindulgence in ultrarefined foods and demeaning activities, can redeem itself through certain new products. Your purchases can save you.

Clearly, these "tableaux" addressed the pressures and maladies of urban existence and upheld certain commodities as the proper antidotes. A brand of yeast was not just yeast but a rectifier of civilization's ills, a particular soap brought romance to the lovelorn, suits from a certain manufacturer were social lubricants, and so on.

The new compound advertisements, so little in evidence before 1910 and so conventional after 1920, were, despite being targeted directly at the vulnerabilities of the urbanizing, middle-class population and so likely to find an attentive if uneasy reception, still not optimally absorbed unless they could be coated with the confectionary of the popular culture of the day. The reader who picked up a copy of a popular magazine for its editorial content would find it difficult to avoid, once within the covers of the magazine, page after page of display advertising for brand-name products. By 1919, such advertising paid for two-thirds of the cost of the periodical (Pope, 1983, p. 136). Readers of the April 13, 1920, issue of *Saturday Evening Post* may have thought they were only getting easily digestible fiction like "Hard-Boiled Mabel" by George Weston or "The Dark Moment" by Perceval Gibbon or "The Book of Susan" by Lee Wilson Dodd, but they were also getting full-page advertising for such products as Ivory Soap, Del Monte vegetables, Fisk Tires, and Hupmobiles ("If there's any one thing, more than another, that the average American family likes in a motor car, it is reliability"). Uneasy and socially aspiring readers could take guidance from depictions for Emery Shirts ("Men who know the art of dress are wearers of Emery Shirts") or Curtis Olives ("Unusual Things to Eat: The Usual Foods in Homes That Know"). The bundling of advertising and popular culture was to serve the requirements of the capitalists in both domains: For those media carrying advertising, it provided a second and steadying source of revenue; for advertisers, likable popular culture proved the best possible companion for their enticements.

Together these two symbol domains, of economic origins, began to override other, more traditional mythologies and belief systems. Their imagery, their messages, their modeling were more appropriate to the remarkable conditions of the times. Individuals had entered urban life throughout recorded history but never in such massive numbers and never to reach such a large proportion of any population. Novel social and economic conditions outstripped the explanatory and ordering capabilities of older belief systems, and into the void came the vigorous, boisterous, vital, touching, relevant content of popular culture and advertising, content which helped individuals in the management of their emotions and behaviors as they strove to negotiate their brave new worlds. Advertising imagery, writes Roland Marchand (1985), offered up "havens of security, intimacy, and simple pleasures [that] would compensate for, and make tolerable, the anonymity and competitive insecurities of urban complexity" (p. 337). Similarly, the images and tastes of popular culture, appearing in films, novels, and magazine stories, helped Americans assume appropriate gender roles and construct their own life stories for a new go-it-alone world.

The triumph of the production/consumption economy occurred with the first appearance in the 1920s of what Stuart Ewen (1976) acidly but accurately labeled "the commodity self" (p. 47), the personage created through the purchase and use of products. Ewen was thinking specifically about physical appearance, about how lips, eyes, nails, hair, breasts, and legs became defined through the commodities bought to alter them—"the ads intimated that anything natural about the consumer was worthless or deplorable" (pp. 47-48)—but clearly the concept of the commodity self extends to all of one's purchases, to pets, vehicles, houses, vacations, education, and on. Such items offer up potential meanings and so help signal identity to oneself as well as to others. Americans have come to inhabit a society where, to some extent, individuals are defined by the sum of their purchases, and moreover, where this is thought to be unremarkable. "The triumph of the commodity form is that we do not recognize its presence at all," complains Robert Goldman (1992, p. 36).

Communicating to the Consumer

Advertising and popular culture have taken on their modern forms as thoroughly economic entities: Advertising links producers directly to consumers, and popular culture is saleable and purchasable entertainment. Media systems have come into existence to realize the efficiencies of delivering such content from a few sources to a multitude of recipients. To endure, the advertising/popular culture/media complex has had to meet on a most rigorous schedule the test of economic viability. Each component has had to return financial profits continuously to those who capitalized it. It is the stringency of this economic dictum that has compelled the entire complex to devote itself unwaveringly to carrying out its mission of communicating deftly and fully with audience members. The conditions of successful reception have always had to be foremost in the minds of those laboring in the culture industries. The advertising and popular culture they produced had to be, in the large, the symbolic material that would be readily accepted in the minds of spectators. It had to speak to audience members in a most attractive way, articulating their impulses and satisfying their needs, or it would not be attended to and the economic dictum would be contravened, with undesirable consequences.

The distinguishing feature of modern audience members has been the extent to which each is constituted as an individual, one in some measure devoid of the social placements and prescriptions that have traditionally lent people their sense of definition and orientation. As a dramatic indicator of the elevation of the individual and the decline of age-old supports, American society has evolved to the point, unprecedented in all of human history, where one-quarter of all households consists of a person living alone (U.S. Bureau of the Census, 1994, p. 59).[7] The gradual unveiling of the individual has heightened private anxieties regarding self-identity and psychological maintenance; it is to these aching concerns that the symbol domains of advertising and popular culture have learned to speak because these are the concerns that audience members long to have treated.

As the two symbol fields have developed, they have come to address different but complementary aspects of the dilemma of the self. These services to the self are detailed in subsequent chapters, but for the moment it can be said briefly that the imagery in advertising works to establish and refurbish ideals for the appearance of the self, whereas the content of popular culture helps in the emotional maintenance of the self. Together the two symbols domains offer up applicable material for the exterior and the interior of every modern person; some of the material may occasionally be appropriated by an individual, as needed.

Attention to the symbol worlds of advertising and popular culture allows the modern individual to participate knowingly in the manifest world of consumer goods. Based on their exposure to, and discriminating appropriation from, the advertising/popular culture mix, people are then able to purchase the items that give off desired symbols. In Grant McCracken's (1986) analysis, potential meanings flow from the culture at large through advertising to consumer goods, and, if purchased, then on to the consumer. "The cultural meaning that has organized a world is made a visible, demonstrable part of that world through goods," he writes (p. 73).[8] Potential meanings actually flow in both directions: from the advertising/popular culture mix to consumers and from consumers back into the symbol fields. Thus when a few people began to buy proto-sport-utility vehicles, and these were taken to radiate an appropriate meaning blend of opulence and ruggedness, then advertising could parlay these symbols into a wider market. Just as individuals contribute symbols to advertising, so advertising adds meanings back to people's lives—at least occasionally and incrementally.

Notes

1. This understanding of the signifying role of goods, the one adopted in this book, contradicts the standard negative evaluation, which Grant McCracken (1988) rightly disputes:

> We "know" from popular opinion and social scientific study that our materialism is one of the things that is most wrong with our society, and one of the most significant causes of our modern difficulties. This familiar, *and entirely wrongheaded*, idea has helped keep us from seeing the cultural significance of consumption plainly. (p. xi, emphasis added)

2. Understanding that, over time, the responsibility for individual identity has shifted from external forces to internal ones leads to the conclusion that David Reisman (1950), in his famous book *The Lonely Crowd: The Study of the Changing American Character*, managed to turn history completely on its head. The historical transformation has not been from 19th-century inner-directed people to 20th-century other-directed ones, as Reisman asserted, but rather from 19th-century other-directeds (suspended in the cake of custom) to 20th-century inner-directeds (questing for self-identity). The fact that Reisman's thesis received such a wide hearing is a comment on the tentative frame of mind of those searching for self-identity rather than on the thesis's accuracy.

3. Although the prime compulsion for the advertising strategy was to smooth out distribution flows, manufacturers acknowledged other reasons, one of which was to even out consumer demand over the course of the year so as to keep expensive manufacturing plants in steady operation. Another was to increase demand not for an entire product category (advertisers then and now recognize that little can be done in this regard) but for a specific brand-name product, and thus steal market share from competitors.

4. One of the powerful advantages of trademarks is that, unlike patents and copyrights, they never expire.

5. For an extended period, advertisers not only sustained broadcasting systems, they also provided the popular culture content for those systems. Beginning in the early 1930s, advertising agencies produced the sponsored radio shows themselves and delivered them to the networks for transmission. This practice continued until the television quiz show scandals in the late 1950s when congressional scrutiny compelled the networks to reassert themselves and take control over programming. The transition from advertiser-controlled to network-controlled content occurred without a fight because it coincided with changing advertising strategies, as major advertisers were deciding not to lock themselves in to blocks of time but to scatter their commercials throughout the broadcast day.

6. However, the earlier business arrangement (of agencies working for the media) survives in the form of the advertising industry's standard compensation system, one of the oddest in the business world. Technically speaking, agencies are still paid by the media in the form of a 15% commission on purchased time or space. Logically, an agency should get paid according to employee hours billed, or sales results, but actually it is paid for something it can take no responsibility for—its client's media budget. The reasons for the survival of this atavistic arrangement are complex; it is only recently that there has been a decline in use of the commission system.

7. According to a *Social Trends* report issued in 1995 by Britain's Central Statistical Office, existence in Great Britain is also evolving in the direction toward solitariness. The percentage of people living alone has doubled since the 1970s, reaching 11%.

8. The concept of the culturally signifying properties of goods, central to this chapter, is often traced to the thought of French anthropologist Claude Lévi-Strauss (1963), who in trying to explain the nature of totemism, wrote,

> The animals in totemism cease to be solely or principally creatures which are feared, admired, or envied: their perceptible reality permits the embodiment of ideas and relations conceived by speculative thought on the basis of empirical observations. We can understand, too, that natural species are chosen [as totems] not because they are "good to eat" but because they are "good to think." (p. 89)

That is, recognizable animal types are used by primitive people to signify invisible but real social categories because the animal types, being visible, help in conceptualizing the social categories. (Primitive people are certainly not alone in this. Many modern athletic teams and most educational institutions are designated by an animal. We bring our symbol inheritance forward with us.) It is no great leap from the symbolizing properties of animals to the symbolizing potentialities of any physical entity. Thus, people can employ any object to make manifest and encapsulate abstract notions that may be overly elusive or diffuse otherwise. Objects, possessions, are "good to think [with]." To this powerful observation, John Fiske (1989a), an explorer of modern popular culture, adds that objects are also "goods to speak with" (p. 31).

3

Flagrant Criticisms

Mediated popular culture and advertising suffer similarly sorry fates at the hands of culture critics, who often seem disposed to drain the lifeblood from both symbol domains. When the two look-alikes might well be glorified as vital and central image flows, lacing the whole of public culture together, such celebration is infrequent and tempered. Contempt toward advertising and popular culture, issuing for the most part from the lofty ground of the Academy (that is, higher education and allied critical circles), has gone on so long and so constantly that it would seem to have obliterated other perspectives. The person who would contemplate advertising and popular culture with regard is working against strongly prevailing opinions. Bearing in mind that the elimination of the twin mainstays of the modern symbol system—should such a thing be possible—would cause contemporary media to dissolve and could jeopardize the modern way of life in its entirety, then the question of why they are subjected to such unremitting attack must be raised.

Two observations should be made at the outset of a study of the critique of advertising and popular culture. The first is to call attention to the vehemence of the attack—that is, to set content aside for a moment and to listen to the scornful tone of the critique. When one critic remarked that popular culture was a "spreading ooze" (Macdonald, 1957, p. 73) and another chastised advertising as "depth manipulation" (Packard, 1957, chap. 1), then clearly dispassionate discussion had been left in the lurch. More recently, when a prominent professor and author refers to popular music as "this gutter phenomenon" (Bloom, 1987, p. 79) and advertising is singled out for "its 'dissolving' influence on culture" (Goldman, 1992, p. 8), then there is little room left for productive debate. The battle against advertising and popular culture is to be one with no holds barred. Exactly why does this high level of enmity exist? What is there about popular culture and advertising that makes some members of the Academy comport themselves in such an antagonistic fashion?

The second observation is this: The voices of the culture critics are not voices in the wilderness. Their points of view can command large audiences; at times, their books top best-seller lists. Why is it that the public, dwelling to all appearances comfortably with these image domains, still is receptive to the slashing critique against advertising and popular culture?

This chapter begins with a survey of representative critics of popular culture. Historically, this critique begins on the right, then loses momentum to the left, before the recent appearance, at least in the Academy if not in the world at large, of a centrist position. Surveyed next is the critique of advertising, one where no centrist position has as yet firmed up. Following these two brief surveys, the chapter turns to the conclusions that result.

The Critique of Popular Culture

Bitter criticism of popular culture is hardly a phenomenon limited to the 20th century. As long as there have been social classes, the higher have demeaned the diversionary tastes of the lower. This disparaging diatribe evinces the exercise of social power, as the ruling classes work to contain the rumbling energies of the underclasses and to maintain the status quo. In Western culture, this snobbery can be traced at least as far back as the ancient Greeks. The philosopher Heraclitus wrote about the general populace,

"For what mind or sense have they? They follow the bards and use the multitude as their teacher, not realizing that there are many bad but few good. For the best choose one thing above all others, immortal glory among mortals, while the many are glutted like beasts" (quoted in Brantlinger, 1983, p. 54). As with the Greeks, so with their emulators, the Romans: The satirist Juvenal condemned the plebians for deserting their civic responsibilities once they had been placated by bread and circuses. The term "bread and circuses," as Patrick Brantlinger (1983) explains, has become a cliché misleadingly employed by culture critics to indicate popular appeasement lulling a citizenry into compliance and supposedly signaling a civilizational decline.

The critique of plebian culture by patricians proceeded strongly in 18th-century England as the British economy began to expand and a middle class prospered. The appearance of popular novels, and their large sales in a growing market, convulsed the aesthetic community (Lowenthal & Fiske, 1957). In the 19th century, the British elite's contempt for popular culture found its strongest voice in the work of poet and critic Matthew Arnold, in particular his *Culture and Anarchy* (Arnold, 1869/1971). The son of the headmaster of Rugby, Arnold had prepared at the exclusive boys' boarding school for his university education at Oxford. Following a term of service as a nobleman's private secretary, Arnold was appointed England's Inspector of Schools in 1851, a position he held for 35 years. After 1857, he also occupied the honorary post of Professor of Poetry at Oxford.

The reader of *Culture and Anarchy* soon discovers what Arnold meant by the "anarchy" he so strongly opposed: It was the loss of authority and the rise of social fragmentation. People, he wrote,

all over the country, are beginning to assert and put in practice, an Englishman's right to do what he likes: his right to march where he likes, meet where he likes, enter where he likes, hoot as he likes, threaten as he likes, smash as he likes. All this, I say, tends to anarchy. (p. 62)

The growing and anarchic power of the underclasses Arnold referred to disdainfully as the "Americanization" of Britain. The answer to "anarchy" lay in what he believed Americans lacked; "a true conception of culture . . . is just what Americans fail in" (p. 17).

But what exactly was "culture" to Arnold? Here matters grow vague. It surely did not mean the description of a particular way of life, as 19th-century German philosophers and early anthropologists were using the term. "Culture," Arnold said early in his book, is

> a pursuit of our total perfection by means of getting to know, on all the matters which most concern us, the best which has been thought and said in the world; and through this knowledge, turning a stream of fresh and free thought upon our stock notions and habits. (p. 5)

Arnold was reluctant to be more specific than this, although it is clear that he esteemed biblical teachings as well as Greek and Roman thought, and at one point added that "culture is of like spirit with poetry, follows one law with poetry" (p. 42). Culture, he said, was to be identified with "sweetness and light," the title of his first chapter. But exactly how one specified "the best which has been thought and said in the world," this "sweetness and light," was left to the discretion of the reader. It would be hard to believe, though, that in Arnold's eyes this content would diverge much from the canon he had studied at Rugby and Oxford.[1]

The menacing unruliness of the underclasses as they sought the advantages of democracy and leisure vexed Arnold. That the underclasses might have a contrasting culture of their own, one as forthright and satisfying as the culture that Arnold sponsored, is a thought that would never have occurred to him; he had, after all, appropriated the word "culture" for his own cause, leaving nothing to label an oppositional force. But as the 20th century began, it became more undeniable that there existed a popular culture in contrast to Arnold's sort of culture (which now had to be retitled "high" culture to distinguish it from the other). The tantalizing draw of motion pictures and the widespread mania for them made it impossible to avoid the vitality of the common culture. Thus the cultural debate, which in Arnold's terms meant noble thoughts as up against the ignoble mob, came to be rephrased in all-cultural terms (although, of course, with strong political implications) as high culture versus popular culture.

Writing near the mid-century mark, poet T. S. Eliot extolled at length the virtues of high culture. In his *Notes Towards the Definition of Culture*, Eliot (1949) took a stand against the "nightmare" of "cultural uniformity." In his scheme of things, "culture and egalitarianism" are necessarily and forever in conflict (p. 14). And what exactly is culture? Like Arnold, Eliot was elusive about this, being at times obscure and at other times nimble, but at one point he ventured, "Culture may even be described simply as that which makes life worth living" (p. 26). It was present in all classes of the "healthily stratified" society that Eliot endorsed, but the varieties were not of equal worth: "This higher level of culture must be thought of both as valuable in itself, and as enriching the lower levels" (p. 36). Yet Eliot deplored any attempt to bring the "higher level of culture" to the general public through education, stating that "whether education can foster and improve culture or not, it can surely adulterate and degrade it. For there is no doubt that in our headlong rush to educate everyone, we are lowering our standards" (p. 111).

Meanwhile, at the other extreme of the ideological spectrum, the Marxist left was articulating its own version of the noxious effects of popular culture. In particular, the so-called Frankfurt School— composed of such thinkers as Theodor Adorno, Max Horkheimer, Leo Lowenthal, and Herbert Marcuse—railed against the products of the "culture industries." These members of Germany's Frankfurt Institute of Social Research had confronted the rise of Nazi fascism in the 1930s and were forced to flee to the United States for the war years. This experience left them fearful of a totalitarianism they believed was incipient in capitalist systems. While in the United States, they honed their analysis of the mass media and the ways that popular culture content snared and misled the proletariat.

The fullest expression of this critique appears in a Horkheimer and Adorno (1944/1972) chapter entitled "The Culture Industry: Enlightenment as Mass Deception." "Film, radio and magazines make up a system which is uniform as a whole and in every part" (p. 120), they argued in an attempt to promote an analogy between repetitious industrial production and cultural production. For them, "all mass culture is identical" (p. 123).[2] The result of such standardized production was to create mindless uniformity among people: "[The culture] industry robs the individual of his function. Its prime service to the customer is to do his schematizing for him" (p. 124). Only avant-garde art, which in their eyes countered mass production, held any true benefit for humanity.

Enlarging on this analysis, Herbert Marcuse (1964) in *The One-Dimensional Man* proposed that "the progress of technological rationality is liquidating the oppositional and transcending elements in the 'higher culture' " (p. 56). The vigor that "higher culture" had once displayed, as Marcuse saw it, had been eradicated by mass communication not so much because popular culture has displaced the "higher culture" of literature and art but because it has simply absorbed it: "This liquidation of *two-dimensional* culture takes place not through the denial and rejection of the 'cultural values,' but through their wholesale incorporation into the established order, through their reproduction and display on a massive scale" (p. 57). In Marcuse's scheme of things, not even the avant-garde could oppose the totalizing and impoverishing effect of popular culture.[3]

In a frequently anthologized article, critic Dwight Macdonald forged a heady synthesis of the elitist and the Marxist positions regarding popular culture. Widespread interest in the piece led Macdonald to rewrite it several times between the 1940s and the 1960s. In the 1957 version, he echoed the elite culture critics in defining popular culture (which he called variously "Mass Culture" and "kitsch") as "a parasite, a cancerous growth on High Culture" (p. 59). The bad kitsch overcame good art because "it is more easily understood and enjoyed" (p. 61). The effect of the consumption of kitsch ("the spreading ooze") from radio, movies, comic books, and television was to create a "homogenized" society where all values are destroyed, as "value judgments imply discrimination" (p. 62).[4] It was not only social strata that were melted down; it was also the division between adults and children, resulting in the infantile regression of the former and the overstimulation of the latter (p. 66). Turning then to the Marxist school, Macdonald approvingly restated their main idea: "Since Mass Culture is not an art form but a manufactured commodity, it tends always downward, toward cheapness—and so standardization—of production" (p. 72). The critic foresaw the future of high culture as bleak and the future of mass culture as bleaker still.

Macdonald's grim fusion of the conservative and the radical attacks on popular culture, however, stands in contrast to another school of thought that has been on the rise since the 1960s. With its origins also in Marxist theory, British cultural studies shared none of the Frankfurt School scholars' assumptions regarding an acquiescent audience. The impetus behind the cultural studies tradition, whose first institutional home was the Center for Contemporary Cultural Studies at Britain's University of Birmingham, was the desire to affirm the audience's power of interpretation within the overall process of mass communication (Storey, 1993, p. 44). Audience members were not simply the dupes of the culture industries, surrendering sheepishly to capitalistic cant; rather, they were active in the process of communication, sometimes tendering meanings that were exactly the reverse of what the senders had intended. The Birmingham Center focused first on working-class culture, their expanded to include the study of feminist culture, then took the analysis further still. Popular culture, as they conceived it, did not have any one meaning and so as an instrument of oppression was a poor one. Writing within this tradition, John Fiske (1989a) affirmed that "Popular culture is made from within and below, not imposed from without or above as mass cultural theorists would have it" (p. 2).

When cultural studies diffused to the United States, it found a welcome among a new generation of intellectuals, many of whom had been active in the counterculture movements of the 1960s and who nurtured an affinity for the oppressed within American society. Concerns about class, still central to British cultural studies, were subordinated here, as attention turned to lifestyles, particularly of marginalized groups as women, blacks, and homosexuals. The disciplinary net was spread wider and wider to incorporate approaches from a variety of established fields, including French and American ethnography, history, sociology, literary analysis, and film studies. This inclusiveness and the intellectual cross-pollination it engendered led Stanley Aronowitz (1993) to write, with only slight hyperbole, "At its best, cultural studies is not interdisciplinary, it is antidisciplinary" (p. 8).[5]

More and more American scholars have been adopting cultural studies approaches and employing them to reexamine popular culture. Intellectual interest in the field is both the cause and the effect of revised attitudes toward the study of popular culture; Chandra Mukerji and Michael Schudson (1991) report, "The legitimation of contemporary popular culture as a subject for study in universities and a subject of inquiry for serious scholars, although far from complete today, has grown enormously in a generation" (p. 3). As the act of scrutinizing popular culture has become more of a serious intellectual endeavor, the object of this scrutiny has become more favorably evaluated.[6] Within the Academy, the condemnation of popular culture from the left and the right is increasingly seen as outmoded and inappropriate (Featherstone, 1991).

However, while an endorsing, spectator-centered position regarding popular culture has been forming in the academic world, within the reading public the age-old deprecation of popular culture continues to hold sway, as the sales of books by culture critics attest. The more the Academy takes the newly inclusive and appreciative view, as if in a balancing act the more the public seems to take solace in the familiar, condemnatory outlook. Neil Postman's (1985) best-selling *Amusing Ourselves to Death: Public Discourse in the Age of Show Business* tapped into this resilient conservative strain in American thinking on popular culture. Postman takes on the entire medium of television, saying that it has become so dominant that "it has made entertainment itself the natural format for the representation of all experience" (p. 87). The once grand discourses of news, religion, politics, and education have all been rendered into amusements, full of "incoherence and triviality" (p. 80). Like Matthew Arnold, Postman looks wistfully back at an imagined golden age: "In the eighteenth and nineteenth centuries, print put forward a definition of intelligence that gave priority to the objective, rational use of the mind and at the same time encouraged forms of public discourse with serious, logically ordered content" (p. 51).

The revival of such reactionary sentiments may account for the unexpectedly outsized readership of two conservative critiques of American education: E. D. Hirsch, Jr.'s (1987) *Cultural Literary: What Every American Needs to Know* and Alan Bloom's (1987) *The Closing of the American Mind*. Bloom finds detestable the core popular culture genre for the young—rock music. "Free sexual expression, anarchism, mining of the irrational unconscious and giving it free rein" (p. 78) are some of the excesses he sees in rock and roll, as he updates the vocabulary of Matthew Arnold. "Rock music," complains Bloom, "encourages passions and provides models that have no relation to any life the young people who go to universities can possibly lead, or the kinds of admiration encouraged by liberal studies" (p. 80). Hirsch (1987) does not mount a direct attack on popular culture as such but does insist on the imposition of a single "national cultural literacy" curriculum, thereby defining culture in the monolithic and bookish terms that cultural studies scholars would likely reject.

The Critique of Advertising

Culture critics' condemnation of advertising has, for them, proved to be a headlong, almost joyous affair, one that has suffered little reproach. A blatantly conspicuous target, advertising remains for the most part completely undefended. Taking stock of the assault on advertising, William Leiss et al. (1990) observed, "It is difficult to think of another contemporary institution that has come under such sustained attack from so many different directions" (p. 17). It is a broad front that advances on advertising, one that cannot be so readily sorted into a right flank and a left flank as can the assault on popular culture. The Marxist critique, stressing the stupefying effects of mass advertising and the retardation of social reform, is a discernible and unified censure, but the non-Marxist critique exhibits little unanimity and stretches over a wide range of accusations. The various non-Marxist criticisms dominated the topic area until 1975, when a surprisingly vigorous Marxist critique emerged, one that has continued to occupy the intellectual foreground.

Surveying the large non-Marxist literature from "all North American authors known to have written on the cultural character of advertising," [7] Richard Pollay (1986) summarized, "What may be shocking . . . is the veritable absence of perceived positive influence" (p. 19). Every writer who has examined the social effects of advertising, Pollay claims, has found those effects to be negative. Even if this assertion turns out to be not precisely true, still the broad range of these authors' accusations is in itself a shock. One of the more frequently cited criticisms is drawn from *The Affluent Society*, a book by Harvard University economist John Kenneth Galbraith (1958/1971). Critiquing the modern economy rather than just advertising was Galbraith's main intent; in fact, the topic of advertising occupies just four pages of his book. But because of the succinctness of his indictment of advertising and the popularity of his book, Galbraith's charge was widely circulated. In his view, advertising's "central function is to create desires—to bring into being wants that previously did not existed" (p. 149). Many readers interpreted his critique of advertising in purely personal terms and wondered if advertising was indeed creating unnecessary "wants" within them.

That the readers of the time would doubt their own strength of character and feel that imperious forces were acting wrongly against them is hardly surprising. Americans had been battered in the 1930s by a economic depression unprecedented in its depth and duration and, on the heels of that, by World War II, a global cataclysm of unmitigated savagery. The conclusion of the war brought not relief but a prolonged Cold War where the unspeakable horrors of atomic destruction hovered in the thoughts of all and wore on the nerves of many. For decades, Americans had been tumbled about by monstrous forces. Thus, when psychoanalyst Erich Fromm (1941) wrote in his *Escape From Freedom* (which went through 24 printings before 1964) that advertising appeals were "essentially irrational; they have nothing to do with the qualities of the merchandise, and they smother and kill the critical capacities of the customer like an opiate or outright hypnosis" (p. 128), readers were quite willing to entertain the proposition that advertising could undo them. By the time Vance Packard's *The Hidden Persuaders* was published in 1957 there was a large and ready audience for his full-scale account of advertising's motivational research and its employment in nonrational persuasion. Packard closed his book proclaiming. "The most serious offense many of the depth manipulators commit, it seems to me, is that they try to invade the privacy of our minds" (p. 266), an invasion that reproduced at the most private level society's real-world dread of a Russian offensive.

In *Subliminal Seduction,* Wilson Bryant Key (1972) took the invasion motif one step further, suggesting that the intrusion was accomplished not by what one could see in advertising but rather by surreptitious things one could not see at all; the enemy, in effect, was landing all the time under cover of darkness. In his book, which is still in print, Key insisted that advertisers insinuate their message at the subconscious level through the use of embedded words, images, or sounds that are below the consumer's level of conscious awareness.[8]

Creating unnecessary wants, sponsoring irrationality, subverting minds—it is quite a bill of particulars that the non-Marxist critique of advertising presents. Richard Pollay (1986) detailed other charges found in less widely read but equally adverse critical works: that advertising promotes materialism, cynicism, debased language, perpetual dissatisfaction, conformity, envy, anxiety, disrespect for tradition and authority, and sexual preoccupation (p. 23). Some of these complaints are echoed in the words of Christopher Lasch (1979):

> In a simpler time, advertising merely called attention to the product and extolled its advantages. Now it manufactures a product of its own: the consumer, perpetually unsatisfied, restless, anxious, and bored. Advertising serves not so much to advertise products as to promote consumption as a way of life. It "educates" the masses into an unappeasable appetite not only for goods but for new experiences and personal fulfillment. It upholds consumption as the answer to the age-old discontents of loneliness, sickness, weariness, lack of

sexual satisfaction; at the same time it creates new forms of discontent peculiar to the modern age. It plays seductively on the malaise of industrial civilization. Is your job boring and meaningless? Does it leave you with feelings of futility and fatigue? Is your life empty? Consumption promises to fill the aching void; hence the attempt to surround commodities with an aura of romance; with allusions to exotic places and vivid experiences; and with images of females' breasts from which all blessings flow. (pp. 72-73)

If the general critique of advertising has momentarily exhausted itself, perhaps due to the overreaching breadth of its attack, the more concerted Marxist critique has been finding ever more vigorous voices (although nowhere near the audience of the earlier campaign). Stuart Ewen (1976), in his *Captains of Consciousness: Advertising and the Social Roots of the Consumer Culture,* subjected the early 20th-century rise of advertising and the development of a consumer economy to a thorough and compact Marxist analysis, one that was to undergird subsequent Marxist treatments. Referring to the 1920s, Ewen wrote, "Advertising raised the banner of consumable social democracy in a world where monumental corporate development was eclipsing and redefining much of the space in which critical alternatives might be effectively developed" (p. 190). The "critical alternative" he had in mind, of course, was a Marxist or socialist economy; it was being held off by big capitalism wielding the foil of advertising. Ewen's ending sentence warned that "social change cannot come about in a context where objects are invested with human subjective capacities" (p. 220). (Most anthropologists would retort that people have always invested objects with subjective meanings, that this is an essential human activity.)

Ewen's historical Marxist analysis was soon complemented by an ahistorical one, Judith Williamson's (1978) difficult and provocative *Decoding Advertisements.* "Advertisements," she began, "must take into account not only the inherent qualities and attributes of the products they are trying to sell, but also the way in which they can make the properties *mean something to us*" (p. 12). Williamson then set herself the difficult task of showing how advertisements appropriate symbols. In analyzing example after example, she established decipherment heuristics useful for future investigators of advertising. Her own mission, however, was to interpret the decodings as support for Marxist ideology: "Advertisements obscure and avoid the real issues of society, those relating to work: to jobs and wages and who works for whom. They create systems of social differentiation which are a veneer on the basic class structure of our society" (p. 47).

Ewen and Williamson's pioneering forays have been extended in more recent work continuing the Marxist critique: Sut Jhally's (1990) *The Codes of Advertising* and Robert Goldman's (1992) *Reading Ads Socially.* Jhally (1990) elaborates on one of Karl Marx's concepts, the fetishism of commodities (which affirms that people in capitalistic societies worship commodities just as tribal cultures worship their fetishes):

> The fetishism of commodities consists in the first place of emptying them of meaning, of hiding the real social relations objectified in them through human labour, to make it possible for the imaginary/ symbolic social relations to be injected into the construction of meaning at a secondary level. Production empties. Advertising fills. The real is hidden by the imaginary. (p. 51)

Jhally, more aware of the anthropological literature than Ewen had been, concedes that people have always invested objects with symbolic properties. The problem nowadays, as he sees it, is that a few capitalists, through their advertising activities, have come to control the symbol codes (p. 12).

Robert Goldman (1992) interprets advertising with respect to another of Marx's ideas, the difference between the "use value" of a commodity (its inherent worth, usually phrased in terms of the labor that went into its manufacture) and its "exchange value" (the excess money it will bring in the marketplace): "Advertising amplifies and reinforces the exchange value of existing goods and services" (p. 15). By being unreflecting receivers of advertising, consumers are implicated in the spread of the false ideology of capitalism and its bogus "exchange values" (p. 2). The fundamentally social nature of people is contorted by advertising: "Sociability is pictured not as a natural outgrowth of the individual's capabilities but as an outgrowth of access to commodities. Social skills become purchasing skills" (p. 24). Advertising's corrosive impact may ultimately be not so much upon individuals as upon the entirety of culture, Goldman (1992) claims: "Whether or not advertising screws us up as individual personalities, its 'dissolving' influence on culture may be advertising's most significant and haunting historical consequence" (p. 8).

In retrospect, it is surprising on how many points the non-Marxist and the Marxist critiques of advertising concur: that advertising manipulates consumers and instills false values, that it extols a materialistic and consumerist ethic, that it deals in emotions and irrationality, that it leads people to buy unnecessary or overvalued items. Behind both critiques there lie similar and remarkable assumptions about the constitutions of the offender and the offended. The offender, conceived of as big businesses or capitalism, is looming, omnipotent, able to exert its will under any and all circumstances. The offended, the misled public, is pliant, supplicating, malleable. Never articulated within the critique of advertising, these underlying conceptions await interrogation. Such interrogation could lead to the missing centrist position, a position devoid of the acute negativity of both the Marxist and non-Marxist versions.

There is some precedence for such a moderate position, despite Richard Pollay's (1986) claim, cited earlier, that the literature on advertising is notable for "the veritable absence of perceived positive influence" (p. 19). Although Pollay lists media visionary Marshall McLuhan among the critics of advertising, McLuhan's (1964) attitude was actually much more complex and ambiguous— and productive. He was capable of the standard critique—"Ads push the principle of noise all the way to the plateau of persuasion" (p. 227)—but he was also capable of seeing advertising as a significant activity—"The historians and archeologists will one day discover that the ads of our times are the richest and most faithful daily reflections that any society ever made of its entire range of activities" (p. 232). Erving Goffman (1976), in his brilliant

analysis of gender representation in advertising, taught a generation of liberal arts scholars to take advertising seriously. Michael
Schudson's (1984) important *Advertising: The Uneasy Persuasion*
was a remarkably full and evenhanded treatment of advertising,
situating it in historical, marketing, anthropological, and artistic
contexts. There are also excellent scholarly histories of advertising
that treat their subject without contempt or condescension.[9] Thus,
a contemplative, unremonstrative literature on the topic exists
that can serve as the platform for the valorization of this symbol
domain. However, for this to transpire, analytical emphasis must
shift from the sending to the receiving end of the communications
channel, from what advertisers care to insert to what consumers
choose to extract.

Analyzing the Critiques

If advertising and popular culture are the twin pillars of
public culture in modern times, why are they subjected to an un-
ending barrage of critical invective? Why are they so embattled?
It is almost heretical to raise this question, so accepted, or at least
tolerated, has the critique become. But if one acknowledges the
towering significance of the two symbol domains and sees the
possibility that the critique is inappropriate, then the task becomes
that of explaining why the critique exists at all.

To do so, one must first return to the tonality of the critique, to
its chastising, bitter register. Figuratively, a stick is being shaken
at advertising and at popular culture; the act suggests its motiva-
tion. The critical voice rises and the lances come out because a
challenge has been perceived. In the final analysis, the threat is
that of social change, of broad transitions under way that elicit
disapproval and a torrent of wordy reprove. The critique swells
then to meet the challenge of the complex of social transformations
occasioned by the rise of what is unique to modern times—the
continuing expansion of the production/consumption economy,
and, within it, of the activities of consumers.

Michael Schudson (1984), referring to advertising, although he could have been speaking of popular culture as well, summarized, "Whatever form the criticism takes, it sees the emergence of a consumer culture as a devolution of manners, morals, and even manhood" (p. 6). The gradual unfolding of a democratized culture, with sufficient leisure for the enjoyment of consumption and popular culture by the many, is feared and resisted. The decline of subordination as a predominant principle of social order, a principle that once legitimated the superordination of the strata of intellectuals and culture critics (whom Pierre Bourdieu [1984] coyly referred to as "the dominated fractions of the dominant class" [p. 176]), is sensed by the critical community to invite the disorder that Matthew Arnold warned about over a century ago. Simmering apprehension is soon converted into a retaliatory condescension. The insecurity that the subculture of social critics experiences is then projected onto the public, and the public is constituted as a tremulous and vulnerable body. To complete the picture and to supply a causative agent for the public's supposedly abject condition, the media carrying the public's popular culture and advertising are rendered as monolithic, invasive forces. The whole mischaracterization is promulgated through the expository skills in which the culture critics have schooled themselves and by means of their privileged and traditional access to the channels of written communication.

While this explanation, premised upon the critical community's sense of eroding authority, may fit the non-Marxist critics, it is uncanny how frequently it seems to apply to Marxist criticism as well. The right's condescension toward the audience can also emanate from the left (Storey, 1993, p. 181). Marxists are supposed to be viewing history from the bottom up, so to speak, with the interests of the underclasses in mind, yet when the public is represented as being stupefied minions of the capitalist class, as they are in the writings of the Frankfurt School, it is hard to believe that this characterization represents a sophisticated understanding of working-class culture or is not elitism in a poor disguise.

It is worth noting that the critique of advertising and popular culture does not extend to older instances of the two, as they recede into the past, but only to instances that exist right now. Why aren't advertisements from the 1910s for Packard cars or Ivory Soap or Coca-Cola (see Figure 3.1) seen as degrading as current ads? Why aren't Tom Swift novels from the 1890s or silent films or 1920s jazz recordings derided like television programming? Older instances have not only become harmless, they have become valuable; they are "collectibles," for which large markets exist. Displayed, they mark their owners as sophisticates, not dupes. This suggests there is nothing intrinsic to the content of advertising and popular culture that makes them contemptible, even though the critique often focuses on content.

Current advertising and popular culture are treated contemptuously not because of what they contain but because of their metamessage about the roiling growth of consumer, middle-class culture. It is the threat that the two symbol domains represent, not their denigrated content, that is what truly instigates cultural criticism. Present instances of advertising and popular culture are seen as the shock troops in the cultural battle, deploying right now, and are treated as such by those who feel under attack.

Yet if culture critics are at odds with the long-term groundswell of social change and the rearrangements and even turbulence that it brings, then why do they not attack that straightforwardly? Why not deal directly with the rise of the production/consumption economy and its egalitarian propensities rather than with its offshoots of advertising and popular culture? Marx centered his attack on capitalism's mode of production and the exploitation of labor—why not continue that approach? Or why not mount an offensive against some other central component of the modern economy, say, the banking system, or that crucial but concealed sector, the distribution system? One reason why Marx concentrated on what he did was that mediated advertising and popular were scarcely emergent in his day and so occupied little of his purview. Had they been more obvious, he would surely have directed more of his attention to them, for they are undeniably the chief *symbol* systems of the capitalistic economy he deplored. The intrusiveness of modern advertising and popular culture might have caused Marx to waiver in his commitment to a purely materialistic analysis.

Figure 3.1. Even the most fervid critic of advertising is unlikely to take issue with an early ad. Older advertisements are treated fondly because they pose no threat. No matter what opponents assert, at bottom it is not the content of advertising which prompts disapproval; it is the immediate challenge of the larger forces which advertising represents.

In any case, subsequent critics have fixed on these two symbol systems in recognition of their centrality to the operations of the production/consumption economy. As public symbol systems, advertising and popular culture have to be highly conspicuous or they would be useless; being conspicuous, they present themselves as inviting quarry to detractors of the economic context that they represent. Because symbol systems are the lifeblood of any societal entity, culture critics are going for a jugular vein when they choose to fix on advertising and popular culture. It is proof of the vital importance of these two domains that for over a century they should be the object of incessant vitriol. Would battalions of critics spend so much time on these matters if they were inconsequential?

As if a goading intuition of a dwindling status were not enough, there is another concern, more subtle but perhaps in the long run more profound, that also propels culture critics. The modality of their critique is the written word; they have trained themselves in the production of erudite text and, through scholarly publishers, control established avenues of dissemination. But print is no longer in command nor the sole means of public communication. The modalities of the advertising and popular culture to which they set themselves in opposition are largely nontextual and manifold. The graphic, video, and sound modalities of the booming domains of advertising and popular culture are usually not within the capacities of cultural critics nor conducive to the sort of discourse they wish to continue using. It is no wonder that culture critics, committed to modes of communication skills that no longer reign supreme, feel uneasy, even resentful. They risk not only losing the culture battle but being stripped of their communication weaponry as well.

Up to this point in the discussion, the analysis of the critique of advertising and popular culture has been conducted in terms of social conflict and of elite resistance to the expansion of middle-class culture. Another interpretation, similar in that it is organized along lines of social power but different in its depiction of the contestants, has emerged from feminist scholars. Viewed in this penetrating light, the issues have now become those of gender rather than class.[10] In his essay "Mass Culture as Woman," Andreas

Huyssen (1986) states, "It is indeed striking to observe how the political, psychological, and aesthetic discourse around the turn of the century consistently and obsessively genders mass culture and the masses as feminine, while high culture, whether traditional or modern, clearly remains the privileged realm of male activities" (p. 191). The dichotomy of an inferior and feminine mass culture in contrast to a superior and masculine high culture continued in 20th-century critical writing until quite recently, Huyssen states (p. 205). However, whenever popular culture is characterized as superficial, emotional, seductive, or easy, one is left to wonder if the gendering and intended degradation has indeed expired as Huyssen suggests.

Feminist scholar Tania Modleski (1986) is among those who see no cessation in the rendering of mass culture as feminine and insufficient. She announces "I want to show how our ways of thinking and feeling about mass culture are so intricately bound up with notions of the feminine that the need for a feminist critique becomes obvious at every level of the debate" (p. 38). Modleski brackets and interrogates the ways that mass culture and the consumption of mass culture, and by implication all consumption, are conceived of as feminine and passive and regressive. While her approach is stimulating, her analysis is modest, leaving her readers to carry forward her line of thinking as they will. Might it extend beyond popular culture to advertising, in that advertising messages are conventionally held by critics to be muscular and manipulative, whereas the absorption of advertising is seen as an act of submission and characteristically done by the female consumer? On these grounds alone, the standard understanding among culture critics of the communication between advertisement and consumer is in need of reanalysis and revision.

Besides class and gender issues, another strand needs to be teased out of the body of antipopular culture and advertising commentary. Just as there is a sociology to the denigration of this mediated content, so too there is a psychology. The two symbol domains frequently depict activities that are exuberant, excessive, indulgent—in a word, pleasurable. Invitations to pleasure are seen by some critics as chancy invitations to licentiousness and hedonism, summons to things properly constrained in the lower reaches of the mind, whose display would challenge propriety and rationality (see frontispiece ad). Such cautions are often labeled latent Puritanism, but doing so only displaces them pointlessly from the moment and does little to help in comprehending their modern strengths or causes. They continue to comprise a formidable critical challenge to the content of advertising and popular culture because they give voice to continuing concerns regarding the exercise of emotions. For many critics, the conscious mind lives uneasily with the subconscious one. As a counterbalance, some working in the field of cultural studies have pledged themselves to appreciating the fuller range of human activity: Cultural studies, writes Lawrence Grossberg (1992), "recognizes not only the existence of different rationalities but the importance of the irrational and arational in human life" (p. 25).

Returning to a question raised at the outset, why do large numbers of people—so large that the critique is the most generally adopted posture regarding advertising and popular culture—find the critique worthy of consideration? The reasons for the consumption of the critique may parallel, naturally enough, its production. Over the past two centuries, the development of the modern economy and the accompanying cultural ambiance has entailed rapid social change, sometimes dizzyingly rapid. The institutions and hierarchies that ensured social order in the past have given way to more amorphous structures, ones less committed to the formal exclusion of ethnic groups, women, the handicapped, homosexuals, the unmarried. Similarly, personal behaviors and emotions once proscribed (toughness in females, tenderness in males) are now less so. These transitions cannot occur without there being a degree of apprehension—those comfortable with or resigned to the old order must wonder what is being lost in return for what is being gained. It is within this climate of persistent uneasiness regarding the social and psychological changes accompanying the growth of consumer society that the critique of advertising and popular culture finds its willing reception. The critique favors the venerable print tradition over electronic communication and favors cultural unity over cultural plurality. For many people, there is great consolation to be found in nestling into spun prose invocations of a fabricated, placid past.

Taking a broad view, it is conceivable that even if the critique of advertising and popular culture is misguided it is still socially functional. On all issues of social importance it is prudent that questioning and reconsideration go on and that debate be engendered. No one would want to argue that everything that transpires is to the greater good. Despite the pleasure that it brings, the practice of smoking tobacco kills people; the extent of this could not have been appreciated if dissenting opinions had not been broached and inserted into public discourse. Similarly, the social changes that spawned mediated advertising and popular culture are indisputably extensive and demand contemplation and interpretation.

When all is said and done, the critique of advertising and popular culture, in essence a conservative, reactionary one, may offer benefits. Even the Marxist version of the critique, which putatively looks forward, often displays an uneasiness with current alterations and a covert appreciation for the apparent stabilities of the past. Harkening backward is like tossing out a sea anchor behind a craft in rough waters; it can help steady the course as, like it or not, the vessel of culture moves forward in time.

In what may be the ultimate comment on the critique, its impact on the production and consumption of advertising messages and popular culture content has been slight. The critique is only minimally reflected in social policy: The Federal Communication Commission (FCC) enters gingerly into periods when it threatens to use its broadcast licensing powers to "improve" television, and the Federal Trade Commission (FTC) has been established as the arbitrator of truth in advertising (a matter of limited importance to most advertisers, who infrequently affirm anything that can be contested). Industry self-regulation has been the chief device in the United States for deflecting the critique. The advertising and popular culture industries conduct their business as if the critique had never existed; hence both symbol domains remain unbridled and vigorous. When the critique *is* acknowledged, it is usually for purposes of conversion into material for the two symbol domains,

Figure 3.2. Impudence is endemic in the advertising/popular culture mix, and one cause of its great vitality. Here, the pieties of the advertising critique are rebuffed as the advertisement playfully incorporates "subliminal" stimuli. (Reprinted with permission of Joseph E. Seagram & Sons, Inc.)

as when *Murphy Brown* incorporated then Vice President Dan Quayle's attack regarding "family values" into the show's story-line, or when the campaign for Seagram's Extra Dry Gin cleverly featured "subliminal" stimuli (see Figure 3.2).

Notes

1. Arnold's (1869/1971) defense of "sweetness and light" and his attack on "Philistinism" employed terms so vague that it is difficult to understand what was being opposed to what. But at moments he could be more precise, as when in his speeches and letters he cast aspersions upon London's *Daily Telegraph*, which, with 175,000 daily readers, was not only England's but the world's largest selling newspaper and thus as much of a mass medium as existed at that time. In 1874, the *Telegraph* counterattacked: "What has he done that he should put on airs and proclaim himself so immensely holier than other men? The answer is simple: he is the high-priest of the kid-gloved persuasion" (Coulling, 1961, p. 175). The battle of high versus common culture was joined.

2. For a contemporary critique of Horkheimer and Adorno, see Collins (1989), who observes that "the nature, function, and uses of mass culture can no longer be conceived in a monolithic manner" (p. 16).

3. The rise of the counterculture in the late 1960s did give Marcuse (1964) hope for the shattering of the oppressive forces of the mass media and popular culture, and for a time he played a prophet's role to that movement. Its ultimate subsistence, however, brought Marcuse back to his previous, despairing position. For a discussion of this, see Brantlinger (1990, p. 232).

4. Macdonald (1957) was playing with semantic distinctions in a very loose and perhaps reckless way. One can, of course, place a positive value on a "homogenized" or, to use another word, democraticized society as against a highly stratified one.

5. If cultural studies in the United States has attempted to incorporate all applicable disciplines, it has not done the same politically. "Cultural studies has not embraced all political positions" (Nelson, Treichler, & Grossberg, 1992, p. 5) but remains firmly ensconced on the left.

6. There are several American antecedents of the new endorsement of popular culture, and considering the intellectual climate prevailing at the time they were written, they deserve mention for their brave iconoclasm if nothing else. For decades, the sole positive explication of popular culture was *The Seven Lively Arts* by critic Gilbert Seldes (1924/1957). Writing before radio became a mass medium, Seldes praised Chaplin films and comic strips, vaudeville comedians and jazz musicians. "My theme," he noted in the preface, "was to be that entertainment of a high order existed in places not usually associated with Art, that the place where an object was to be seen or heard had no bearing on its merits" (p. 3). However, Seldes later wavered in his allegiance to this egalitarian approach: In 1950, he

published a mild retraction, titled *The Great Audience,* in which he expressed misgivings about popular entertainment.

In 1970, Russell Nye, Professor of English at Michigan State University, published his survey and history of popular culture, *The Unembarrassed Muse: The Popular Arts in America,* and in doing so established the foundation for the serious American popular culture scholarship to follow. As others did before and since, Nye (1970) distinguished between folk art, elite art, and popular art. The folk artist works anonymously, with simple materials; the elite artist creates work within a certain aesthetic tradition, works which are exclusive and individualistic; for the popular artist, "the criterion of his success is contemporary, commercial, measured in terms of the size and response of his public" (p. 5).

In his book *Popular Culture and High Culture: An Analysis and Evaluation of Taste,* sociologist Herbert J. Gans (1974) further subdivided the public into five distinct "taste cultures." Gans's work remains a strong and effective polemic in favor of the validity of popular culture. His book, he stated clearly in his preface, is "an argument for cultural democracy and an argument against the idea that only the cultural expert knows what is good for people and for society" (p. vii).

These three staunch books stood virtually alone until the arrival of the cultural studies paradigm.

7. Pollay (1986) notes with evident satisfaction about the authors of the works he consulted, "All have terminal academic degrees, and those still active continue to accumulate distinctions" (p. 20). Like the elite critics of popular culture, they are certified members of the Academy.

8. Advertising practitioners are forever astonished by the fact that the public believes that techniques of subliminal persuasion are used routinely. From the perspective of advertising agency personnel, the counterarguments against such usage are overwhelming: that subliminal stimuli, being vague as well as vaguely received, have never been proven to direct consumers to an advertiser's specific product; that discovery of such stimuli would irreparably harm an advertiser's reputation; that in three decades no disgruntled advertising agency employees (and there are many of them) have come forward and demonstrated that they have done this frequently and under instructions; and that the well-known psychological mechanism of "projection" easily accounts for all that is held to be embedded in advertisements. For discussion of the absence of subliminal stimuli in advertising, see Beatty and Hawkins (1989), Rogers and Seiler (1994), and Rosen and Singh (1992).

9. Competent histories of advertising include Atwan et al. (1979), Fox (1984), Marchand (1985), Norris (1990), Pease (1958), and Pope (1983).

10. John Fiske (1987b) comments, "The primary axis of division was originally thought to be class, though gender may now have replaced it as the most significant producer of social difference" (p. 255).

4

The Dynamics Behind the Advertisement

Although similar long-term economic forces have ushered in mediated advertising and popular culture, and similar cultural criticisms have berated them, and similar modes of personal selection and interpretation greet them, advertising and popular culture remain two distinct symbol domains, requiring separate consideration. The next chapter discusses the nature and function of popular culture, while in this one the focus in upon advertising—in particular, upon the concealed, subsurface, upwelling forces that influence the construction of ads.

The typical advertisement or commercial is the professional product of highly skilled and exacting craftspeople and, as such, presents a perfectly polished, opaque surface to the reader or viewer. Yet such perfection is only an illusion, a camouflage so well wrought that it deflects scrutiny of the churning dynamics lying below and beyond. Any advertisement is the product of contesting forces and battering vectors operating just out of sight, just beyond hearing. In the end, an advertisement is a temporary truce, offering a cease-fire for conflicts that are inherent and ultimately unresolvable. Conceivably, advertisers may find advantages in the fact that such conflicts and tensions can never permanently be laid to rest because they can infuse the advertising message with some of whatever penetrating energy it is to possess.

The Client Versus the Agency

*Any advertisement represents a temporary armistice between the adver-
tiser and its advertising agency.* Those unfamiliar with the practice
of advertising may be astonished at the amount of tension, however sublimated, that exists between the independent advertising
agency, on the one hand, and its client advertiser, on the other.
From a distance it would appear that the two are such born allies
that they are fused; thus the word "advertiser" is commonly applied
to this joint entity of the client and the agency. Properly speaking,
the advertiser is the firm with goods or services to sell, and the
agency is the outside company hired to execute the creation and
placement of the advertising portion of a total marketing effort.

In the agency world, it is commonplace to observe that advertisers know little or nothing about advertising. That is, the advertiser (from the agency's perspective, its client) has demonstrable
ability at manufacturing goods or delivering services but lacks
skills in the generation of advertising messages and the purchasing of appropriate media time and space, and so must contract with
a specialist, the advertising agency. Each of the two parties has its
own delimited area of expertise, yet problems habitually arise
when the client fails to respect this division and overly intrudes
into the efforts of the agency.

There are several reasons why this occurs with near guaranteed
regularity. The advertiser has typically entered into dozens of external business contracts, as with raw material providers or office
maintenance firms or distribution services, but of them all, it often
appears to the advertiser that the relationship with the advertising
agency could be the one most yielding to efforts to stimulate sales.
The client is frequently anxious to see a rise in sales, or should
sales be dropping, an end of the decline; this urgency translates into
pressure, both subtle and overt, on the hired agency. There is an
underlying divergency of worldviews that discourages mutual
understanding; the advertiser deals with and is familiar with items
that are countable and manifest, such as cartons of cereal or airplane passengers, whereas the finesse of the agency lies with the
subtleties and ultimately invisibilities of communication with

large populations. Even though the intricacies of mass communication are not within the competencies of the advertiser, this does not stop the client's personnel from having and offering opinions about the agency's creative work. Clients insist they are consumers too and so should have important contributions to make about proposed creative executions. From the agency's point of view, however, client executives are very atypical consumers, and their purported contributions to the creative process often have a deadening effect, resulting in a stillborn execution—a co-option of the agency's stock-in-trade, its creativity. Agency resistance to a client's intrusion is weakened through recognition of the client's right to sever the contractual relationship, a right all too frequently exercised.

It should not be implied, however, that the agencies themselves are always blame free; their creative efforts can be stale[1] or their departments understaffed, as they try to carry out their several obligations—to service the largest number of clients with a minimal number of employees while at the same time putting together speculative proposals to attract new clients. As a result of client versus agency tensions, when a campaign or an individual advertisement is approved by client personnel and agency personnel and is delivered to the media to be run, it is a de facto compromise between the aspirations of the client and the aspirations of the agency. All this contesting, none of it inconsequential to those involved or to the final production, has been done out of sight, behind the scenes.

Research Versus the Creative

Any major advertising effort embodies an unresolved conflict between research information and creative execution. Within an advertising agency, advertising messages are produced in spite of the clashing, dialectical forces of science and art. The communicative arts, which are dependent on symbolic elements, and the scientific research, which is dependent on numerical measurement, always stand in juxtaposition; the chances that the two can enjoy a smooth and reciprocal relationship are slim.

Although research departments in agencies have dwindled in size over recent years, they are still active contributors to the advertising process, ladling in voluminous data on the demographics of target markets, nature of the competition, consumer attitudes toward the product and toward past campaigns, and other tabular marketing information. Data vendors outside the agency provide more statistics, as required. Such numerical material is often advantaged by the client's appreciation of it because it resembles the kind of information used in making conventional business decisions. Scientific data, however, are notoriously poor informants on efforts at human communication. The nuances, styles, and fluctuating symbolic codes of successful communication cannot be prescribed or even implied by data collections.

The data that researchers present to the creative department of an agency will be essentially at odds with the temperaments of the art directors and copywriters in that department,[2] but they will grudgingly consult the data, perhaps aware of past errors when they have let their imaginations wander too far afield. The ideal balance occurs when the data are allowed to suggest an armature onto which an imaginative appeal—the "creative," so called—is then fashioned. Too often, though, the proportions of science and art are not in proper balance. Perhaps the statistical profiles are allowed to intrude and to stifle the creative effort so that the final product is a sterile one. Advertising for Procter and Gamble's products, for example, is sometimes criticized as being too unimaginative, too data based. Or, less likely, the creative team is given free rein and, unresponsive to the measurements, produces an inappropriate campaign. Perhaps this is what happened in the case of Joe Isuzu, the comically deceitful salesman who repelled new car buyers in droves and who may have been responsible for the demise of the product line.

The Product Versus the Appeal

Within the advertisement or commercial, tension will exist between the product and the appeal. That is, the commodity material (depictions of the product and descriptive copy directly pertaining to the product) and the noncommodity material (all the rest of the message—the imagery and words that are extraneous to the product) are dialectically posed. Any compound advertisement is, as previously noted, an invitation to transfer the content that is not integral to whatever is being sold onto the advertiser's goods or service. Thus, the roguishness of Dennis Hopper's berserk NFL referee, representing a breakdown of authority, may add devilry to the image of Nike footwear. The transfer of meanings from artful imagery to a product constitutes the labor of the advertisement. As always, not all labor is successful and produces desired outcomes. The lack of a flow from symbolizing imagery to product, the failures of this effort, afford an opportunity, a chink in the surface, to observe the workings of the advertising substructure. The noncommodity imagery might not be found appealing or, if appealing, may not transfer to the product because of some perceived disjuncture between the imagery and the product, or may transfer but then render the product jarring or unattractive in some unanticipated way. It is easy to set a product and an appeal within the frame of an advertisement, but there is no guarantee that a transfer of meaning will occur (see Figure 4.1). The lack of an unconditional flow indicates that a border exists between product and appeal, a border that needs to be crossed.

The endless rift between the commodity content and the noncommodity content lies behind the frequent happenstance when everything is recalled from an advertising message *except* the product. The transfer of meanings has been rejected, and memory of the product has been obliterated while memory of the appeal has not. For advertisers, this may be the cruelest fate of all, for the carefully constructed enticements seemingly have taken on a life of their own, abandoning the products they were supposed to wed and honor. In the advertising world this is sometimes referred to as "vampire creative"—the creative execution has drained the blood from the featured product. If the viewer remembers that Jason Alexander, the actor from *Seinfeld*, parachutes from a plane with a pet dog in his arms and lands in the middle of the 1995 Super Bowl but forgets that Jason was eating a Rold Gold snack at the time, then the "vampire creative" has struck.

Figure 4.1. From *Elle*. Many of the young women targeted by this ad will appreciate its depiction of unconventionality. However, for at least one person the imagery inspired resistance. "Riding a cow backwards on the beach—that's ridiculous," she complained. For this consumer, the non-commodity appeal did not glide over onto the commodity; there was an irresoluble breach between the two orders of content. (With permission of Sanofi Beaute Inc.)

There is another impediment to the transfer of meaning, one that exists in the very foundation of the advertising strategy. The symbolic appeal is often a perfected *condition* that is personally sought after but unlikely to be obtained in full (such as beauty, or love, or transcendence), whereas the commodity is a *thing* that can be readily purchased and possessed. The ideal and the lesser actuality are yoked in a sometimes uneasy union, a linkage of inherent dissatisfaction. One is being proposed as a surrogate for the other, but it is a substitution the consumer knows can never be completely equivalent. The more satisfying and the less so dwell warily within the same frame.

When imagery does successfully impart meaning to the product, then the surface of the ad closes back in again and the undercurrents are no longer visible. Yet sometimes the concealed contests are reflected artfully at the surface of the advertising in well-wrought symbolic creations that are complex and even self-contradictory—as much like the human minds that come to accept them. Thus, our friend the Energizer bunny is, on the one hand tough, resolute, and strident and, on the other, cuddly and warm; the battery can take on both sets of allusions. Similarly, the Virginia Slims "You've come a long way, baby" campaign features a female personage who has developed into a solo, independent woman while at the same time remaining a dependent "baby"; for some, the cigarette will incorporate the polarity. McDonalds has managed to position itself as an institution of homey, personable, rustic values while also being young, with-it, hip, and urban.

Words Versus Images

Far below the surface of the ad, the communication modalities of words and imagery rub up against each other. The interpretive words of an advertisement come normally in the textual copy of a print ad or in the announcer's voice-over for a commercial; their function is to constrain the range of possible meanings that might be found in the pictorial matter and to facilitate the transfer of meanings from the pictures to the product. This verbal material was at the beginning of the 20th century the greater portion of an ad, but as the decades passed, its employment dwindled (Pollay, 1984). Today, some advertising does without it altogether. Text lent itself to an assertive, even authoritarian tone that, in a democratic century, consumers found increasingly disagreeable. Assertions could always be controverted, and advertisers soon learned that this sort of parrying with consumers had to be avoided. Images conveyed richer, less contestable meanings—to be tuned with just a few words—and so were employed more and more. This strategy was both the cause and the effect of American's swelling vocabularies of common visual referents (see Figure 4.2). Nonetheless, copywriters still find employment, and interpretive text still exists in advertising.

The heart of any advertisement or commercial, however, is the visual imagery redolent with symbolic properties that the advertiser hopes the consumer will find significant. Because images are one kind of symbol and words are distinctly another, a deep, modal tension exists between them within advertising. Words are completely arbitrary creations; whether we call the domesticated pet *dog* or *Hund* or *chien* makes absolutely no difference so long as those with whom we are most likely to converse are willing to employ the same symbol. An illustration of a dog, however, is another matter; it is a similar figure irrespective of the local language and thus is not an arbitrary but a naturalistic representation. But is the naturalistic image not only different from but also superior to the arbitrary word? Is the image so superior that it has no symbolizing or metaphorical properties at all but a one-to-one correspondence to its subject? In his discussion of the difference, philosopher of aesthetics Ernst Gombrich (1981) takes pains to point out that the word and the picture do not exist in pure contradistinction; rather, there is a continuum whereby the word is a learned and arbitrary or conventional symbol and the image is a partially learned and partially naturalistic one (p. 24). People have to have had some associations with dogs, built up some meanings regarding dogs, to make sense of the depiction of a dog. There is a unavoidable tension between the two symbolic orders: the higher naturalistic component in the visual imagery that makes it more approachable pitted against the greater precision of the

Figure 4.2. In the execution of advertising, words—in the form of print copy or an announcer's voice—have dwindled over the course of the 20th century as images thought to be of interest to the consumer have usurped the purchased time or space. This strong and representative ad, from *Glamour,* is almost completely given over to imagery. The few words—"Be brilliant"—are at once a light-hearted pun and a serious injunction, and cue the intended response to the picture. The product substitutes for personal expression, disclosing a beauty within. What happened to this woman's cranium? Images that at first look simple can turn out to be laden with unstated, undebatable implications. (With permission of Swarovski Jewelry U.S. Ltd.)

verbal symbols that, in the hands of the advertiser, make them more purposeful and, as a result, more cautiously greeted by the consumer.[3]

An important aspect of the symbolizing imagery in modern advertising is that it is not artwork completely created by hand, although the talent is certainly available, but is photographed on film, either still or moving. Over the course of the 20th century, advertising shifted from hand-drawn artwork to photography, which proved much more suitable for advertising's mission. The explanation for this lies in the nature of photography itself and of the struggle it contains between truth and falsity. It was important for the advertiser that there be no impediments between the advertising message and the consumer. A reproductive process that appeared guileless, which over 100 years' time had accrued an enormous equity as a truth recorder, would serve the advertising effort much better than a process that was acknowledged by all as artifice—and proudly so. What stamped the imagery created by hand as interpretive and individualistic for artistic purposes ruined it for purposes of persuasion.

Photography, venturing under its reputation as a truth teller, could turn out lies in a wholesale fashion, and permissibly so. That is, the manner of recording was so accurate that it disappeared as a recognized artifice in the transaction between advertising message and receiver, even though exactly what was recorded had been artificially established, a synthesis of symbolic features which the creators of the advertising had purposefully assembled, arranged, lighted, and filmed so as to convey a predesignated message. The surface is accurate (or, allowing for manipulation and retouching in the laboratory, close to accurate), but the subsurface, the preparatory effort, is a thorough fabrication. Although the surface can be so lustrous and precise that the receiver has no sense at all of any tension between truth and falsehood, or chooses not to acknowledge any tension as the emotive responses elicited override such reservations, photography clearly walks a line between the true and the false. Bill Nichols (1981) commented, "The camera, like a magician, appears to read our mind, and our own act of reading, our necessary act of collaboration in this deceit, goes unnoticed and unnoted. Photographic realism, then, works to naturalize comprehension; it hides the work of perceiving meaning behind the mask of a 'naturally, obviously' meaningful image" (p. 35).

Most American advertising contains a so-called product shot,[4] often at the bottom of a print ad and at the close of a commercial, capturing the product, its containers, and labels with the brand name, in a still shot that seems perfectly noncommittal or natural but, on analysis, is recognized as stylishly and bewitchingly lighted and photographed. The product shot, combining words with pictures of things, encapsulates the entire advertisement, containing in the small the same communication modalities that the advertisement contains in the large, and so attempts to establish an equivalency between the product and the rest of the advertising message as it also attempts to resolve any modal disparities (see Figure 4.3). The advertisement is to the product shot as a child is to a doll; what is vital in the first is intended to recede metaphorically toward the second.

The Contested Frame

The frame of any advertisement is problematic and contested. The advertising surface looks polished and placid and, by all rights, so should its borders. The print ad occupies a precise space on the page, and the commercial occupies a precise amount of time, measured to the split-second. But the edges are much more ragged than this sort of accounting can suggest, for the advertiser is always pushing against perimeter constraints, just as the consumer may be pushing back. Commercials defy their frames acoustically, raising their volume levels to challenge household hub-bub, whereas for print ads the pressure at the border is done graphically using the widely employed "bleed" technique. A majority of print ads do not have borders, but instead bleed the imagery all the way up to, and in intention beyond, the edge of the page. In tests, bleed ads have higher readership than nonbleed ads, as if the imagery had overflowed the page and filled the consumer's sphere of vision (see Figure 4.4).

Figure 4.3. From *U.S. News & World Report*. The product shot, in the lower right corner, is the only portion of the original ad in color. The job of the advertisement is to have the appeal imagery—the magnificence of the animal, the magnificence of the Canadian wilderness—recede to the product shot, implying a congruity of the two. (Courtesy of Brown-Forman Beverage Co.)

The raggedness of the frames pertains to the content also, for the advertiser, in trying to highlight some symbols while ignoring

ANNE KLEIN

ANNE KLEIN II FOOTWEAR

Figure 4.4. A bleed ad. The sands extend forever, enveloping a willing reader in their texture and timelessness. (© 1993 Anne Klein II® Footwear for Schwartz & Benjamin.)

others that are related but confusing or devaluing, will carefully frame in some content and frame out other. Sometimes, an ad will be constructed with, in effect, an opening in the frame that the spectator is enticed to enter, perhaps to complete a refrain or supply a noticeably missing visual element (an example is J&B's Christmas season ad stating "ingle ells," which invites the reader to supply "J" and "B"). At other times, the advertiser will stoutly delimit a composition, trying to compel the spectator to be merely an onlooker. In such instances, only the most thoughtful viewers or readers are going to ask "What is missing here? What has been framed out?"

The tension between the frame and the nonframe, between the contained and the uncontained, can never be resolved for long, and continues from one advertising message to another, from one reading to another.

Intertextual Strains

An advertisement or commercial does not stand alone but enters into a number of intertextual relationships, which supply further dynamics to the message. Varda Leymore (1975) observed that "individual advertisements are meaningless till they are put into a system of relationships with each other, from which the individual significance of each may emerge" (p. 127). The individual entreaty may make diminished sense, for example, if the previous commercials in a campaign are unfamiliar and so not available for intertextual reference and comparisons (Wernick, 1992, p. 92). It is difficult to withdraw the fullest meaning from a later Taster's Choice commercial if the earlier vignettes were never seen. But the same contextualizing principle is true even if the commercials do not exist in serial form. A present Oil of Olay commercial takes on reflections of past, unconnected campaigns; a Listerine spot can inadvertently harken back to preceding ones. Consumers cannot help but absorb present overtures in the light of exposure to past ones.

This diachronic mode of intertextuality, though, may pale in comparison to the synchronic variety, in which a commercial or advertisement is interpreted relative to other contemporaneous ones—in particular, ones for the competitors. Thus, a Pepsi ad takes on meanings in relation to a Coca-Cola one, and a Nike commercial message is perhaps subconsciously compared to a Reebok one. For a particular product category, adept consumers are constantly, if unreflectingly, comparing all the appeals with all the other appeals, testing out the variety in the search for the one appeal and the one set of symbols (and the attached product) that best suit their own needs. Each individual campaign takes on overlays of allusions from its relationship to other, competing campaigns, as the advertiser tries to advantageously position its product vis-à-vis other products in the mind of the consumer.

The immediate context for an advertising message also has implications for intertextual interpretations. All the other advertising on the television program or in the magazine will influence the reception for one particular advertisement and, to the extent that the advertising agency is attuned to this, will also influence the makeup of the message. Thus, if it can be predicted that all the other print advertisements will be bleed ads, perhaps a composition with a white border will get a higher readership, however antiquated this is from a graphics perspective; or if no other ad is going to use reverse type (white text on a darker background), perhaps this agency's ad should. Such stylistic choices, made with reference to the surrounding advertising, will have an impact on the ad's content.

Similarly, if six other automobiles are going to be advertised in a magazine issue, perhaps a seventh is futile; or if it is to run, its creative execution must be a stand-out. Also, if it can be anticipated that all the perfumes advertised in an issue will feature escape fantasies, then a different approach is warranted. Or, most radically, assuming that all the other ads will be compound ones, incorporating imagistic appeals, perhaps an ad without an appeal will capture attention (see Figure 4.5). The reader of a magazine or the viewer of a program may well be playing off one advertising message against another in an intertextual spot.

Another sort of intertextual play is also going on, one that advertising agencies have some but not much control over, and

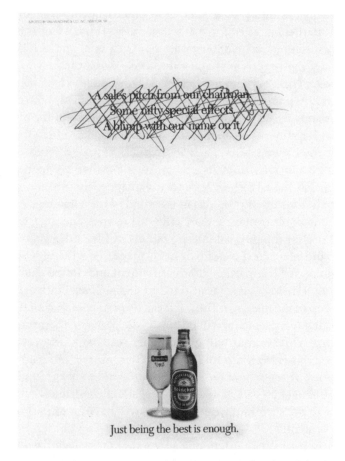

Figure 4.5. A rarity in national consumer goods advertising—a commodity without noncommodity appeal imagery. This ad would work only intertextually: The reader must know how this ad stands out from all other ads, and the reader should have previous exposure to the product. (With permission of Heineken USA, Inc.)

which has a subtle but undeniable influence upon the receptivity of their handiwork. The advertising they have worked so hard to create is going to be served up in a context not of their making; for the most part, it comes embedded in popular culture content.

Agency personnel may not always affect this perspective, but from the receiver's point of view, the advertising and the medium's content come bundled together, and it is pointless to bother to studiously disentangle them. Thus, advertising is consumed with a flavor of nonadvertising content and, in the opposite direction, the advertising content seeps into the program or articles. The two types of content, so separate for those at the sending end of a channel of communication, are at the receiving end interwoven and contrapuntal.[5]

The Advertisement Versus the Consumer

A tension exists between the advertising message and the individual consumer, a tension reflected in the composition of the message. All the application of the advertiser and the advertising agency amounts to nothing if the message being sent is not received. Successful communication takes the work of advertising's receivers as well as its senders. However, in this system, successful communication is at times resisted by the consumer because successful communication is not always seen as being to the individual's advantage. Since no one can purchase everything that is advertised, the responsibility of an adept consumer in the production/consumption economy is to husband financial resources (wealth or credit) until one's needs are matched up with the most assuaging consumables. Confronting resistance and skepticism, what advertisers must try to do is to move their own offering up the ladder of purchase options, from the least assuaging to the more. To have the greatest chance of doing this, the messages of the advertiser must be constructed so as to make the fullest contact with the mind of the consumer. The human mind has two components of interest to the creators of advertising: One is the area of the mind governing the individual as a social creature, and the other is the area of the mind housing basic instincts, impulses, drives, and needs. The most successful advertising will incorporate symbolizing appeals to both.

Commodities exist as items external to the self, as purchasable cultural markers by which the purchaser constructs desired signals. Commodities pertain to both the outer social self and the inner emotional self, but of the two, commodities are more relevant to the former, due to their signaling properties. Thus, the imagery in advertising, trying to stimulate the consumption of a particular commodity, will concentrate more on social appearances than on emotional invocations. (The emphasis in popular culture is just the opposite.) The noncommodity material in an advertisement, striving to put forward the cultural symbols that the consumer is most likely to transfer willingly to the commodity itself will, on balance, reflect more social information than emotional information, will show more faces devoid of emotion than animated by it. Yet considering the nature of the creature to whom the message is directed, emotional referents are never entirely absent (see Figure 4.6).

The One Versus the Many

Any advertisement or commercial overtly appeals to the individual consumer at the same time that it is covertly and contrarily appealing to the masses. This tension between beckoning to the one and beckoning to the many ripples the subsurface currents of the advertising message. The maker of the advertising is striving to sell a commodity to multitudes of buyers but recognizes that these sales can only happen one by one. The advertiser knows the advertising message is a comprehensive denial of the individual, yet must conceal this knowledge behind imagery that the individual might feel speaks to him- or herself alone. The advertiser attempts to put forward a symbol set that most of the target market will find meaningful and in the nature of a personal affirmation. In the worst case, from the advertiser's point of view, the duality in such imagery can cancel itself out; that is, in trying to appeal to all, the message may appeal to none.

The duplicity on the sender's end regarding the one versus the many is matched by a similar duplicity on the receiver's end of the

Figure 4.6. Although popular culture is much richer in emotional invocations than advertising, emotionality is never entirely absent in ads as all symbols have an emotional quotient. Here is an uncommonly strong emotional appeal, pitched to assertive or vengeful feelings. This is a deceptively complex ad (the taped "change the game," the ambiguity of "right back at you," "reflections" of what?, the shattering product), but its aggressive thrust is clear. (Created by FCB/LKP Advertising for Fila U.S.A.)

transmission. The individual looks at advertising imagery and the associated commodity in the attempt to find those pleasing signs that will define oneself in distinction to others. Still, those signs *must* be readable by others, so what the solitary consumer is buying is not so much self-definition in isolation as participatory symbols. The shopper buys for others who, while they may not possess the sign, at a minimum can read it and impart meaning. (In fact, when the exact same signs do appear in the same time and space, it is too much of a good thing. The symbols then call attention to themselves and desert their claim on meanings. This error of symbolic obliteration occurs when two women show up in the same dress at a party or when identical new knapsacks are brought by two different hikers to the start of a camping trip. Caught in such contretemps, people work quickly to individualize whatever is identical and to shift them back to their crucial symbolizing function.)

Viewing this strife between allegiance to oneself and allegiance to the many, as played out in advertising, Gary Day (1990) reluctantly finds some societal gain: "Advertising appeals to the self and not the community but the image it offers of the self fits everyone and so it manages to hold the social structure in place" (p. 7).

Proselytizing

Advertising messages are acts of propaganda, challenging the faithless and the relapsed as they confirm the beliefs of the committed. This commercial or that print ad, innocent as it may seem on the surface, is at bottom an active proselytizer for the faith of consumerism. When the solitary ad joins into the army of its fellows, together they constitute an ideological force of great magnitude. The consumerist belief system is based on a conviction that sacred symbols and meanings exist in the form of purchasable commodities. It is through one's purchases, perhaps more than in any other way, that personal definitions are constructed, and it is by means of one's purchases that those definitions are relayed to others. As a result of the supremacy of commodities, the focal activity of each individual who wishes to fit into this belief system without distress has to be that of consumption. Adherents must regularly devote time to the activity of consumption, first by being familiar with the constantly updated Holy Writ of advertising and then in an act of Communion by effecting purchases. Moreover, consumers must understand that the commodification of areas of human activity that lay previously uncommodified is in the natural order of things, and indeed if noticed, perhaps the source of some satisfaction, derived from the propagation of the faith.

The consumerist faith is superimposed upon earlier belief systems, which it resembles in important ways: those of religion and of magic. Magic, found among primitive peoples (and certainly not extinguished in the present day), is premised on convictions that people dwell in a world infused with living, amorphous spirit, and that certain special individuals, whether through training or natural endowment, can at moments intercede in the spirit world, perhaps with the aid of special objects or rituals, and cause one thing to happen rather than another. The belief system of magic was partially superseded by the formalized belief system of religion, where usually a single godhead was established, a lore written down, and worshipful practices codified.

All three belief systems maintain control by mediating perceived scarcities, in the perspective of adherents: Only occasionally will the spirits do what is asked of them; not everyone will have a place in Heaven; not all goods can be afforded. All three systems dominate by monopolizing communication: the loquacious spirit world demanding interpretation; the ubiquity of religious texts, imagery, and practices; the incessant shower of advertising. All three systems invite the adherent to reach out: to hear the spirit world more clearly; to become freer of sin; to obtain through purchases a more satisfying personal definition. In the ongoing human enterprise of making the invisible palpable and comprehensible, all three are highly materialistic: primitive people's fetishes; religion's shrines, treasures, raiments, and houses of worship; the commodities of the capitalist ideology. What changes over these three stages is the location and extent of the sacred: everything, for the tribe member; a few places on earth and some sites in the other world, for the devout; personal possessions and experiences for the consumer. Mike Featherstone (1991) asserts about the new ideology that "the sacred is able to sustain itself outside of organized religion within consumer culture" (p. 126). While the sacred grows smaller and more particularized over these three stages, for better or worse the individual looms larger.

Each of these belief systems is potentially totalizing and shows little tolerance for the challenging existence of the other, so it is not surprising that frictions can occur when they confront each other. Tribe members were hostile and resistant to the arrival of missionaries; religions treat consumerism scornfully, projecting onto it their own materialistic fascinations. The old, though, is never eradicated by the successor, and so all three of them exist side by side in the modern world. In fact, all three belief systems can coexist in one mind—and frequently do.

As the capitalist ideology manifested in advertising has come to the fore, it has sustained itself in part by feeding on the previous belief systems. Religious imagery, such as a halo around a product or a shaft of light from above falling upon a commodity, was common in advertising of the 1920s and 1930s, according to Roland Marchand (1985, p. 282). Such iconographic devices are rarer now, perhaps because religious symbolism is not as commanding as it once was. And being rarer, commercial appropriation of such symbols may stand out as sacrilegious and elicit reproval. Sut Jhally (1989) points out that the otherworldly allusions in contemporary advertising do not reference any established religion with an "articulated moral code" but, rather, draw closer to primitive fetishism (p. 226). Jhally likens the consumer commodities in advertising to tribal fetishes that were thought to magically enhance an individual's power over others or over the spirit world. Judith Williamson (1978) asserts that "all consumer products offer magic, and all advertisements are spells" (p. 141). When products are animated or anthropomorphized—for example, when the cleanser sings—it is the residual belief that objects can live that is being plucked at. With those products for which it is not explicitly claimed that they work "like magic," the connection is often implied (see Figures 4.7 and 4.8).

Tabasco® brings out the unexpected in food.

The lively taste of Tabasco® sauce. Don't keep it bottled up.

Figure 4.7. Advertisers may send symbols of magical power and control, but symbols lie dormant until a consumer lends meaning to them. A woman who found the imagery in this advertisement to be "very strong" turned out to be a regular user of Tabasco pepper sauce; the ad confirmed, and perhaps strengthened, her cooking preferences. "It's cute, and in a way it's true," she reported about the ad. "That sauce makes food lively"—a taste sensation she found well rendered visually by means of snake charmer imagery. (With permission of McIlhenny Company. Tabasco®.)

THERE ARE TIMES WHEN MY MUSIC LEADS ME FROM THIS WORLD OF PARKING FINES AND IDIOT DRIVERS.

I JUST POP IN A DISC AND HEAD OUT, FREE FROM CARE. UNWINDING IN BUMPER TO BUMPER MUSIC.

BUT HOLD ON TIGHT WHEN I CRANK IT. THIS HIGH POWER JENSEN CD RECEIVER'S 6 AUDIO OUTPUTS LET ME EASILY ADD EXTRA AMPLIFIERS. PLUS SUBWOOFERS FOR BASS THAT QUAKES THE BONES.

I NEVER KNOW WHEN I'LL HAVE TO ESCAPE WITH MY MUSIC AGAIN. COULD BE TONIGHT. COULD BE TOMORROW. I'LL BE READY. BECAUSE WITH A DETACHABLE FACE JENSEN, NO ONE CAN TAKE THE EXPERIENCE FROM ME.

FOR SOME FREE INFO ABOUT JENSEN PRODUCTS AND THE DEALER NEAREST YOU, CALL 1-800-67-SOUND.

JENSEN®
THE MOST THRILLING SOUND ON WHEELS.

© 1993 JENSEN IS A REGISTERED TRADEMARK OF INTERNATIONAL JENSEN INC IN CANADA. CALL SCL PRODUCTS 604-273-1095 (VANCOUVER); 416-890-0298 (TORONTO).

September 1993 Details   237

Figure 4.8. Magically, this CD player gets people and automobiles airborne. (Reprinted with permission of International Jensen Incorporated.)

Explaining the prevalence of magical allusions, agency executive Howard Gossage (1967) stated that advertising messages, in the interest of reaching the largest number of people, had to incorporate appeals to "the most common denominator of all, magic" (p. 364). Acceptance of (or more cautiously put, a lack of rejection of) magic, animism, fetishism and the like is the most widespread and enduring belief of people; it would be odd if the new belief system did not carry this forward and exploit it for its own aims. The fetishes used in the new ideology are purchasable commodities, and the new ritual activity is personal consumption.

Advertising imagery constitutes the iconography of this new, infusing consumerist ideology. Referring to an artistic style that Erving Goffman (1976) called "commercial realism" (p. 15) and Michael Schudson (1984) labeled "capitalist realism" (chap. 7), Roland Marchand (1985) explained, "Like the paintings and murals of Socialist Realism, the illustrations in American advertising portrayed the ideal and aspiration of the system more accurately than its reality. They dramatized the American dream" (p. xviii).[6] However, just as the predétente Soviet citizen might sometimes feel that Socialist Realism artwork was an overstatement and stretched to the bursting point the sphere of meanings it was trying to reify, inviting skepticism and even ridicule, so the capitalist consumer will also at times find advertising imagery exaggerated and repellent. Like a Russian peer facing exortative poster art, the Western consumer enters into a complicated negotiation with advertising iconography, not always accepting its lessons. Even when they are accepted, they are usually taken to represent the world not as it is but as it might be. The imagery defines the further range of existence, not the nearer. Thus, the consumer, like the Soviet citizen, accepts art known to be deceptive and misleading because it has utility in limning an ideal.[7]

The capitalist belief system promotes itself strenuously through advertising—not strenuously in the sense that any one advertisement or commercial shrilly tries to drive home the total ideology, but strenuously in that the total accumulation of advertisements creates a heaving surround of symbolizing material. Why does the advertising effort need to be strenuous? The answer, of course, is that it meets resistance. Proselytizers are not always welcomed. Most consumers believe in moderation, some enjoy periods of nonconsumerist relapse, and a stalwart few refuse to convert at all. In the end, the outsized volume of advertising art testifies to the reserve of the consumer.

Notes

1. An uninspired "creative" (as agencies refer to the concept behind a message and the execution of that concept) happens all too often. A glance at the advertising in any magazine or television program will confirm this. For all of its vitality, advertising is not exempt from the regression towards the mean which occurs in most human endeavors, when conventions and norms evolve and come to dictate.

2. David Ogilvy (1983), whose career was primarily on the creative side of agency work, had bitter words about researchers: "They take three months when I only have three weeks. . . . They are natural slowpokes, and too frightened of making mistakes" (pp. 36-37).

3. The large communicative difference between pictures and text is captured in Starch Readership tests (conducted by the research firm of Starch INRA Hooper). In these recognition tests, an interviewer goes page by page through a magazine issue the interviewee has previously looked at and asks for that person's recollections of each ad. On average, 45% of the readership will say they have *seen* a four-color, one-page ad, but only 9% will claim they *read* the copy.

4. Occasionally, especially in fashion advertising, there is no product shot. Only the initiated can know what the advertising is for. Robert Goldman (1992) categorizes these as "this is not an ad" ads.

5. Spectators' intermeshing of advertising messages and popular culture content is the subject of Chapter 9.

6. An earlier statement of the idea that advertising is capitalism's official art, just as the Soviet Union had its official art, was Raymond Williams's (1960/1980) observation: "Advertising is also, in a sense, the official art of modern capitalist society" (p. 184). It is possible that all subsequent uses of this analogy stem from his trenchant thought.

7. Soviet Realism was unable to stave off the spread of the competing ideology and iconography. After noting that recent Russian immigrants were mesmerized by the commercials on American television, Martin Esslin (1982) went on to express a sentiment that turned out to be premonitory: "There is a vast, unexpressed, subconscious yearning in these people, not only for the consumer goods concerned but also for the hidden forces and miraculous action of the spirits inhabiting them" (p. 273).

5

The Dynamics of Popular Culture

On his first foreign foray, Shaquille O'Neal strained to render his personal complexities simple and clear for European reporters. The 7'-1" center of the Orlando Magic basketball team explained, "I'm a combination of the Terminator and Bambi. Sometimes I'm a killer and sometimes I'm nice" (Lane, 1993, p. 87). It is to the established domain of popular culture referents that everyone, even a new inductee into that domain, can resort to when trying to constitute meanings. Advertisers, attempting feats of communication no less difficult than Shaquille's, are no different.

The symbol domain of popular culture—consisting of the mediated figures of the Terminator and Bambi and Shaquille and all the rest—offers lavish pickings to advertisers trying to construct attractive messages for reticent consumers. Advertisers will appropriate such popular culture material as celebrities, music, comedic styles—anything that can drape their products in accepted and enhancing symbols. The overriding question, however, is why the domain of popular culture, this repository of much-appreciated lore, exists in the first place. What does popular culture, greeted more enthusiastically than advertising, possess to attract its spectators? Why is popular culture popular?

Why Is Popular Culture Popular?

To understand the popularity and centrality of popular culture, there first must be agreement that it is received by *individuals*; to insist that it is received by *audiences* is to perpetuate its denigration and miscomprehension. There is no such thing as a productive conceptualization of "mass communication," of mediated communication received by masses. Indeed, there are no masses, as Raymond Williams (1958) determined decades ago:

> I do not think of my relatives, friends, neighbours, colleagues, acquaintances, as masses: we none of us can or do. The masses are always the others, whom we don't know, and can't know. . . . Masses are other people. There are in fact no masses; there are only ways of seeing people as masses. (p. 299)

It is only within the mind of the individual spectator that symbols are turned into meanings, that the welcomed content finds its purpose. The level of analysis must at bottom be that of the individual.

Moreover, the reception of popular culture content ought not to be seen as "passive"—yet another misnomer in the effort to depict popular culture as inconsequential. Attendance to popular culture is a highly active process, although not one muscle may visibly move. The individual first selects, even if by default, one medium rather than the others, one offering rather than its competitors. To the chosen production the viewer then attends fully or not so fully, depending on personal inclination. Popular culture productions, writes Michael de Certeau (1984) are

> confronted by an entirely different kind of production, called "consumption" and characterized by its ruses, its fragmentation (the result of the circumstances), its poaching, its clandestine nature, its tireless but quiet activity, in short by its quasi-invisibility, since it shows itself not in its own products (where would it place them?) but in the art of using those imposed on it. (p. 31)

The "art of using" popular culture, as Certeau calls it, encompasses the labor of reception, the labor of making meanings. Reception is an exercise leading to wide-ranging nuances of interpretation and wide-ranging shades of gratification, all variations that depend upon the proclivities of the individual.

The individual undertakes the labor of reception in learned anticipation of, above all, sensations of pleasure. Pleasure is the most important attribute of the reception of popular culture; no consideration should be allowed to conceal or color this fundamental fact. There is an element of coercion in other human activities such as work and education; people go to work to sustain themselves in the near term and go to school in hope of bettering their employment options in the long run, but they might do neither were they relieved of economic obligations. Yet whether in school or out, whether employed or not, whether endowed or not, they would be sure to attend to popular culture offerings for the enjoyable diversion experienced. Participation in popular culture, an entirely voluntary activity, is entered into willingly for the gratifications it brings.

What is the nature of the pleasure that calls audience members to popular culture? Sigmund Freud (1924/1959) explained that pleasure can commonly result from the discharge of psychic tension, but that it can also result from an increase in tension (sexuality was the example he offered) (p. 256). Pleasure is the sensation of emotional correction—through the discharge of psychic pressure when it is too ample and through the excitation of it when a desired feeling is too scant. Thus, when the symbol domain of popular culture offers pleasure, it is offering emotional compensation by proxy.[1]

Human emotions are continually being inflated by the pressures of everyday life or by material welling up from the deeper unconscious, and they are often being deflated by the removal of their stimuli or by the simple passage of time. Popular culture artfully presents material that invokes insistent or unfulfilled feelings, and offers an imaginative space for their play and restitution. It is a sportive, rollicking space, one that allows for the vicarious discharge of the somatic components of emotions under conditions that (being symbolic, not actual) are more or less safe and controlled. It is the space of emotional reparations; it is the welcome opportunity for the indirect release of psychic tensions or, in other cases, for the augmentation of feelings. This is the primary source of popular culture's great allure.

Mediated popular culture, then, offers its audience the elixir of emotional management, so needed for the maintenance of successful lives in the modern world. Norbert Elias (Elias & Dunning, 1986) states that leisure activities like popular culture "can mimetically evoke fear and sorrow as well as triumph and joy, hatred as well as affection and love. By allowing these feelings to flow freely within their symbolic setting, . . . they lighten the burden of people's all-around restraint in their non-leisure life" (p. 44).[2] The continuing expansion of the domain of popular culture over the course of the 20th century and of the time that individuals allocate to it stems from increased needs for this psychological tonic. Social behavior today is less likely to be directed by traditional external protocols, and more likely to take account of the emotional make-up of the individual. Emotional energy is to be used and adjusted so that social transgressions are minimized and social congress can transpire satisfactorily. As a result, it is ever more incumbent upon people to manage and redirect their own emotions in ways that are acceptable (Elias, 1982, p. 232). Under these conditions, the use of popular culture to remediate emotions can only increase.

Critics of popular culture who fix on the prominence of sex and violence in the media do so with much justification, for these are the emotions that individuals find the hardest to manage, that they are in the greatest need of fictive content to treat, and that popular culture offers up in abundance. Excessive and unseemly exhibition of the desire to fornicate or the impulse to aggress against others can only occur at the expense of the social fabric. These urges are genetically imprinted on individuals and play decisive roles in the success of any animal species, ours included, but for a society to hold together they must be channeled carefully and displayed appropriately. The task of restraining such impulses, traditionally the proscriptive work of strong institutions such as religion, community, extended families, and marriage, has in recent times devolved to the individual. Entering imaginatively into the realm of popular culture, individuals can acknowledge their own sexual and antagonistic feelings and experience progress toward their resolution.

One of the reasons why individuals today spend hours with popular culture is that they have learned over years that such exposure brings with it sensations of equanimity and resolution, that harbored but unwanted drives are somehow, if not vented, at least diminished, and that desired but unfulfilled feelings are supplemented. Increasing demands to personally manage emotions and behavior have led to increasing needs for the popular culture content that accomplishes precisely this.

If the popular culture offering occurs in the shape of a narrative, as with prime-time television programs or theatrical films, there are additional emotional benefits to be anticipated and derived from the format alone. Among humans, stories are the universal form for encasing and, in a tantalizing way, relating affective content. Structured with a beginning, middle, and end,[3] a story starts with the invocation of emotional issues that, the implication is, will be satisfactorily resolved in the end: family bonding, romantic love, social acceptance, frustrating impasses, the conquest of evil. In the middle come the plot's entanglements and enigmas that pleasurably forestall the resolution promised at the beginning. "What supports delay over a stretch of time as cables support of suspension bridge over water is our investment of desire. Narrative dangles a lure before us; it promises to unfold in time, yet not run down or dissipate; to take form, to inform," writes Bill Nichols (1981, p. 74). As a narrative pulls viewers forward through the widening and sequencing of the plot elements, prompting wonder about the next happenstance, it also provides a temporal analog to change within the real world of the spectators. Dramatic change shapes interpretation of the mysteries of change in real time, the underlying vector of human life. Should the expected conclusion take place at the end of the narrative, then the emotions stimulated within the viewer may find their pleasurable appeasement.

Thus, the dramatic form of the narrative, beyond lending attractive shape to the popular culture material that directs interior feelings toward pleasure, has exterior implications, in providing patterns for making sense out of the world. This dual allegiance can be generalized to all of popular culture, nominating the domain's second function. Not only does popular culture help in the adjustment of affective energy, it also provides secondary satisfactions through the familiarizing of the individual with the abstractions of the social world. By the dramatized portrayal of norms, beliefs, values, ideologies, and so forth, popular culture encourages the acknowledgment of those tenets and the private rehearsal of them.

A story's spectator can have certain emotions stimulated and then gratified thanks to the framework of the narration but can also have certain operating beliefs reconfirmed: that change in time is the mainstay of human life; that resolution of the inharmonious is conceivable and good; that human experience is not inchoate but can have form—and having form, has meaning. Lawrence Grossberg (1986) affirms, "The popular produces our internal and external horizon" (p. 186); that is, popular culture offers the means both to work on interior feelings and to work on the exterior alignment of the individual to the social world. Thus, sexual desire is recast as the more responsible romantic love, and the viewer is encouraged to recast it in this mode also; aggressive behavior is recast as a justifiable attack on wrongdoing, or as the surrogate and regulated combat of televised sport. The reason why popular culture is so popular is due to its completeness in addressing the two abiding concerns of the individual: one's interior of emotions, and the exterior of the norm-governed social world.

But because popular culture works constantly on two fronts, operating on two dimensions of personality that are often not well reconciled at all (those of personal feelings vs. social standards), then the material of popular culture is inherently and thoroughly contradictory.[4] First, it offers content that relieves emotions, and second, simultaneously and conversely, it offers content that affirms the operant social codes. For example, popular culture can give the audience the opportunity to rebel angrily against authority and also to define and adjust to authority. In fact, both opportunities can be present in the same piece of popular culture, as in such films as *The Wild Ones* or *Natural Born Killers* or in many rap music songs. That popular culture serves two often contradictory purposes at the same time is part of what lends it its great complexity and richness of alternative meanings. This duality explains why popular culture can depict dramatized violence as a tableau for the spectator's projection of aggressive feelings but, considering the outsized volume of mediated bloodshed, does little to teach violence as a mode of everyday behavior.[5] "The monster who watches television and then goes on a rampage is a *metaphor*, a creation of criticism," John Hartley (1988, p. 236) notes as he dismisses the concept of television-inspired aggression.

Popular culture is readily comprehended because these internal and external concerns are represented in symbols that for the most part are of some standing, having long been accepted by spectators. Thus, guns and gun wielding stand for aggression, and bikinis and intergender kissing stand for sexuality. Members of the audience have grown up learning not only their mother tongue and the prevailing social codes but also the lexicon of popular culture symbols. The task of the popular culture industries is to reassemble these customary symbols into entertainment discourses that are familiar enough to invite predictable reactions but not so overly familiar and trite as to elicit boredom. The industries cannot, while maintaining their financial mandates, hope to generate in a wholesale fashion new symbols with new referents.

Although popular culture creators are largely confined to an established symbol vocabulary, they do have some degree of latitude as they move material from the plane of emotions to the plane of norms; they can even under changing social conditions aid in the creation of new norms. For instance, over the course of the 20th century the popular culture industries have not led, but still have helped, in the generation of new perspectives on blacks in American life. At the beginning of the century, blacks were often depicted as despicable and so were grafted onto feelings of hatred; by the 1920s and 1930s, black characters were featured humorously and so served the conflicted feelings of curiosity and ridicule; by the 1990s, popular culture creators had reconstituted blacks as friends, partners, neighbors, and household members, constructing them as vehicles for the white audience's kindled, if still ambivalent, feelings of fellowship. The creators were able to change the depiction of blacks by shifting its anchor to other audience emotions. Beneath all symbolic representations in popular culture are the emotional summons that invite the audience to affectively invest in the production; the symbolic material itself enjoys some slight didactic leeway, to be used at the discretion of its creators.

A widespread misconception of the dynamics of popular culture, one prevalent in all schools of thought, is that there is no return flow in this communication activity, that is, from the receivers of popular culture back to the producers. As with any successful communication effort (and, overall, none is more successful than popular culture), feedback is a stabilizing force, with information about reception moving back to the senders so that they can try to readjust in the interest of a more targeted product the next time out. All the popular culture industries hang tensely on the extent of the audience's welcome of their offerings, for it is on the matter of acceptance or rejection that their profitability, and hence their well-being, depends. Thus, feedback data in the form of television ratings, ticket grosses, and book and recordings sales are scrutinized avidly when they arrive in the offices of the culture industries. This information on popularity gives the culture producers a general sense of the content that audience members currently find to their liking, and helps creators and receivers stay in tune with each other.

However, even if the feedback data are good in broad terms, they are poor in being able to finely predict which specific products are likely to find favor with audience members in the future. Nevertheless, without these data, the products of the culture industries would more resemble shots in the dark than they presently do. Audience members speak loudly to the culture industries about their general wants and preferences, and the culture industries listen as attentively as they possibly can. Omission of this feedback cycle in discussions of popular culture only serves to distort the relationship of creators to audience members, rendering the creators more powerful and the spectators less so than is actually the case.

The cycle of communication—from the industries to the users in the form of popular culture material, and back again in the form of feedback data—is suggestive of the dynamics that govern the whole domain of popular culture. The domain is never static; in fact, its agitated nature may be its definitive characteristic. New, ephemeral material is constantly being offered up in the attempt to engage the fickle and partially obscured tastes of the public. The onrushing sea of content is a churning one, with a thick froth to it. Creative minds in the culture industries fabricate much of the offering, but other disquieting material is added in from subgroups generating their own particular local cultures in opposition to the general variety, taking on self-definition in their resistance. The whole domain is roiling with energy as fads come and go, formats thrive and dwindle, particular content has its day, songs are on everyone's lips and then no one's, stars peak and disappear, new symbols and new meanings advance and retreat. Popular culture is a swirling, rich, nutritious assemblage of symbolic material. According to M. Thomas Inge (1989), "Popular culture shows man at his best, as his most capable and creative, and in his most liberated state. Thus the health of a society is directly reflected in the liveliness and quality of its entertainment" (p. xxiv).

In underscoring the incontestable vitality of popular culture, however, there is the danger of overstepping critical propriety, a danger that Chandra Mukerji and Michael Schudson (1991) sternly warn about when they observe, "We can happily celebrate discoveries in popular culture of sociability, fellowship, and creative resistance to exclusionary cultural form; but that should scarcely blind us to popular traditions of racism, sexism, and nativism that are just as deeply rooted. This is popular culture, too" (p. 36). Although popular culture can be overpraised, it can scarcely be overestimated. It is nothing less than a major instrument by which contemporary individuals learn to make sense out of themselves and of the cultural world around them.

To communicate with consumers, advertisers thus have a fertile, ample melange of purchasable symbolic material to draw upon. They can turn to a popular culture that is pleasurable, emotional, noncoercive, accessible, normative, confirming, polysemous, and every so often slightly didactic. To further detail the rich lore of popular culture that advertisers find usable, two leading genres are examined: situation comedies and popular music.

Situation Comedies

The emotionality that is the core of popular culture's appeal, with its attendant visceral (if vicarious) component, often goes unacknowledged. Academic discussion of popular culture may mention its ardent and bodily qualities only discreetly and then rush on. Even genuine fans can overlook the emotionality: Asked about a movie, they recite a plot; asked about an athletic event, they give a score; asked about a rock concert, they are often speechless. Because much of the response to popular culture is interior, with the viewer or the novel reader or the theatergoer sitting immobile, this can mask the emotions at root. When audience displays suggesting emotionality do occur, they are often immediately forgotten; many people do not recall laughing during a situation comedy episode. Yet were you to walk into a room where others are watching television and laughing, before you too succumbed to the comedy it would be clear that the physical response of laughter was occurring and did reveal the affective nature of the experience. "What's so funny?" you might ask as you sat down, traversing from one sort of discourse (perhaps an interior one) to another (the television discourse). Laughter is the particular sort of emotional release that situation comedies specialize in.

It is difficult to get people to laugh, especially an unseen and heterogeneous audience numbering in the tens of millions, but the better creators of situation comedies have learned to do it almost routinely by inserting jokes in the dialogue and then cuing the audience response with a laugh track. The laugh track is the easy part; the jokes demand great care in their creation and delivery. Jokes, in Sigmund Freud's (1905/1960) analysis, are succinct invocations of repressed feelings, feelings that are tricked into appearing through an adroitly incongruous verbal or nonverbal expression. An appropriate subject is positioned, pacing is established to ready the audience for the appearance of a joke, and then the snappy punch line or pratfall occurs. In private, in millions of living rooms and bedrooms, out come the bursts of psychic energy, temperate or not, that signal the joke has hit its target and a certain amount of constrained mental material has been discharged. After a half hour of regular laughs, snickers, and guffaws, the audience has experienced a sufficiently pleasurable release of tension that people may be inclined to tune in again next week.[6]

The restorative jokes in a situation comedy punctuate a dual narrative structure, one that creates a doubly secure frame for "controlling an enjoyable de-controlling of feelings," as Norbert Elias phrased it (Elias & Dunning, 1986, p. 49). The biformity of the structure is suggested in an ambiguity surrounding the genre name: The word *comedy* is clear enough, but does *situation* refer to the ongoing situation of the same characters in the same setting week after week, or to this particular episode's singular "situation" that introduces the requisite tension and begs for resolution within 24 minutes? The ongoing structure is virtually invincible, short of cancellation: Although infrequently a new character might be introduced, what sustains the program is the same characters entwined in the same relationships and located in the same few settings. In outline, the episodic structure is even more solid: Stability will be challenged by forces originating either within the characters themselves or externally; dramatic tension will be produced through a short series of events; resolution of the issue and the reestablishment of a stable group will occur at the end. It is a cozily crafted imaginary world that situation comedy viewers find themselves in, an exceedingly safe place to let down one's guard and laugh.

There is more to the emotional services provided by situation comedies than the satisfying jokes, venting minor irritations, that are embedded in the dual structures. The fictional milieu invariably exposes viewers to a nest of warm, sustaining human relationships. Momentarily, the spectator experiences the affirmation of a caring, primary group—the program's family, semifamily, pack of friends, or work team. Thus, a surrogate group offering surrogate membership and surrogate fellow-feeling is part of the reward for

watching. Situation comedies offer symbolic, affective compensation for the go-it-alone lives (either fully or partially) of most
Americans. For a population whose solitariness is unmatched in
history, such secondhand sociability is hardly inconsequential.
Beyond this psychological service, the prevailing emphasis upon
the group carries with it broad-stroked normative implications.
The values of cooperation, thoughtfulness, charity, forgiveness—
these are all made to glimmer during a typical half-hour episode, and may be taken by the viewer to be more praiseworthy
than they might be if the exposure (or, more realistically, season
after season of exposure to the saccharine world of situation comedy)
had not transpired.

The pleasures of situation comedies—from the discharge of
laughter, from the surety of the dramatic framework, from the
provision of a surrogate and sustaining group—are reinforced
through the (by now so usual as to be overlooked) pleasures of the
television experience itself. More so than any other form of mediated communication, television is intimate (being domestic), multi-
modal and multisensory, transmitting voice, music, sound effects,
graphics, and imagery to eye and ear. The delivery of moving
images to the home—historically and technologically the most
difficult feature to activate, the most awaited, the most influential—
allows television to match up with the sensory capacity that biological evolution had decreed to be the primary one for humans,
that of mid-range vision. Before viewers' eyes dance phantasmic
scenes, an ever novel kaleidoscope of symbolic activity, a presentation that invites some to churn constantly through the channels
via remote control. Television strains to put forward a stream of
appetizers for the visual sense and, by delighting the eye, to hold
attention. Along with other engagements of the mind, the television viewer is seeking and finding pleasure at a fundamentally
sensory level.

The gratifications of situation comedy can be illustrated with a
representative program from the now-syndicated *The Cosby Show*.[7]
The plot mechanisms of this particular episode center on son Theo,
who, believing his father's pledge that the Huxtable townhouse
will be at his disposal, has come home to cook a romantic dinner

for his girl friend Cheryl. Dr. Huxtable, however, is a presence throughout, both when he is on the premises and when he is not, for the character of Theo has matured into a facsimile of Dad—a warm, steady, and reactive personage. Theo's plans are hampered (but, given the genre, not thwarted) by the unexpected appearance of his friend Dinty's girl friend, Ellen, and by the surprise return of his parents from an aborted ski trip. The circulation around Theo of these four characters—Ellen and Dinty, Clair and Cliff Huxtable—provides the currents of the plot.

The key contretemps that upsets decorum and launches the plot occurs when Ellen, stopping by to enlist Theo in a surprise she has planned for Dinty, drinks a glass of wine on top of the antihistamines she has taken for an allergy, becomes groggy and ill, and unknown to Theo flees upstairs to vomit. There she changes from her soiled dress into one of Dr. Huxtable's bathrobes. It is in this condition—stuporous, robed, and in the bedroom area—that Theo finds her; he must scramble to prevent her discovery first by his friend Dinty, who has dropped in to discuss what he believes is a fractured romance with Ellen, and then by Theo's returned parents.

Concealing Ellen, as she wanders from bedroom to bedroom, provides the occasion for much physical comedy. The laugh track sizzles as Theo narrowly gets her hidden in first one room, then another, and as Cliff emerges from his bedroom with a perplexed expression. The string of verbal jokes in the show turn on mellowed tensions between generations and between genders. Cliff—the lovable, sage, bumbling Dr. Huxtable—confides to Theo that he recognized he was in love with Theo's mother when he began cooking for her; Theo dismisses his father's sentimentality by saying playfully, "Dad, that was in the olden days," and the studio audience cackles. Other jokes touch on the relationship between marrieds, between Cliff and Clair (who is mad at her husband for allowing a rainfall to end their ski trip). Cliff, delighted to be home, says, "We put 300 miles on those skis. 'Course, they were on the top of the car." More guffaws.

The human setting of friends and family, within which the jokes and the plot are worked out, becomes denser as the episode proceeds, adding complications but also warmth. Theo's two older sisters and their husbands appear; his grandparents stop by to pick up a table saw. At one point, Dinty and Ellen's misunderstanding is situated within three generations of interacting Huxtables. Resolution arrives when Ellen comes to her senses, rushes around to the front door just as Dinty is about to storm off, and pretends that it was Theo who obtained the tickets for her surprise date with Dinty. They exit happily, Cliff and Clair have already left for Chinese food, and Theo is finally able to begin a peaceful dinner with the arriving Cheryl. Order has been restored.

The willing viewer of the episode has been able to laugh along with the studio audience and the laugh track at the mild gibes, has experienced the joys and consolations of an extended surrogate family, and has felt the satisfaction of having disorder and impropriety righted, and of having social norms—of romance, of friendship, of trust, of maleness and femaleness—affirmed one more time. It has been a pleasure.

Stars

Bill Cosby, for years the most highly compensated entertainer in the United States (and, with an annual personal income frequently above $50 million, the most highly compensated person in any field anywhere), represents another quality of popular culture that is of great interest to advertisers: namely, that popular culture is the seedbed of those few personalities, the stars, who can command general recognition from a diverse population. The idea that mere performers could and should be cultural figureheads is a historical novelty, largely localized to the 20th century and to the context within which mediated popular culture and consumer advertising arose (Fowles, 1992a, chap. 2). In other times and places, notables emerged from such institutions as the polity, the military, religion, universities, the arts, and, infrequently, commerce; entertainers were lowly and unremarkable figures, rarely known by name, and if known to city dwellers, certainly not known in the countryside where the majority of the population lived. There, entertainment took the form of homespun folk culture and depended on whimsy, musicality, bravura, or derring-do—but certainly not on stars. The word "star," as applied to performers, was not in use before 1830, and not in general use until near the end of the 19th century. The appearance of this new cultural centerpiece has much to suggest about the social changes accompanying the rise of the production/consumption economy.

As discussed, popular culture is correctly understood as the domain that provides individuals with the symbolic material they can use to help normalize their lives. "Normalize" as employed here has two referents: interiorly, to normalize or correct emotions through the discharge of certain surplus feelings or the satisfaction of certain emotional deficiencies; and exteriorly (and secondarily), to remeet social norms or codes in a dramatized and behavioral form and to relearn operant beliefs and values. The individual's need for exposure to this normalizing symbol domain is hypothesized to have grown over the 20th century in response to what Cas Wouters (1986) calls the historical process of "informalization." In ever more informal, egalitarian times, suggests Wouters, people have to learn (and have learned) to channel emotions into inoffensive outlets and to be more considerate of others. As individuals increasingly turn to popular culture for help in meeting these obligations, it is little wonder their attention would center upon the element in that domain that most closely and thoroughly approximates their own condition—the solitary personage, the individuated star. The attention of enough audience members upon certain select performers grants those performers the widespread popularity that defines the star.

The individual spectator regards the star in several intensely personal ways. First, it is the star in a production who encapsulates and personifies the normalizing services of popular culture. The performance of the star—whether on a movie screen or a television set, at an athletic contest, on a stage, in a concert—is likely to deliver the emotional material the spectator is looking for and inculcate the feelings sought after. The behavior of the star will exemplify the relevant social norms in ways comprehensible by the spectator.

Second, drawing from a series of performances, the spectator will abstract and reapply to the performer a particular, defined personality. The spectator both knows, and does not care to know, that the personality is constructed from performance behavior that is unlike real-world behavior. The performance behavior is highly perfected—it has been practiced or rehearsed until it can be executed as flawlessly as possible, or it has been manipulated in the studio or editing room until it is a highly refined presentation. From these perfected performances the spectator constructs a rounded personality that takes on iconic significance. To give orientation to the development or maintenance of one's own personality, the spectator needs iconic personages and so fabricates suitably ideal types from the highly visible performances of stars. Grant McCracken (1989) submits that the star is "a guide to the self-invention in which all consumers are engaged" (p. 318).

Third, the fact that the star is known to many is itself advantageous because the spectator can use the star's personality and behaviors as conversational coin, and conduct informed and satisfying discourses with others. Stored star knowledge thus serves the spectator in yet another way in the aligning of the individual to the world beyond.

Last, and more broadly, the spectator senses the star to be a champion of the entire domain of popular culture. It is a domain antithetical and antidotal to the real world where doubt and distress reign; it is the pleasurable domain of play. Popular culture, the mythic land of gratification and compensation, is validated by the welcome personage of the star.

Because stardom is composed of a great range of personality types (Fowles, 1992b, chap. 4), the meanings that stars offer can serve a variety of purposes for the spectator. Stars can depict the perfectly normalized behavior that most modern people aim for. In a study of the imaginary social relations that spectators enjoy with stars, one of the respondents expressed admiration for Bill Cosby by saying, "He exhibits self-control. I try to exhibit this attribute and I hope to be as successful as Bill Cosby" (Alperstein, 1991, p. 49). But the meanings associated with other stars can conversely detail the borders of abnormality and deviancy, as for some the apparent androgyny of Michael Jackson did. In service to their audience, stars can range bravely and publicly into risky cultural areas. Although stars serve both as norm definers and norm defiers, even those traits that challenge norms (and, for an outlying few, become personality ingredients) are taken by most spectators to specify and reaffirm norms through their oppositional stance.

Large with imparted qualities, the constructed star can be extracted from the popular culture context to be a shadowy companion to the spectator in real time (Caughey, 1984, p. 41). Either as a love object or as a model of appearance and behavior, the star exerts an imaginary but actual presence in the conduct of the individual—sometimes strongly but more often only referentially. This symbolic accompaniment is more likely to occur among the young, who are seeking assistance in the stressful negotiations into adulthood and through the difficult development of the self-identity that will sustain them in decades to follow. A conspicuous feature of the condition of youth, as opposed to many other human conditions, is that it is unavoidable and universal. Everyone goes through the stage of being young, and every modern person brings into adulthood the residue of a devotion to particular stars—indeed, to stars in general.

The investment that spectators make in their popular culture stars represents a sort of equity that advertisers can only eye covetously. The solemn, heartfelt stature that stars enjoy with spectators, even if in the passing of years it has trailed off to mere familiarity, waits to be exploited. Because, luckily for advertisers, most stars are for hire, it is only a matter of time before the star takes on a secondary, commercial role as spokesperson.

Popular Music

The genre of popular music more clearly illustrates popular culture's primary appeal. Because music is largely devoid of narrative devices, it represents popular culture stripped to its emotional core. "Music has the ability to stimulate extraordinary emotional feelings," summarizes James Lull (1992, p. 12). The list of feelings that music can invoke is lengthy and remarkably varied: passion, affection, devotion, patriotism, aggression, rage, calm, nostalgia, fear, warmth, exhibition, happiness, sadness, pride, hope, delight, and so on. There is an undeniably somatic aspect to the reception of popular music, causing the body to relax or, in the opposite direction, become excited. The sounds and tempos of music penetrate the mind's defenses and partitions, and reach deeply into the subconscious strata, and to the associated kinetic sensations. Those who hum along with the music or mouth the lyrics are incorporating the music into themselves and themselves into the musically defined terrain where emotions are doctored. Succumbing to the evasive and invasive pleasures of music, the listener is inviting the currying of snarled feelings.

It is only logical that the sector of society in greatest need of emotional adjustment and remediation would be the sector most devoted to popular music. Whereas situation comedy is the preferred popular culture genre among the general population, music is the preferred genre among the young. Adolescents' use of popular music in the management of emotions has been explored in a survey by Alan Wells and Ernest Hakanen (1991) of 1,500 youths, aged 11 to 19. They report that "most respondents were able to identify strong links between music and emotions" (p. 449), the three emotions most frequently connected to music being excitement, happiness, and love.[8] The quest for excitement through music probably had more to it than the higher energy levels of the young; it served additionally to distinguish this age group from its elders, and from everything that elders represented. In Lawrence Grossberg's (1986) analysis of this demarcation as formed by rock music, "For the fans, one of the primary functions of the music was to create boundaries segmenting 'them' from 'us'—i.e., constituting differences. . . . Boredom was associated with both adulthood and the world it constructed. The celebration of pleasure and the body functioned to reinforce and redefine the separation of 'them' from 'us' " (p. 191).

The second emotion sought, that of happiness, would compensate for some of the unhappiness and turmoil that accompanies the maturation of individuals. To develop adult identities calls for much bumping against the impositions delivered by parents, schools, and peers. Adolescence is a tentative period, with great opportunity for psychic bruising; music can alleviate some of the distress. That, third, feelings of love would be sought and found by adolescents in music is hardly surprising since they are engaged in the transition between familial love and the adult variety, and must learn about the characteristics and conditions of the latter, as well as experience the sensations of it.

The emotional pleasures that adolescents derive from musical choices as individuals are then compounded into the musical tastes and the identity of subgroups (heavy metal fans, rappers, rockers), and even to the musical definition of a generation (the rock and roll generation). Popular music, beyond delivering emotional gratification to a listener, also serves as a ticket to membership in a group with similar tastes. Participation in the sphere of popular music is never a solo experience, even if done in a solitary fashion; it carries with it implicitly the bonus of integration into a coterie of the like-minded. This is not just a temporary coterie, but rather one that will spin on through the years, across time, tracked and incidentally strengthened by radio broadcasters attempting to create audiences for advertisers. In its own way, then, popular music reconstructs the social orientation which the lack of a narrative structure appears to discard.

Deriving emotional benefits from popular music and developing taste in particular types and instances of music are practices that live on in the minds of adult consumers. They endure as pleasurable and ever renewing experiences, ones that advertisers, seeking less defended entrances into consumers' minds, will exploit.

Notes

1. The assertion that popular culture serves in the management of emotions receives empirical support from a study by McIlwraith and Schallow (1983). Among a sample of 219 adults, viewing habits were correlated to interior mental

states; those who were the most distressed were the most likely to turn to television fantasy. The authors conclude that scholars "ought to regard the use of the media as one active means that individuals may employ to control their own awareness of or attention to their mental images and fantasies" (p. 86).

2. Elias (Elias & Dunning, 1986) was referring in particular to the pastime of spectator sport, but it is clear from his comments here and elsewhere in his book that his observations can be generalized to all leisure activities, including attending to popular culture.

3. It ought to be pointed out that the idea that narrative structure should proceed in a linear fashion, with a beginning, middle, and end, is a conceit of the literate mind. Preliterates (which humans have been for most of their 60,000-year span) do not tender stories in such a fashion; their stories dart from point to point, add overlays, jump to another perspective, proceed backward (as we see it), and so forth.

4. The contradictions rife in popular culture are here interpreted in psychological terms, as popular culture is seen in service first to personal emotions and second to perceived social norms. Among cultural studies scholars, it is more common to interpret the contradictions along social or political lines, as emblematic of class struggles. Thus, when Stuart Hall (1981) refers to popular culture's "double movement of containment and resistance, which is inevitably inside" (p. 228), the "double movement" he sees is the result of political or class acquiescence and contention rather than of the two front (emotions vs. norms) psychological struggles stressed here.

5. For a more complete discussion of viewers' use of television violence, see Fowles (1992a, chap. 7). See also Fowles's (1984) analysis of the academic misreading of television violence's utility.

6. Among those who would testify that situation comedies can produce a release of tension and a sense of relaxation is the Dalai Lama, the supreme spiritual leader of Tibetan Buddhists. During his 2-week tour of the United States in 1994, he told reporters that his favorite program was *M*A*S*H*, whose syndicated episodes he viewed daily. "It comes on at 5:30 p.m., in time for my evening tea" ("Couch Potato," 1994, p. A26).

7. For an exploration into the polysemy of *The Cosby Show*, see Jhally and Lewis (1992).

8. The 12 possible selections on the survey's checklist were love, hope, fear, pride, grief, anger, sadness, passion, delight, happiness, excitement, and confidence.

6

Exchanges

Michael Jackson is estimated to have personally earned $26 million in 1992 (Newcomb & Chatzky, 1992), putting him among the few most highly compensated entertainers and thus among the most valued individuals both economically and culturally. Worldwide, he might well have been the best known and most admired living person. He regaled millions upon millions of people through the video and audio sales of his music, supplemented by his global tours. Seeming to exist at a distance from the usual distinctions between genders, between ethnicities, between sexuality and asexuality, he floated somewhere above earthly categories, freed of the constraints that bind most mortals. His persona, active and randy when in performance, passive and bland when not, invited emotional projections from all sorts of people in all sorts of situations. When, just a year later in 1993, he began a free fall from grace, a global audience gasped in disbelief. The world's boy-warrior, the rock and roll angel, stood accused of pederasty, a heinous crime that not only affected those involved but also betrayed the image of perpetual youthhood, the state of innocence and awakening from innocence, that Jackson had so vividly personified. What had been idealized as pure and rare was now felt by many to be rancid and corrupt.

Jackson's millions of fans were not the only ones distressed by the turn of events. Executives at the Pepsi-Cola Corporation, which for a decade had had Jackson under contract as a product endorser, may well have been beside themselves with dismay. Beyond the enormity of the charges against Jackson and the transferred blotch onto Pepsi-Cola, Jackson had managed to implicate Pepsi more directly. When he terminated his "Dangerous" tour and dropped out of sight, he claimed that he was not fleeing prosecution but was seeking treatment for an addiction to painkillers prescribed after a scalp burn he received during the 1984 filming of a Pepsi commercial (Gleick, 1993). The soft drink executives were quick to exercise an escape clause in their agreement, and in November 1993 they severed their connection with Jackson, their longest lasting and most visible spokesperson.[1]

Michael Jackson was not the only celebrity endorser Pepsi had under contract, nor indeed the only one whose career had taken a turn that would seem to leave the bottler exposed to public derision. The company had experienced this vulnerability several times over ("Another Pepsi Star," 1993). In 1989, Pepsi had been contractually linked to the heavily promoted release of Madonna's "Like a Prayer"; a commercial containing scenes from the video was to be aired concurrently. But when the video proved to be too bawdy for some segments of the public, the soft drink company was forced to distance itself from the famous performer. After Mike Tyson was sentenced to a lengthy penitentiary term following a conviction for rape, Pepsi had to release this endorser too, and when Magic Johnson disclosed he had tested HIV-positive, Pepsi had little choice but to ease him out as a spokesperson. With an extensive record like this, why does Pepsi continue to use popular culture icons, notoriously fallible, as celebrity endorsers?

Stars' propensity to lose credibility in dramatic ways is epitomized in the saga of O. J. Simpson, a long-time Hertz spokesman. If such catastrophes were not enough, there are yet other liabilities to the association of entertainment figures with commodities. Leading performers are expensive to hire—ranging from hundreds of thousands to millions of dollars (Michael Jackson's 1984 contract with Pepsi was reportedly for $5 million)—and can represent a sizable portion of any promotional budget. Once hired, they bring to the promotional effort a set of meanings that enhances the marketing goals—but often other meanings that do not. The late actor John Houseman lent connotations of propriety and stead-fastness to the campaign of the Smith Barney brokerage firm, but when he was placed in a McDonald's commercial the same al-lusions undermined the chain's self-depiction as a site of escape and relaxation.

It is also entirely possible that the celebrity, who is often better known than the product, will overwhelm the sales message. For example, 70% of an audience sample correctly recognized that Joe Montana had appeared in a Super Bowl commercial, but only 18% remembered that the product he had endorsed was Diet Pepsi (Shani & Sandler, 1991). The celebrity, being an independent per-son, may harm the product's repute in more direct, disclosive ways. Cybill Shepherd has the distinction of doing this twice: when she undermined her contract with the National Live Stock and Meat Board by stating that she avoided red meat, and when she antagonized her advertising partner, L'Oreal Cosmetics, by affirming to an interviewer that she never colored her hair (Gabor, 1987). The majority of consumers now feel that stars in commer-cials are "less than credible" and that their appearance is due solely to financial considerations (King, 1985). In what would seem to be a decisive judgment of the worth of stars in advertising, an extensive study of persuasiveness in over 5,000 commercials determined that the presence of celebrity endorsers neither helped nor hindered success at communication (Hume, 1992).

The question asked of Pepsico readily applies to all advertisers: If stars do not make a difference and represent great expense and some risk, then why are they used in advertising? By count, celebrities appear in 22% of magazine advertisements (Stout & Moon, 1990) and, by estimate, in 20% of television commercials (Misra & Beatty, 1990).[2] The short answer is that sometimes stars do have a discernible effect on sales; Pepsi-Cola experienced a satisfying 8% rise in sales during 1984, the first year of its contract with Michael Jackson (Gabor, 1987). Advertisers know that, like it or not, they will have to take some chances if they are going to have any hope of enlarging their share of a particular market, such as the one for soft drinks. The use of popular culture stars in advertising represents a closely monitored gamble on the part of advertisers, one whose potential gains are seen to be worth the risk involved.

It is popular culture's appeal that advertisers are trying to exploit as they strive to stimulate interest in their products; their essential strategy is to get the familiar connotations of the popular culture material to shift onto the commodity. This chapter looks at several common types of symbol transfer from popular culture to advertising—iconic stars, popular music, and the conventions of humourous productions. Acmes of personal attractiveness also shift but do so in more of a back-and-forth fashion, as will be seen. Two varieties of apparently blatant intrusion in the opposite direction—from advertising into popular culture—are then discussed: product placement in movies and infomercials on television.

Stars as Endorsers

The growth in consumer-ingratiating advertising after 1920 immediately intersected another 20th-century trend: the nation's increasing awareness of and devotion to popular culture stars. Advertisers were quick to appreciate the sacred relationship between popular culture idols and spectators, and quick to hire stars as their spokespeople. Leading entertainers such as Joan Crawford, Clara Bow, and Janet Gaynor had their personal incomes handsomely enlarged from promotional budgets (Fox, 1984, p. 89). Stars lent themselves to the advertising agenda because of their fame, fame to an extent that had been inconceivable before the arrival of film and then of radio. What advertisers thought they were getting in celebrities were figures familiar to the public who could in turn make the product familiar; the star was performing the social tasks of an introduction and a recommendation.

More contemporary advertisers perceive the celebrity endorser as someone who can penetrate the commercial clutter on television and hold viewer attention for a few milliseconds longer.

What an advertiser hopes but may not articulate is that because people consume the image of a star they will consume a product associated with a star. People consume star images because they ascertain meanings in them, so whenever a celebrity endorsement communicates it is because there has been a successful transfer of meanings from the established performer to the commodity for sale—and then, ideally for the advertiser, from the commodity to the consumer in the form of a purchase (McCracken, 1989).

That this flow of meaning—at least the portion of it from celebrity to product—is not merely a theoretical concept but can go on in a measurable way was demonstrated in a 1991 experiment by Mary Walker, Lynn Langmeyer, and Daniel Langmeyer (1992). One hundred individuals were asked to rate the meanings of products and endorsers on a semantic differential scale consisting of 25 word pairs (such as Exotic/Ordinary, Attractive/Unattractive, High Quality/Low Quality) with seven possible gradient choices between each pair. Respondents were asked to evaluate Madonna or Christie Brinkley, then to evaluate one of three product categories (bath towels, blue jeans, or VCRs), and finally to evaluate the product when endorsed by the celebrity. The study's conclusion was "that the two endorsers are perceived very differently and that this perception difference does indeed affect product meaning" (p. 70). Each of the three products picked up the distinct characteristics of the specific endorser. For example, in comparison to Christie Brinkley's VCR, Madonna's VCR was judged "unattractive, risky, unreliable, unpleasant, low class, useless, disliked, rugged, nasty, unsophisticated, revolutionary, and silly" (p. 74).

Advertisers' choice of leading entertainers as spokespeople (as opposed to choosing, say, lesser known people with clearcut expertise pertaining to the product) carries with it certain valuable contextual inferences. These performers have found their fame within the domain of popular culture, and when they reappear in the domain of advertising, they to one degree or another bring with themselves an aura of entertainment and diversion (see Figure 6.1). When Candice Bergen testifies to the advantages of Sprint telephone service, the much enjoyed "Murphy Brown" is testifying also; when the retired Larry Bird appears in a Nike

Figure 6.1. Is this man an opthalmologist? Promoting a brand of dark glasses, his credibility derives from his stature as a player within the domain of popular culture. It is his expertise as a sports hero and a public figure that consumers want to rely upon. Dark glasses are a signature item of celebrities; consumers who choose this brand may want to share the spotlight. (Courtesy of Vuarnet-France Optical®.)

commercial, the active Larry Bird, memorable leader of the Celtics, is there too. When Lionel Richie or Ray Charles plays his own music in Pepsi commercials, the sensation of listening to one of his recordings or being at one of his concerts is rekindled. Comedienne, athlete, musician—it makes no difference: Each can reacquaint consumers with successful performances in his or her own corner of popular culture. Because the viewer is invited, when remeeting known stars, to remeet the known territory of popular culture, the advertisement loses some of its crassly persuasive nature and takes on diversionary highlights. The advertiser can only hope that this referential nimbus will cause consumer resistance to weaken and the advertising message to be greeted more favorably than it would be minus the celebrity endorsement. The more that the line between popular culture and advertising is blurred, the better are the advertiser's chances for successful communication.

When the transfer of meanings from the endorser to the product and from the performance to the advertisement works well, it works well indeed. Nike came to "mean" Michael Jordan, Bruce Willis is credited with moving Seagram's wine coolers to the top of the market by giving them a wry "with it" image, and Candice Bergen made Sprint stand out from other long-distance carriers—a Sprint executive reflected, "Using Candice in our TV spots has allowed us to break away from the competition by coming across as witty, different, smart, and even a little bit sassy" (Fitzgerald, 1993, p. S12). (A reversal of this approach is shown in Figure 6.2.)

However, when the endorsement process does *not* work, it is perhaps more revealing about the dynamics at play. The list of failed endorsers is long. For example, Suzanne Somers could not sell the services of Ace Hardware stores, Dom DeLuise could not interest consumers in NCR personal computers, Ringo Starr created no run on Sun Country Classic wine coolers, George C. Scott watched sales of Renault automobiles drop, and John Wayne chased buyers away from Datril painkillers. Even Bill Cosby, the master salesman for Jello and Ford, failed when it was his turn to tout E. F. Hutton. In these cases, the meanings that the celebrity presented to Americans did not transfer onto the commodity. Resistance to the transfer occurred because consumers could sense no congruity between

Figure 6.2. This advertisement makes sense only when readers recognize the well-known performer Tiny Tim. In this instance, however, the famous personage is being used antithetically: Consumers are invited to situate themselves in opposition to the star. (With permission of Kenwood Electronics Inc.)

the well-known celebrity and the less-well-known product; the breach between them was too great for meanings to flow easily, and was left unremedied in the creative execution of the advertising. Endorsements succeed only when consumers feel that meanings can shift along unimpeded paths from performer to product—either because of an inherent affinity between the two or because of the ingenuity of the agency's creative team, or both.

Whether it succeeds or fails, any celebrity advertisement constitutes further information about the star for the consumer. According to Neil Alperstein's (1991) analysis of consumer responses to celebrity spokespeople, informants "used commercial appearances in a dialectical manner in order to adjust their knowledge and beliefs about celebrities" (p. 53). Ed McMahon's personality takes on one more facet when he tries to sell insurance; Charles Barkley's aggressiveness is fine-tuned when he growls for Nike, "I am not a role model." As the star's image cycles back into popular culture, it does so with the new accretions of inferences from the commercial detour. Sometimes, the star has lost credibility due to the temporary role as a hawker of goods, and the image has been slightly flattened; if it is to be resuscitated, the star must retake a position within popular culture and deliver the enjoyable performances of before. Alperstein's respondents were often troubled by stars' appearances in commercials—"What does Jack Klugman know about copiers?" asked one, and another was appalled to find his hero Orson Welles advertising wine—but they were able to forgive these transgressions: "Paralleling relationships in real life, viewers can balance positive feelings for celebrities with negative or neutral attitudes towards their appearance in commercials" (p. 55). Such is the high regard and willing indulgence the American public showers upon the meaningful stars of popular culture.

Music in Advertising

In one study of over 1,000 television commercials, music was incorporated in 42% of them (Stewart, Farmer, & Stannard, 1990,

p. 40). The utility of music is commonly acknowledged within the advertising industry, even if music is usually among the last items specified for a commercial execution (Dunbar, 1990).[3] Background music can establish a mood with targeted consumers and also lend an emotional dimension to a brand (Bruner, 1990). Music is a great asset in the important task of delineating time and place, transporting viewers to, say, the Greek Isles, the World War II era, or the Christmas season. At some moments, for some of the audience, the music track can modify the meanings of the verbal or visual content.[4] Lyrics can deliver a straightforward sales message, and carefully selected notes can be the musical signature of a particular brand. There is substantial evidence that the music in advertising is more memorable than the words (Stewart et al., 1990). There is also a belief among advertisers, a belief that enjoys prima facie support, that a message can be repeated more times without exhausting itself if that message is musical. All in all, music can establish a congenial acoustical space within which an advertiser can grandly display whatever is being offered for size.

Although much of the music in advertising is original material composed expressly for a given campaign, an increasing proportion of it consists of reused popular culture hits (Rosenbluth, 1988). There are several strong reasons why advertisers might want to pay the higher fees for rights to a once popular song instead of commissioning new music from a jingle house. As television commercials have become briefer, the advertiser has had less opportunity to establish a new musical connection with viewers; songs already familiar to the audience have enhanced value under these foreshortened conditions. The meanings that established music inculcates with viewers are going to be more stable than the vaguer, flexible meanings of new music and, consequently, can be more accurately tested by the agency. When Nike purchased the right to use the Beatles' "Revolution," the company and its agency knew precisely the sorts of meanings they were buying. By selecting hits from a certain time and for certain fans, the advertiser expects to make connections with an older version of that same audience and so is able to target its commercial expeditiously. In the attempt to reacquaint that group of fans, and perhaps an even larger group, with a particular time and place, no music is likely to work better than a popular hit from that point in time. Just as stars do, hit music also conveys implications of the entire domain of popular culture and the pleasures and satisfactions of that domain (see Figure 6.3). The chances of the advertising message striking home can only increase if audience members let down their guard to welcome back a treasured piece of popular culture.

The use of popular music for commercial ends carries with it a particular contradiction, however, one with some potential for undermining an advertiser's grandiose design to be loved by all and rejected by none. The music may have initially achieved its sacred standing because of its oppositional stance to mainstream culture. Music can be embraced most fervently by the resentful young and the marginalized groups in greatest emotional need of it, using it to allay feelings of estrangement and to secure the perimeter of a subordinate but sustaining subculture. This music then defines the true, nonexploitative camaraderie of the like-minded, speaking to and reflecting sincere needs. Once that music is expropriated and applied to commercial purposes, to the extraction of the consumer's money, then it has violated its covenant with those who originally possessed it and gave it meaning. This violation may be great or small, but in any case, it represents a potential liability for the licensee. When in 1994 Bob Dylan, a long-time hold-out, finally licensed (the appropriately titled) "The Times They Are A-Changing" to a major accounting firm for its corporate advertising, more than a dissenting murmur was heard. "I'm shocked . . . I'm stunned," his biographer stammered ("Dylan Goes Commercial," 1994, p. 36). When "Da Doo Ron Ron" was used to sell Heinz Ketchup and "Tired of Waiting for You" to sell Nivea Shampoo, rock critic Jon Savage (1988) grew furious

> because those songs were originally part of an enfranchising social process. Their very success gave a voice and a face to the dispossessed: whether, in these cases, West Indians, white working-class punks or pure mavericks. Today, that success is turned against them

Figure 6.3. From *Rolling Stone.* Popular music can even be invoked in print advertising. This ad would establish a series of connections for those readers who recalled the famous rock band Sex Pistols. (With permission of Yamaha Motor Corporation, U.S.A.)

as they are reemployed to prop up an oligarchic, outmoded but highly powerful value system. (p. 32)

But not all those involved are so indignant. When Crosby, Stills, Nash, and Young licensed "Teach Your Children" to Fruit of the Loom underwear for $1.5 million, songwriter Graham Nash casually remarked, "I'm not that precious about my music. We're not talking Mozart here" ("Just in Case," 1994, p. 23). For the most part, advertisers are similarly nonchalant because they have found the number of the truly offended is typically small and the number of those engaged by the recycled hits enormous. When questions were raised about putting Pepsi's lyrics into Michael Jackson's "Billie Jean," a Pepsi executive responded plainly, "It's not like Tchaikovsky, writing for posterity. This is pop music, and it's written on a commercial basis" (Schwartz, 1988, p. 49).

The appetite of advertising for successful popular music is so great that it can devour whole genres. There is hardly a more alienated form of popular music than rap, originally the property of young, angry, urban, black males. Emerging in the South Bronx in the 1970s, rap had by 1990 been used in a number of campaigns, being intoned not only by Bart Simpson and Joe Pepsico but also by—in some sort of twisted cultural apotheosis—the Pillsbury Doughboy.[5] By the time the genre was deployed so far from its original locus, it had lost much of its resistant force and had become assimilated into the dominant culture; unless it was to be replenished at its root tips, it would soon be desiccated (Blair, 1993).

A similar co-option occurred with country music, which until 1992 had been considered outside the fold by most advertisers. Yet once they noticed it was the fastest growing segment of the music business, they began to hire one country music star after another. Willie Nelson signed with José Cuervo tequila, Clint Black with Miller Lite Beer, and George Strait with Wrangler jeans (Morris & Holley, 1992). Country music, which had previously circumscribed redneck culture and given definition to rural, underclass life, was losing some of its adversarial status and was being embraced more widely as a form of generic white blues. Singers were leaving behind their country accents and Western hats. As country became the most popular radio music format in 1993, Barbara Mandrell narrated the virtues of Sunsweet prunes, Eddie Rabbitt hawked Adidas shoes, and Tanya Tucker became a spokesperson for Black Velvet Canadian Whiskey (Kanner, 1993). Advertisers were falling over themselves to climb on the country music bandwagon, hoping it would not grind to a halt.

The alliance between advertising and popular music is so strong, as advertisers attempt to drape their products in the same meanings that greet popular hits and genres, that no one should have been stunned when Chevrolet, trying to find the appropriate hyperbole to announce its redesigned Camaro in 1993, reared back and brayed, "What else would you expect from the country that brought you rock 'n' roll?" What else indeed.

"Is It on Straight?":
Humor in Advertising

Little Caesar's Pizza, struggling to increase its share of the highly competitive pizza market, has successfully forged an identity based on humorous advertising. In a representative commercial, a chunky boy about 11 years of age grabs a slice of Little Caesar's Cheeser Cheeser Pizza as he darts down a jetway to a departing plane. The cheese pizza topping stretches out behind him. In the air, an elderly woman[6] says to her equally elderly male companion, "I just want to freshen up my lipstick." The shot of her in the washroom is through the mirror; she is puckering her lips and preparing to apply lipstick. Then the plane begins to jerk about crazily, for it is still tethered to the airport by the elastic pizza cheese. The nose of the plane bobs up and down; the nose of the lady is mashed against the mirror glass. The plane breaks free, and the woman, lipstick smeared over her lower face, is next seen asking her companion, "Is it on straight?" The man stares back incredulously, as does the boy from the next row (the same one who had brought the pizza slice on board). Cut to the sales message—Cheeser Cheeser Pizza is $7.99.

When Connie Feldman, the woman who played the airplane passenger, was asked by an interviewer what the skit had to do with pizza, she responded, "Nothing. Nothing. There wasn't any connection at all" (Fulford, 1993, p. 15G). Well, yes and no. It might seem that lipstick application and pizza are not related; it would especially seem so to an adult woman who does regularly wear lipstick and who does not regularly eat pizza. But if the two are not directly related, they are indirectly yet strongly connected through a third element—the preadolescent lad (who, it just so happens, represents the largest demographic segment of the target market). What looks like a small role to an older person is, to any boy or girl, the largest role in the vignette and the point of meaningful entry into the commercial, the gateway to the path that may lead to the eventual purchase (or, harassing for the purchase) of the product. It is the boy who frames the commercial, being present at the beginning and the end, and more important, it is the youngster who is the agent of the action, the commercial's protagonist, for it is he who brings the cheesy pizza slice on board and it is his double take that certifies the humorous mishap that has resulted.

The essence of the humor in the commercial, the cause of laughter for those viewers who did laugh, lies in the contention of the subordinate against the superordinate, the young against their elders, the mischievous against the decorous, the pizza-eaters against the non-pizza-eaters.[7] Humor, if artfully wrought (as it is here), is the means by which this contention is acknowledged and the contentiousness of the struggle is mitigated. The agency and the commercial director it hired have skillfully employed several comedic devices: the conventional quality of the establishing scene in the airport, the casting of the pudgy lad (jolly, prankish, playful, excessive), the casting of the elderly woman as the laughingstock, the visual hyperbole of the looping plane held by the strands of cheese, the physical comedy of the nose squashed against the mirror, the incongruity of the askew lipstick and the proper lady asking if it was "on straight," the double take of the old man and the boy, and the editor's skillful pacing throughout. The agency personnel may have convinced their client that the commercial would be good because it provided memorable testimony to the cheesiness of their product (the commercial ran during the fall season when Americans' caloric intake is on the rise), but what the agency really accomplished was something more difficult and significant—the construction of a bridge of meanings between the product and the targeted consumer.

Let's disentangle the humor a bit more. The woman featured, Connie Feldman, was 88 years old when this commercial was made; the casting director remarked that he had been instructed to find someone "very senior" (Fulford, 1993, p. 15G). By situating their character so far along the age spectrum, the creators of the commercial made her into a distant "other" and opened up the broadest chronological territory for the "non-others," those who could be in on the joke. The commercial is designed to appeal to not simply youngsters but to the mischievous child in almost everyone. The commercial taps not only viewers' resistance to propriety but their resistance to aging and ultimately to death, the greatest impropriety of all. Connie Feldman signified all this. What precipitates the discharge of laughter toward her "otherness" is the artistic adeptness with which she is made to commit a social mishap, a small death. In and of itself, the setting of the airplane in flight introduces a note of jeopardy. The social calamity is constructed by first establishing her as a social creature; she is witnessed in a social setting (the airplane aisle) making a social comment (regarding her departure from her companion) about her social appearance (her lipstick). Then she composes herself in private for her social reemergence, establishing conditions for social success or failure. Next, she sports the makeup of someone who is outside the pale; she has lost face. When she dies a symbolic death, viewers' fear of their own deaths are lessened through their laughter at her.

The entire vignette is begun, elaborated, and concluded in just 22 seconds. This would hardly seem enough time for what is, on analysis, a very complex tale. Life (in the spontaneity of the boy) and death (the social humiliation of a person near the end of her life span) have occurred in miniature.

The reason why the commercial works, that it can be easily absorbed, is that all the ingredients of it are well known to viewers through their exposure to, and expertise in, the humor offered up in popular culture. The character of the mischievous boy whose actions challenge the adult world is well established: Kevin in the film *Home Alone,* the comic strip's "Dennis the Menace," and TV's Bart Simpson. The slightly befuddled older person is also a stock character: cartoondom's Elmer Fudd, Coach on *Cheers,* and Rose on *Golden Girls.* The gyrating airplane is reminiscent of the excesses in the movie *Airplane,* and the amazed, speechless double take is a staple of American video humor. The four-part structure and pacing of the joke is also a standard format: the introduction of the characters and their actions, the hyperbolic premise of the stretched pizza cheese, the second comedic cue of the nose pressed against the glass (decorum rendered ridiculous), and the climax with its incongruities.

Viewers, wanting to enjoy the release of laughter, come to commercials highly trained in the conventions of American humor and primed to "get it" (that is, to supply meaning). The schoolhouse for their expertise in what is a very intricate and sophisticated activity has been their years of contact with popular culture. Acknowledging the audience members' desire to laugh, advertisers raid the precincts of popular comedy for renditions that will arrest audience attention as they stimulate laughter and create a postrelease contentment that might be transferred to the product.[8] By count, 30% of radio advertisements and 24% of those on television are intended to be humorous (Weinberger & Gulas, 1992).[9]

Cycles of Attractiveness

Regarding the complex modern vocabularies of iconic celebrities, music, and humor, it is clear that, for the most part, meaning-eliciting material is cultivated within popular culture and then expropriated by advertising. On the matter of establishing ideals and representations for physical attractiveness, however, the symbolic transactions are more dialectical, with ideations from popular culture and ideations from advertising impacting each other. Although attractiveness is held to lie solely on the surface, it does not; it refers to other human qualities that lie below. By empirical demonstration, attractive males, compared to those less so, are judged more intelligent, more controlled, self-accepting, sensation seeking, and resilient, whereas attractive females are decreed more socially adept, understanding, achieving, enduring, and inquisitive (Lakoff & Scherr, 1984, p. 132).

How do such attributes get established? In no small part it is through the provision of popular culture that visible personal surfaces get attached to invisible personal qualities. The spectator sees attractive males and females in performance and, through close observation of behaviors, learns to match up certain exteriors with certain inferred interiors. What advertising does, since on final analysis it is wholly given over to the merchandising of the palpable, the visible, the commodified, the superficial, is to strip the surface off personalities and present those surfaces in their most purified form as epitomes of beauty. Those ideations of attractiveness then flow back into popular culture (occasionally with actual people attached, as models try to become actors) to influence the new selections for stardom. The cycle of attractiveness defined in popular culture and then refined in advertising repeats again and again as personalities are reduced to surfaces and these surfaces are turned back into personalities.

The emphasis on attractiveness in both symbol domains, and the constant traffic in ideals of attractiveness between them, is a reflection of the preoccupations of audience members. Standards for physical attractiveness are arguably more crucial to the operations of current culture than they ever have been in human history (Banner, 1983, p. 290). Over the course of the 20th century, the increasing informality of social relations and the decreasing sovereignty of social categories and traditional institutions have compelled the individual to become responsible both for an interior personality that adjusts the emotional contours within to the prevailing social norms and realities, and for the exterior appearance that makes portions of the personality publicly manifest and accessible. People have to put their best face on and negotiate on their own

Figure 6.4. From *Seventeen*. Testimony to the rising importance of personal appearance, the legend here—"Your face is the first thing people see when they meet you"—could be the maxim of 20th-century life. (Courtesy of the Procter & Gamble Co.)

behalf (see Figure 6.4). Because of the rising importance of appearance, there has been concomitantly a rising interest in exemplars of physical attractiveness. Where else are the many to find the few perfected templates of attractiveness than in the highly polished and widely disseminated imagery of the mass media?

The criterion of physical attractiveness has grown so important over the century—applying first and formidably to women, later and less to men—that the likelihood that it would provoke a reaction could only increase in time. It was also perhaps predictable that the adverse response would fix on the most extreme depictions: those in advertising. It was not only committed feminists who resisted the imagery but also less ideologically focused women who began to find in advertising's females first something unachievable and perhaps misery-making, and then something worthy of resentment. When portions of the consumer population slide from a posture of envy to a posture of indignation, the advertising mission would appear to be compromised. The feminist critique of images of beauty is more cerebral and potentially more devastating because it strikes at the ideological roots of the portrayal of women. The argument, in brief, critiques advertising "in the way that it deploys images of women, constructs and reaffirms stereotyped and limiting views of women's lives and capabilities" (Betterton, 1987, p. 19). The stereotypes are held to serve paternalistic sensibilities, in that beautiful women are represented as objects to be ogled and possessed, humans converted into commodities, painted and decorated, slight, vulnerable with limbs and chest exposed, wobbly on high heels.

But in spite of the reaction to advertising's portrayal of distilled beauty, consumers' need for stereotypes of appearance has proved active enough to discourage much experimentation. In fact, over time, the stereotypes have become even narrower. In a survey of magazine advertising between 1950 and 1980, the proportion of heavy models dropped from 12% to 3% of all women featured, whereas the use of very thin models rose from 3% to 46% (Gagnard, 1986). Another content analysis found that "women's roles as decorative objects in advertising have continued to increase over the years, despite social changes brought about by the feminist movement" (Busby & Leichty, 1993, p. 258). That is, women are ever more commonly portrayed not as producers (either at home or on the job) but as beautiful empty objects.

Advertising Overtakes Popular Culture?

Other symbolic material besides ideations of attractiveness also cycles between the domains of popular culture and advertising. A frequent route occurs when content with low salience in popular culture but still resident there gets employed in advertising, enjoys wide display, and subsequently reemerges in popular culture but on a much broader plane. The "Simpsons" enjoyed a few minutes of airtime on the *Tracey Ullman Show,* became spokespeople for Butterfingers candy bars, and went on to star in their own television program and their own movies. Bob Uecker was a major-league baseball player of sorts, developed a comedy routine based on his short-lived career and found a small audience for it, became a spokesperson for Miller Lite Beer, and reemerged with his own situation comedy. Max Headroom and George Foreman took the same circuit. Spike Lee, known in limited circles as an independent film director, received wide exposure in Nike commercials as Michael Jordan's alter ego, and reemerged in the culture industries as a recognized and powerful figure.

Less common is a one-way flow from advertising, the more dependent domain, to popular culture, the mightier one. Elle Macpherson began as an advertising model and then, after gaining prominence in a *Sports Illustrated* swimsuit issue, went on to garner movie roles; Jim Varney's character, Ernest, was first an advertising figure and then had movies built around him; a Coca-Cola jingle became a pop tune; and directors of commercials have gone on to try their hand at Hollywood films, bringing some of their techniques and stylistic flair with them. On occasion, however, the movement from advertising into popular culture is a brash, generic one, forcible enough to be met by resistance from those offended by it. Two flagrant instances of this are the appearance of brand-name goods in films (known as "product placements") and the development of the "infomercials" which have displaced half-hour segments of televised popular culture.

Owing to the commitment of multi-million-dollar budgets and the contributions of perhaps the grander talents of the times, the medium of the movies is the artistic capstone of 20th-century popular culture. Few would deny that the stories told in that medium are the most encompassing and well-wrought fables of American civilization. That the medium, purportedly not an advertising one, could be tainted by commercial content is anathema to many. "Commercialization debases the art medium, whatever its form, by compromising its producer's integrity and the audience's trust," complained a contributor to the *New York Times*, who found within the film *Bull Durham* some 50 brand-name references (Jacobson, 1988, p. 39).[10]

The product placement subindustry has grown vigorously over the past two decades as Hollywood producers have sought additional sources of income to offset rising production costs, and as advertisers have searched the media horizons for underused and less resisted venues for their promotions. Some observers may be upset, but few are surprised when Tom Cruise conspicuously drinks a Bud in *Top Gun*, Meg Ryan sips Snapple in *Sleepless in Seattle*, Kevin Costner downs Stolichnaya in *The Bodyguard*, and Woody Harrelson gulps Coca-Cola in *Natural Born Killers*. Nor when Sylvester Stallone and Wesley Snipes race millions of dollars worth of GM products through *Demolition Man* and a fleet of Ford Explorers stars in *Jurassic Park*. Nor when the Flintstones chow down at McDonald's "RocDonald's" and Taco Bell is the only surviving fast-food chain in the 21st-century setting of *Demolition Man*.[11]

Elsewhere, the recent appearance of television infomercials might constitute bolder evidence of an untoward invasion by advertising into the domain of popular culture. These segments represent the capitulation of some of television's less contested temporal territory to the forces of commodification. Beginning in 1984, when the FCC relaxed regulations against the wholesaling to advertisers of television time previously reserved for entertainment, half-hour infomercials have become commonplace on smaller channels and in late-night broadcasting. From its tawdry beginnings with get-rich-quick schemes and condo sales, the genre quickly developed to the point of attracting highly regarded advertisers like Braun and Volvo. Further compromising a separation between popular culture and advertising, some of the entertainment world's best-known figures are finding infomercials a bully pulpit for stirring up consumer fervor: Roseanne sells her line of large-size clothing, Vanna White plugs Perfect Smile tooth whitener with great success, and Cher touts a line of cosmetics.

Although evidence of a current ascension of advertising content within the sphere of public communication looks compelling, what is seen more likely represents a change in presentation than a change in volume. Since the late 19th century, the communication media have always been friendly to the advertising agenda, often even more openly than at present. When magazines developed as a dedicated medium for advertising, the editorial content had to be generally favorable toward advertisers and often specifically so. Half-hour single-advertiser programs, as congenial to the sponsor as possible, were the stable of radio and television broadcasting until the 1950s when advertisers, in the aftermath of the quiz show scandals, began to find it prudent to scatter their messages throughout the broadcast week. And product placement in movies, as contemporarily challenging as the practice may seem, actually has an extended history, at least as far back as 1945 when Joan Crawford conspicuously consumed Jack Daniel's whiskey in *Mildred Pierce* (Nebenzahl & Secunda, 1993). It is not clear that advertising's intrusion into popular culture is any more widespread today than it was decades ago.

The greater or lesser prevalence of advertising aside, what is clear is that the public does *not* consider the amount of advertising overwhelming. For audience members, the advertising domain remains manageable and of undiminished utility. A study of product placement determined that most people do not object to the practice; when asked to complete the sentence "In my opinion, product placement is _____ and should be _____," 70% of the moviegoers' responses in the first blank were positive in nature as were 66% of their responses in the second one (Nebenzahl & Secunda, 1993). The appearance of products in movies, paralleling the appearance of products in real life, may make a film seem more realistic and vivid. Viewed within the extended narrative of a film, the products featured provide spectators with a full set of candidate meanings; the spectator has more information for making purchase choices. Moreover, the public's perception of television commercials is generally not unfavorable; according to one viewer survey, "Of the total mentions, 72 percent would be considered favorable and 28 percent negative. . . . These overall positive impressions are surprising and very likely at variance with the popular view influenced by critics of television advertising" (Aaker & Bruzzone, 1981, p. 17).

Advertising is not depleting or obliterating popular culture, nor has the advertising effort, no matter how subtle or shrewd, managed to eradicate general recognition that advertising is advertising and popular culture is popular culture. Audience members willingly tolerate the interpenetration of the two domains and even at times encourage it so that highlights from one will add luster to the other. The spectator is always on the lookout for symbols and meanings, and sometimes certain enhanced symbols, reverberating back and forth between the two domains, are appropriate and useful.

Notes

1. The relationship between Pepsi and Michael Jackson had been a strange one from the start. A Jehovah's Witness, Jackson did not drink the product himself and was not willing to fake it for a commercial nor even to say anything that directly pertained to the soft drink. Still, the company made extensive use of Jackson in its advertising and promotions.

2. Furthermore, according to Stout and Moon's (1990) data, the use of celebrity spokespeople is on the rise, climbing from 44.1% of all endorsers in 1980 to 58.2% in 1986 (p. 542).

3. Advising advertising practitioners on the use of music in commercials, David Dunbar (1990) offers, "The best place to study both the use and the effectiveness of music in communication is in big screen feature films" (p. 200), and so directs them back to the font of popular culture.

4. In a demonstration of the utility of music at modifying meanings, Dunbar (1990) and his colleagues took attractive but meaningless film footage and paired it with six different musical tracks. The films were then shown to focus groups.

"With different music tracks, the original film, peaceful *without* music, became in turn exhilarating, serious, expectant, menacing, frightening, sinister, insecure" (p. 203).

5. The Doughboy was breakdancing as he rapped. According to an agency executive, "Originally we wanted the Doughboy to moonwalk, but it was a problem because he doesn't have knees" (Berger, 1991, p. 27).

6. The person playing the female airplane passenger was not a professional actress but a retirement home resident and a near accidental choice. She later reported, "I didn't know anything about the casting being done. I just came downstairs and everybody was all lined up. They said, 'You're the chosen one.' " Despite the modicum of fame that greeted her performance, Connie Feldman was not interested in repeating the experience: "I wasn't bitten by the acting bug" (Fulford, 1993, p. 15G).

7. Among the contentions addressed by the Little Caesar's Pizza commercial is the contest between genders. The female is the butt, and males are the cause of and testifiers to her faux pas.

8. That some viewers will perceive themselves as identical to the laughing-stock of a humorous commercial is virtually the only risk an advertiser takes with this presentational mode. People do not like being the objects of ridicule, a fact that is telling about both the nature and the strength of humor. Italian Americans, computer hackers, owners of cocker spaniels—any group will retort if fun is made of them. The female character in the Little Caesar's commercial belonged to a group without much power, which may have been an unacknowledged factor in the creative development of the commercial. The strategy of an advertiser then must be to, first, create a butt familiar enough that it elicits laughter but not so familiar that millions will place themselves empathetically in the butt's position, and second, not run the commercial so long that an opposition has the chance to crystallize.

9. In contrast to the prevalence of humor in radio and television commercials, Weinberger and Gulas (1992) report that only 10% of print ads have a humorous intent. Humor has the best chances of working when it can be carefully sequenced in time.

10. Among the 50 brand names sighted or mentioned in *Bull Durham* were 21 for Miller beer and 7 for its arch-competitor, Budweiser. One is left to wonder who is toying with whom—are advertisers gulling audience members more or less than movie producers are playing fast and loose with advertisers, pitting one against the other?

11. Actually, Taco Bell is featured only in the American release of *Demolition Man*. Outside the United States, it is Pizza Hut. Stallone's lips mouth "Taco Bell," but the words heard on the soundtrack of the international version are "Pizza Hut." The producers felt this lack of a lip synch was no problem because in most foreign markets moviegoers see a dubbed or subtitled version anyway (King, 1993).

7

The Surface of the Advertisement, Composed and Consumed

In directly contributing recognizable and appreciated ingredients and then in establishing a congenial setting, popular culture is providing great services to its boon companion, the domain of advertising. Important as these contributions are, however, it is only further investigation that can uncover the general thrust of advertising communication. What essentially is the content that is laid out on the surface of the advertisement? At the start of this chapter, concern is not with the totality of the compound advertisement but with the symbolic material that is left once notice of the commodity itself is subtracted from the message. That is, we are reaching for generalizations regarding the kinds of cultural symbols that advertisers strive to attach to their products, no matter what those products are.[1]

Scrutinizing the surface of the advertisement for what is presented there invariably leads to the problem of "meaning." The meaning that one person takes from an advertisement is certain to differ from what another person does.[2] How then is the content of advertising determined? The only answer is through a collection of approximations, all of them more or less imperfect but yet all of them an improvement over blanket ignorance or, worse, ascertainable untruths.

The Dominant Theme in Advertising Imagery

It is a surprisingly small palette of imagery that creative directors in advertising agencies typically turn to. The criteria for inclusion on this palette are severe, although they are not so rigid that they cannot slowly evolve in time. The imagery must be potentially meaningful to the audience, of course; the expensive display of meaningless material has no earthly purpose here. The imagery should usually be congenial, as its meanings are often intended to glide over onto the product. Unpleasant imagery is risky and hence rare (see, for example, Figure 7.1).[3] Ordinarily, the images must be pleasant to the greatest number and offensive to the fewest; the chosen pictures must, as Andrew Wernick (1992) wrote, "reach over the heads of the combatants and beyond their incompatibilities to whatever, nevertheless, can be expected to unite them all" (p. 43). Because the task of the messages is to change behavior, and the easiest, least resisted change in behaviors is in the direction of ideals, the images should usually be idealized depictions. These idealized depictions cannot be sanctimonious or insincere, or they are sure to be shunned. The number of possible themes dwindles.

Because advertisements are trying to inculcate meanings and because meanings exist only in a human context, it makes sense that the majority of advertisements contain images of people. In a study of advertising in men's and women's magazines, about 75% of all ads featured humans (Masse & Rosenblum, 1988, p. 129). The percentage is even higher in commercials—an analysis of both morning and evening network commercials determined that 87% contained human beings (Bretl & Cantor, 1988, p. 600). Because advertisements are messages designed to instigate sales, a visitor from another planet might well ask if they are selling people, since images of people typically occupy more of the purchased time and space than do images of commodities. Advertisers make this allocation because the harder job is not the display of the inert product but the display of a human context that may or may not lend singular meanings to that product (a product sure to resemble all the other competing products in its class).

Figure 7.1. One of the rare unappealing figures in advertising, exaggerated so as to be comedic, this gentleman is not the centerpiece of the Logitech campaign but a peripheral, change-of-pace character and so perhaps a relief. The computer users targeted by this ad may enjoy its collegiate whimsy but have little inclination to allow the image to color the product. Then again, isn't there a little larceny in everyone? (© 1993 Logitech Inc. Used by permission.)

The people portrayed in American advertising are often engaged in pleasurable, leisure, off-hours activities. Swedish scholar Gunnar Andren (1978) conducted a content analysis of a carefully composed sample[4] of American print ads and found that less than 5% of the 300 ads examined showed scenes of employment (p. 130). Of the 162 ads he coded for some depicted activity, 110 (or 37%) contained leisure-time activities (p. 140). In a Canadian study, leisure was featured in just 1% of the 1930s' ads but almost 20% of the 1970s' (Leiss et al., 1990, p. 272). Using perhaps a narrower definition of leisure, Richard Pollay found leisure in evidence in 14% of his 1975 sample, still a gain from the 8% found at the start of the century (Belk & Pollay, 1987, p. 55).

The pleasures illustrated in advertising are commonly tamer and slighter than those available in popular culture; the brevity of the advertising presentation and the requirement not to violate the definitions of comportment held by potential customers dictate this. However, for one kind of pleasure—sexuality—the opinion is widespread that its depictions in advertising are on the rise. A 1986 study explored this by comparing a sample of 1964 print ads with a comparable sample of 1984 ads; the finding was that "the percentage of ads with sexual content has remained constant" (Soley & Kurzbard, 1986, p. 53). Then what can account for the general perception that the use of sex in advertising is expanding? Soley and Kurzbard (1986) provide two clues: First, although the proportion of sexual ads remained the same, the number of ads per magazine issue had climbed, which meant more sexuality in the advertising environment; and second, although the proportion of sexual ads remained constant, the sexual depictions within that percentage had become more overt, which also meant more sexuality in the advertising environment. Proportions had stayed the same, yet sexuality had increased. However, to put this into perspective, American advertising remains conspicuously prudish in contrast to its European counterpart; only 2.5% of Soley and Kurzbard's 1964 sample and 4.3% of their 1984 one were suggestive of sexual intercourse (p. 51). Fowles (1976) found strong sexual appeals in only 2% of print ads (p. 92); Pollay, studying 1975 print ads, found also that just 2% contained what he labeled "eros" (Belk & Pollay, 1987, p. 133).

Of interest is the fact that the social settings and personages characteristic of post-World War II advertising in the United States do not advance class distinctions and status markers as prominent themes. The comparative absence of class depictions has been especially clear to European observers, for in their home countries such social clues infuse advertising. "It is surprising that status does not play a major role," Andren (1978, p. 139) reported about American ads, expressing an incredulity that a native-born observer might not be susceptible to; only about 10% of the ads in his sample contained obvious status symbols. In a 1991 comparison of British and American print ads, the hypothesis that the U.S. ads would overwhelmingly depict an idealized upper-middle-class consumer and the British ads would reflect more class consciousness through a range of class portrayals was borne out in the data: Only 1% of American ads featured working-class people, whereas 24% of British ads did (Frith & Wesson, 1991, p. 222).

The relative classlessness of American advertising does not capture social reality, for every American senses that different social classes do exist, nor does it parallel popular culture offerings, where class placements and class markers are frequently conspicuous, contributing an important scale to the dramatic action in many programs and films. The muting of class information in advertising serves to eliminate an unpleasant social reminder from the message. Its removal also responds to a democratic American ideal, further confirming that advertising is the symbolic domain where ideals are advanced. The absence of class distinctions shifts the calibration from social definitions to personal definitions, from society to the individual.

Advertising imagery may be relatively free of the categorical impositions of work and of class, but just the reverse is the case with gender depictions. The liberated individuals within American advertising are sure to be highly delineated prototypes of maleness and femaleness. When Alice Courtney and Thomas Whipple (1983) complain that "women and men in society today clearly are far different from their portrayed images in advertising" (p. 24), they are unquestionably correct: Advertisers are certain that images of people as they are "in society today" will draw no more attention in advertising than do average people in the real world, whereas highly stylized paragons will attract the same fascinated gazes they would if they were spotted walking down any street in America. Thus, normal or unattractive people are rare in advertising (see Figure 7.2); only 1 of the 300 ads that Andren (1978) studied depicted a body deformed by work, sickness, or age (p. 125).

For females in ads, appearance was most commonly the totality of their persona, Andren determined; if any character trait shone through pictures of women, it was most likely to be "niceness" or "tenderness" (p. 128). Male appearance was most frequently and stereotypically linked to "toughness" or "expertise" (p. 128). The women in advertising conform to, as Andren says, "a very narrow ideal of female beauty" (p. 123). About half of the featured females are going to be noticeably thin (Gagnard, 1986, p. R46).[5] They are more likely than male models to be smiling (71% vs. 49%) (Choe, Wilcox, & Hardy, 1986, p. 125), a sign of amiability and acquiescence. They are also many times more likely than males to be partially or completely undressed (Andren, 1978, p. 132; Soley & Kurzbard, 1986, p. 53; see Figure 7.3).

The presence of so many lithe and less-clothed women represents advertisers' attempt to project certain meanings onto their commodities. The objectified women are redolent in possible significations: They are vital, warm, accessible, pliable, consumable. They are the apples of many men's eyes, and some of their desirability can slide over to the inert product they are linked with. Such depictions may work with male consumers, but advertisers are convinced they work with females as well; according to Soley and Kurzbard (1986), in the 1984 ads they reviewed, the depiction of partially clad or nude models was 50% greater in women's magazines than in men's (p. 50). The implication would have to be that men are drawn to a certain portrayal of femininity and women are drawn toward occupying that portrayal; for women as well as men, a favorable disposition to the portrayal might then shift to the product.

Both males and females in advertising are certain to be youthful. This feature is so conventionalized that it may be overlooked, but

Kotex understands what it means to be a woman.

Presenting the Kotex SecureHold Maxi.
With a wraparound tab from Velcro USA.

It stays in place better than an
ordinary maxi. So it protects you better.

For protection that really stays in place. **Kotex Understands.**

Figure 7.2. The normal, the average, is uncommon in advertising, so uncommon that, intertextually, it can make one ad stand out from all the rest. The rarity of the ordinary confirms that advertising deals almost exclusively in the extraordinary, removed from the plane of everyday life. (© 1994 Kimberly-Clark Corporation. Used by permission.)

Code Bleu Jeans 1466 Broadway NYC 10036

Figure 7.3. Nude figures in advertising are much more likely to be female than male. This advertisement, which because of the strong presence of the unclothed woman looks to be simplicity itself, is actually somewhat complicated. In the original ad, the spiral around her is blue, signifying the missing product. Thus, her body and the product are intertwined, and meanings are meant to flow from one to the other. Her body signals both liberation (nudity, dancing) and control (a choreographed movement), and her ethnicity may well signal social change and the avant-garde. (Courtesy of Code Bleu Jeans.)

it should not be, for it is suggestive of the ultimate function of advertising imagery. Busby and Leichty (1993) found that over 70% of the women in both 1959 and 1989 ads were judged to be between 18 and 34 (p. 259). There has been no discernible broadening or raising of age stereotypes over the decades for females, and the same is likely the case for males. Males' age in ads has always averaged several years older than females' (England, Kuhn, & Gardner, 1981), but there is no evidence that, as time has passed, this average has increased.

The greatest change in advertising since World War II has been the ascendant motif of the solitary figure. Andren (1978) found that illustrations of individuals occurred far more frequently than couples, families, or friends. He wrote, "When we read advertisements, we get the impression that people live completely isolated from one another in a social vacuum" (p. 142). Leiss et al. (1990) discovered that individualism rose steadily over the 20th century in their sample of Canadian print ads (p. 272). Similarly, in Fowles's (1976) study of motivational appeals in a sample of American print ads from 1950 to 1970, the sharpest climb was in the need for autonomy (p. 92). A single human figure was the most prevalent element in Masse and Rosenblum's (1988) sample of 564 print ads from 1984, prompting them to reflect about advertising that "this utopian world sustains an idealized, narcissistic self" (p. 131). A comparison of 1988 American and British print ads found that 57% of the American ads contained a single person, whereas 45% of the British advertising did (Frith & Wesson, 1991, p. 220).

A summary statement does a disservice to the outlying content in the expressive domain of advertising, but can capture the central themes. More than anything else, the imagery in advertising is that of idealized human beings. There is no requirement that this be so (advertising could feature abstract colors or pictures of ferns or no images at all), but it happens because advertisers have learned over time that this is what consumers want to look at. The people featured are largely devoid of employment and social locus and increasingly devoid of family and, in fact, others altogether (see Figure 7.4). This fascination speaks to our situation in history, to the present need to observe paragons of the self. It can be inferred that the imagery that lies on the surface of the advertisement is pertinent to the newly all-important concern for construction of the self. The imagery depicts young people because youth is the stage most given over to the formation of self-identity.[6] It shows leisure activities because those are the hours devoted to the self. It is gender-ridden because gender lies at the core of self-identity. Advertising imagery fixes on what individuals fix on, converting their needs into its forms in the hope that acceptance of these figurations will lead to acceptance of the commodities offered.

Social Values and Advertising

The imagery that lies on the surface of advertising is often subject to debate regarding whether it creates social values or simply mirrors social values already in existence. Critics of advertising usually hold the first position; defenders find solace in the second. Stuart Ewen (1988) appears to believe in the former, for he claims that advertising style is "a process of creating commodity images for people to emulate and believe in" (p. 91). Bruce Brown (1981), however, defends the latter, arguing that "advertising can be said to *reflect* middle-class cultural values" (p. 12).

Considering the fact that this debate has been raised countless times in virtually every serious treatment of advertising (including here), why is it that it has never been conclusively settled? The question is possibly a good (even if unanswerable) one, drawing out quickly and succinctly any observer's position regarding advertising. But there is also the possibility that it is a duplicitous question, appearing to address the issues but actually concealing them in such a way that they cannot be productively confronted. In truth, the relationship between advertising imagery and social values is unlikely to be a simple cause-and-effect one nor one conducted on one plane—both of these being implications in the query as originally formulated. Advertising imagery may not "cause" social values and existing social values may not "cause" advertising depictions, in any way that resembles simple causation. Nor, given the discrepancy between the heightened idealizations prominent

Figure 7.4. What Americans primarily want to gaze at in advertising are exemplars of the individual, shorn of social trappings and pure in self-containment. They want to study the surfaces of those idealizations, first, to view acmes of attractiveness, and, second, to catch any glimpses of integrity, self-respect, and contentment. (Courtesy of Bestform Foundations, Inc.)

in advertising imagery and the typically routinized lives (necessarily) of spectators, is it likely that communication would occur in a direct and level way according to the information flow presumed to exist in both arguments.

Advertising cannot create social actualities out of whole cloth, and it is folly to think it could. To believe it can impose stereotypes of its own making upon the public is to hold demeaning and, in the end, unsupportable views about the nature of the public. Consumers do not all accept the idealizations in advertising and then pattern themselves determinedly on them, or there would be much more uniformity in taste and appearance than there is. Resistance to advertising messages, or indifference to them, is revealed in the uneven marketplace successes of the commodities promoted within them. Conversely, it is clear that only a fraction of social actuality is captured in advertising; selection on some basis accounts for what is a highly circumscribed set of images. Even that selection is unlikely to mirror social realities. Attention to ads depicting what is already abundantly evident in the cultural world would be lower than the marginal attention currently paid to advertising.

Only when one reconsiders the imagery that actually lies on the surface of the advertisement can one begin to understand the relationship between advertising, consumers, and the creation or mirroring of reality. To repeat, what is seen on the surface are renderings of people in the prime of life, stripped of occupational roles, stripped of class allocations, stripped of ethnicity (an increasing number of Black and Asian models have Caucasian features), stripped of age considerations, and constituted as paragons of their genders. Missing is most of human life—work, duty, routines, small kindnesses as well as unpleasantries, not to mention the extensive variation in gender confirmation. Advertising distills from the variety of human appearances the few that will be accepted as apotheoses and returns them in perfected form to an audience desiring to see such singular renditions.

To trace this movement, the shift is from the plane of normal existence (the consumer's life, with a full cultural quotient except for nonpareils of attractiveness) to the out-of-this-world plane of

idealized states (the flawless depictions conjured by advertising
personnel) and back to the plane of this world (now armed with
useful—perhaps even useful for purposes of rejection—epitomes
of attractiveness). In circling from the quotidian to the idealized
and back to the quotidian, not all of the idealized "information"
will be adopted and brought back; it is the nature of ideals that
they be recognized as distant and abstract, perhaps not to be
incorporated but only to be acknowledged as points of cultural
reference. Thus, advertisers respond to vague preferences with
certain specific figurations that settle back into consciousness to
both reify and vary standards of attractiveness. Advertising does
not, and cannot, create these stereotypes from sources that exclude
the public, nor does advertising passively mirror stereotypes; it is
actively involved in the dialectical process of making and remak-
ing them.

If the primary dynamic at work is not a shuttling of cause and
effect in one direction or another, but rather a spiraling of need
and image, that of refined preferences and further refined images,
this still does not explain why the imagery consists in exactly what
it does. In a national survey, 2,200 adults were asked to select their
two most important personal needs from a list, and the results (in
percentages) were these (Kahle, 1984, p. 78):

- Self-respect 21.1
- Security 20.6
- Warm relationships with others 16.2
- Accomplishment 11.4
- Self-fulfillment 9.6
- Being well respected 8.8
- Sense of belonging 7.9
- Fun/enjoyment/excitement 4.5

Self-respect tops the list, it can be presumed, because being at
peace with oneself, feeling that the person who has been created
is a person worthy of creation, remains elusive for the atomized
population of Americans. In a period when the burden of identity-
creation has fallen upon the individual, people are often trying to

improve who they are and, accordingly, require idealizations of the self to respond to.

How Consumers Exploit Advertising

What is encoded into advertising is far from identical to what is decoded. The consumer now comes to center stage. In the face of the large literature on the subject of advertising, which Richard Pollay (1986) says is notable for "the veritable absence of perceived positive influence" (p. 19), the treatment here undertakes to valorize both advertising and consumers. The scope is thus widened to take more explicit account not only of advertising's composition but also of its reception, and the scope is further widened by reincorporating the commodity-related material into the advertising message and into consumers' consideration.

Just as a valorization of popular culture by cultural studies scholars depended on the recognition and appreciation of the powerful, interpretive role of the *user* of popular culture, so the valorization of advertising awaits acknowledgment of the truth that advertising does not exploit consumers, but, rather, that consumers exploit advertising. David Mick (1986) enjoins that "we must move beyond conceiving advertising in terms of what it does to people and view it more in terms of what people do with advertising" (p. 205). Consumers are, on the whole, adept social creatures, working to get the most from their resources in the interest of fulfilling their responsibilities and pleasures. To see consumers otherwise, as sheepish or foolish, is to do a disservice not only to them but to oneself both as a representative consumer and as a social observer. According to Mary Douglas, "Theories of consumption which assume a puppet consumer, prey to the advertiser's wiles, of consumer jealously competing with no sane motive, or lemming consumer rushing to disaster, are frivolous, even dangerous" (Douglas & Isherwood, 1979, p. 89). A position held by some feminist scholars is that a condescending view toward consumers is yet another instance of the patriarchal effort at the subordination of women, as it has long been held that production is men's work and consumption women's (Myers, 1986, p. 103). The sexist treatment of consumption would thus parallel the sexist treatment of popular culture (Huyssen, 1986).

In making selections for purchase, consumers do not rely extensively on advertising either consciously or inadvertently. Far more important are the opinions of friends and family members, the consumer's own experiences with the brand, and the price found in the store (Schudson, 1984, chap. 3). When consumers are unavoidably in the presence of advertising, as when reading a magazine or watching television, only a limited amount of the advertising is permitted to enter through the aperture of their minds. For those few advertising messages that are allowed in, many are either misunderstood or rejected outright. In one study of print advertising, 20% of the responses (from a national sample of 1,347 adults) to factual questions regarding a just-read ad evinced either miscomprehension or rejection (defined as occurring "when the receiver of the communication extracts meanings neither contained in nor logically derivable from the communication and/or rejects meanings contained in or logically derivable from the communication") (Jacoby & Hoyer, 1989, p. 437).[7] In an earlier study regarding television commercials, the average level of miscomprehension per commercial was 28% (Jacoby, Hoyer, & Sheluga, 1980, p. 73).

Decoding, the act of attaching meaning to the symbolic material of the advertising message, is clearly highly complex and interactive, with consumers bringing deeply personal readings to the process. Following the three-part scheme that Stuart Hall (1980) applied to popular culture, the meaning received could be the "preferred" one of the advertiser: for example, the consumer already thinks favorably of Candice Bergen and will consider using Sprint. Or the commercial could produce an "oppositional" meaning: the consumer finds Candice Bergen insipid, now and always, and will never use the long-distance carrier. But most likely the meaning is a "negotiated" one: perhaps the consumer has an amorous interest in Candice Bergen or has a sister who looks like Candice, perhaps the household dog is named Candy. These and a million other meanings come forward and greet the commercial.

For those advertising messages that the consumer does receive and supply meaning to, the content of the message will now be used for entirely personal purposes. The appeal associated with the product first takes up its place within the sphere of stored meanings, either affirming an old one or creating a slightly altered one. The young actor who poses as a doctor or a Chinese relative in the Bud Light commercials ("Yes I am!") lends playful nuances to concepts of imposture and pretense. The image of the accompanying product may or may not be allowed to register at all ("Was that for Bud Light or Miller Lite?"). If the product is accepted, it may be mentally situated near the meaning of the appeal: The beer takes on meanings of impudence, and impudence comes to imply the beer. Or the beer may be lodged somewhere in the concentric spheres of widening meanings: defiance, self-assertion, youthfulness, fun.

For each ad that enters the mind, the consumer has chosen to reconfirm or add to the massive symbol vocabulary necessary for the conduct of a well-managed life. The appeal imagery may endorse a notion of what constitutes the good life, for example, and the product image may take on inferences of an item useful toward the realization or communication of that good life. The consumer does not in any way "believe" the ad's implied equation that the product will necessarily result in the depicted tableau of the good life. Michael Schudson (1984) calls advertising "the art form of bad faith" (p. 11) in that neither advertiser nor consumer literally "believes" the message. Yet the imagery of accepted ads has credibility because it is performing the crucial service of establishing ideals and anchoring scales of evaluation. For the consumer, the ad takes vague notions of important states and lends those a form, an image. The consumer does not want advertising to deal in realities, which already abound in the consumer's life; the consumer appreciates advertising that offers gossamer. Only a culture critic, employing inappropriate discourse standards, would rebuke advertising for being unreal.

The act of creating appropriate idealizations through the discovery of evocative imagery in advertising and may well be a pleasurable one for the consumer. There is intriguing quantitative evidence in support of this: In a carefully controlled study by Myers and Biocca (1992), college-age females who were exposed to commercial television footage edited to feature idealized female body images felt more euphoric afterward. Moreover, they judged themselves as *thinner* than they had on pretests. Trying to explain these unexpected findings, Myers and Biocca write,

> The commercials invited them to fantasize themselves in their future ideal body shape. The significant drop in depression levels suggests that subjects exposed to the body-image commercials felt better about themselves immediately after exposure to the 15 ideal-body ads. The commercials' cumulative message of "You can be thin" may have developed greater feelings of self-control in the young women. (p. 127)

By this reasoning, exposure to an ideal had invited pleasurable fantasizing of movement toward that ideal.[8] To a slight but discernible degree, the young women had permitted meanings taken from the paragon to be incorporated into the self and the self into the paragon.

As further indication of the integrity and purposefulness of consumers, it is not often that the absorption of advertising leads to actual purchases.[9] The consumer is ruthlessly selective in what will or will not be bought. Economist Stanley Lebergott (1993) has data showing that 86% of the 85,000 new products advertised in the American market over the 1980s did not survive beyond the end of 1990 (p. 18). The few advertised products that are purchased are highly likely to provide the meanings sought. When Marxist critics Max Horkheimer and Theodor Adorno (1972) complained, "The triumph of advertising in the culture industry is that consumers feel compelled to buy and use its products even though they see through them" (p. 167), they were correct—but in an unintended way. Products are linked to meanings, and if consumers see through products, it is to those meanings lying around and beyond.

The way that consumers make use of advertising—in the search for idealized states to which a meaning connection can be made, with a passing interest in the products that may be associated with those states—has become decisive in the construction of that advertising. Advertisers and their agencies respond to the preferences of consumers by offering up first and primarily the desired depictions and then by insinuating a connection between the appeal imagery and the product the advertiser is trying to sell. The appeal imagery is not what the advertiser wishes to impose on the consumer nor what the advertiser thinks there is even a chance of imposing but, rather, what the advertiser prays will give form to the proclivities of the consumer. Leiss et al. (1990) confirm that "in the consumer society the consumer, not the product, is the core of the message system about the sphere of consumption" (p. 295).

As it plays to the extraordinary discretion, even power, of the consumer, advertising may now be reconceptualized as almost the reverse of what the authors of the advertising critique insist upon. Advertising is not a hail of commercial barbs inflicting damage on huddling consumers and their culture. Advertising is a buffet of symbolic imagery that advertisers hope will prove tempting and lead to the more difficult exchange of money for goods. Consumers pass down the table of displayed appeals, glancing here and there, but stop only infrequently to oblige a felt inner need for a symbol and a product—and to buy. It is their favor that advertisers are assiduously courting.

Notes

1. It can be difficult at first to separate the product from the pitch. When beer drinkers are asked why they choose Budweiser, they sometimes respond, "Because it's the King of Beers." Yet, in short order, one learns to mentally subtract all the information factually related to the product, leaving the nonproduct material ready for inspection. Once again, there need be no logical link at all between the commodity and the noncommodity material in an advertisement, and frequently there is none; mere association is sufficient for the transfer of meaning.

2. For a restricted yet emphatic empirical demonstration of how interpretations of advertising can differ, see Sentis and Markus (1986). In their study, they asked groups of males to judge depictions of aftershave lotions and found that judgments varied according to the respondents' self-descriptions, leading Sentis and Markus to conclude that "consumers take very different ideas from advertising and other brand communication depending on the organization and content of their self-concept" (p. 146).

3. Leiss, Kline, and Jhally (1990) indicate that fear appeals have fallen off in Canadian advertising since the 1930s (p. 268); the same is certain to be the case for advertising in the United States.

4. Andren (1978) and his colleagues took their sample from the 11 largest circulating magazines of 1973. The 300 ads in the sample were chosen after allowing for the various magazines' circulation sizes and annual numbers of issues. Issues were selected randomly from throughout the year, and within each of these issues ads were picked randomly.

5. Howard Gossage (1967) thinks he knows why models are so thin: "They are supernatural representations and I defy you to account for them in any other fashion" (p. 366). Their ethereal, unearthly quality levitates the associated products from the plane of the real to the plane of the magical.

6. On the prevalence of the young in advertising, and this feature's link with spectators' concerns for self-identity, Diane Barthel (1988) concurred, "It is no wonder that advertising stresses the appearance of youth and the values of youth. It is caught up with youth's crises and concerns, namely, finding identity and managing intimacy" (p. 187).

7. It is important to note that in the study by Jacoby and Hoyer (1989) respondents were handed a print ad and instructed "Please read what it says and tell me when you've finished" before being asked comprehension questions. Clearly, miscomprehension rates would have been much higher under normal reading conditions.

8. A study with contrary findings was reported by Richins (1991). Results from groups of female undergraduates suggested that "exposure to highly attractive images can negatively affect feelings about the self" (p. 81).

9. If advertising does not lead to (many) purchases, then why do advertisers advertise? There are fundamentally two reasons. The economies of mass communication mean that the cost per consumer contact is small considering the enormous number of consumers reached; if only a tiny percentage of these inexpensively contacted consumers go on to effect purchases, the effort will still be profitable. But even if the cost of advertising does not seem to be directly paying out, to pull back from this type of marketing when competitors do not is to risk extinction. Advertisers advertise to stay abreast with competitors, who are also advertising.

8

Deciphering Advertisements

In pursuing a mission to make manifest the most deeply felt needs of the broadest number of people, and thereby attempt to hold them in thrall, advertisements take on the status of fascinating cultural documents. The symbols appearing in advertisements reflect a remarkable width and depth of communicative effort. The symbols must be comprehensible by the many, since the advertising strategy strives to enlist multitudes, and so must be composed of familiar elements that articulate commonalities within the society. Yet by the same token, the symbols must not be so overly familiar, so banal, that they elicit indifference or even rejection from consumers. The work of the advertising industry is to scratch away at the psyche of the public, to uncover deeper veins of sentiment, and to produce fresher symbols with improved chances of striking newer chords with consumers. Products of the strenuous efforts of the advertising industry to communicate both widely and deeply, of this industry's excavating powers and creative drives, advertisements can reveal many of the inner workings and secret protocols of American culture. In this expressive domain, in a wondrous shorthand, one finds symbolized the personal assumptions, the operating beliefs, the aspirations, and the plaintive wants of those who populate what is currently the most dominant culture on earth.

But deciphering this rich cultural material is an arduous task, at least at first attempt and without guidance. Some students of advertisements may find themselves "in the beam" of an ad and blinded by it; the ad is aimed directly at them, and they are fully engaged by it to the point of having little perspective and little power of discernment. To such an investigator, the ad seems totally natural, and the levels of signification thus collapse to form an obdurate, impenetrable surface. "It's all so obvious," this observer might feel, "and not worth discussion." In the opposite direction, others may be so far out of an ad's beam that they cannot recognize the symbols used or make sense of them, or they may be nearer the beam in that they recognize the symbols but reject them, perhaps disparagingly, as people of one gender sometimes dismiss ads aimed at the other.

Deciphering, as the term is used here, is not concerned simply with describing what is encoded by the creative personnel at the advertising agency. (Art directors and copywriters, by the way, are not usually good informants on content. When asked about the composition of their messages, agency employees typically respond in terms of marketing objectives, using the jargon supplied to them by their client, or offer up vague approximations of creative intentions, ultimately invoking practiced intuitions and little more.) Nor is deciphering focused solely on the decoding process, even when the primacy of the interpreter is upheld. Much more material is contained in any advertising message, and much more is absorbed, than any one individual is likely to be conscious of.

Instead of aligning oneself exclusively with the encoding side of advertising, as might semioticians, or with the decoding side, as might cultural studies scholars, the more acute decipherer of advertising adopts a position somewhat removed from the exchange and, like the person granted height (as from an airplane) over watery depths, can see what is concealed within. The decipherer of advertising is looking for the layers of signification embedded in even the simplest versions of compound advertising.

An early, now-classic deciphering of a French print ad conducted by French scholar Roland Barthes (1964/1977) has served as the foundation for much subsequent analytical effort.[1] At first glance, the content of the ad Barthes selected is thoroughly plain: In his words,

> Here we have a Panzani [an Italian food products company] adver-
> tisement: some packets of pasta, a tin, a sachet, some tomatoes, onions,
> peppers, a mushroom, all emerging from a half-open string bag, in
> yellows and greens on a red background. Let us try to "skim off" the
> different messages it contains. (p. 33)

Barthes finds three message levels: the linguistic (the few recognizable words in the ad), the denoted image (exactly what has been photographed), and the connotative. Because "all images are polysemous" (p. 44), the linguistic material serves to fix or anchor the imagery. Photography, as the mode of denotation, "naturalises the symbolic message" (p. 45) by making it appear uncontrived. The meanings suggested by the imagery are extensive and, in the end, individually determined (p. 47); Barthes is more concerned with exploring the semiotic theory of imaginal communication than in detailing possible meanings. However, he does offer one key connotation as an example of how meanings can be elicited: "Italianicity" (his coinage) is suggested by the colors chosen (those of the Italian flag) and the Mediterranean vegetables (especially the tomato). He also touches on the connotations of freshness (the vegetables associated with the packaged goods), of plenty (the items tumbling out of the bag), and of a nonindustrial way of life (the string market bag). He mentions that the composition is a still life but does not cite this painterly convention as a prestigious marker. Had he cared to delve further into potential meanings, he might also have reflected on the cornucopian form of the bag (connoting abundance and Greco-Roman classicism). Yet, as a start into the process of deciphering the cultural material layered in any advertisement, Barthes indicated the intellectual vistas.

Before beginning this process, some fundamental concepts require review. Every compound ad, whether print or electronic, is involved in a quadratic relationship: There is the sender, offering preferred meanings; the two components of the ad (the commodity information and the noncommodity, or symbol, appeal); and the person receiving the advertising message. The advertiser wants the symbolic meanings of the usually idealized appeal to drift onto the commodity so that it will take on favorable connotations in the consumers' conception of the product. The mere association of commodity and appeal, no matter how disparate the two are, is sufficiently a precondition for the transfer of meaning. Just as physiologically there exists the phenomenon of "persistence of vision," in which an image lingers in sight for an instant after the stimulus has been removed, so it can be said by analogy that there exists a "persistence of meaning," in which symbolic meanings are carried over as attention shifts from appeal to product. The decipherer of all this aims primarily at unfolding the cultural material that has been (wittingly or not) folded into the appeal imagery.

The process of deciphering is more insightfully and more satis- factorily accomplished if it is done not as a solitary activity but in the company of others. No one individual can recognize the totality of possible referents included in an ad nor of the mean- ings that might be taken away from it. A symbiotic effect often results from the exchange of opinions, as individual reaction is piled up against reaction. Under these communal conditions, there is no such thing as a correct or incorrect interpretation of an ad. Some readings are more common and others less so—a degree of con- gruence that can be determined by poll but should never be taken as a determination of "truth." To begin, a commercial should be shown several times to the group; if a print ad is the focus, it should be continually displayed via an overhead projector (or better, converted to a slide and projected).

The following deciphering guidelines are offered as tools for separating out the layers of signification included in any com- pound print ad or commercial. Phrased as a set of questions, the guidelines proceed through three main divisions. The first, the context for the ad, attempts to establish the important elements of the background that may help in situating the ad and may facili- tate probing it productively. This is the extramessage information (to be gathered quickly from those in attendance or not gathered at all) that may impinge upon the message. The second division entails close scrutiny of the advertising composition itself. In the third division, the attempt is made to widen the discussion and to raise questions about the culture within which this advertisement and its commodity are lodged.

Although the guidelines proceed in a numbered sequence, deciphering an ad is generally not so clearcut and may involve circling back to some items in the light of subsequent discoveries. Progress through the guidelines is rarely linear and more often of a rocking sort. Care must be taken that the guidelines never become too stringent and thus foreclose inviting avenues of exegesis. The same guidelines that open territories of thought can also, if adhered to with excessive rigor, close off productive insights.

Deciphering Guidelines

Context for the Ad

1. What *product category* does the advertised commodity fall into? What are the names of some of its *competitors*? Comparatively, how are the competitors faring? Are there any noticeable advertising campaigns we should be aware of? Have any of these commodities been in the news lately for any reason?

2. Which *medium* did this ad appear in? Specifically, in which magazine or television program? Time of the year (and day)? Any thoughts about the *placement* of the ad? Why might it appear where it does rather than someplace else?

3. Judging from the ad's placement, what can be inferred about the *intended audience* for the ad? Describe them as carefully as possible. (It is very important to view the ad through their eyes, to the extent possible, and to decipher the ad from this vantage point.)

Looking at the Ad

4. Considering the *aesthetics* of the composition, is there any reason why the ad is structured as it is? Describe the layout (if a print ad) or the scripted sequence (if commercial). Any reason for

this particular structure? Why this typeface, or that caliber voice-over? Do these items "say" anything? Comments about color (or lack of it), about the musical score or the sound effects? Do any of these considerations help establish an overall mood for the ad?

5. Is the artwork in the ad *photographed* or drawn? Why might the agency art directors have specified the mode they did? Why did the photographers (or illustrators) use the particular lighting they did, select the particular angle on their subjects? Why the particular shot (long, medium, or close-up) or the particular focus (sharp or not sharp)? Any retouching in evidence?

6. In the imagery, what is being pushed into the *foreground*, and what is placed in the background? Why?

7. Precisely what is the *commodity* that is being sold? This needs to be stated as dryly and factually as possible. Once it has been described, it should be *subtracted* from one's conception of the ad for the time being. The pictorial material that is left con-stitutes the ad's *symbolic appeal.*

8. We need to create the longest possible *list of the various elements* pictured in the symbolic appeal. It helps to pretend that we represent a combination of property master and casting direc-tor. What would the items be, or the individuals, that are required for the creation of this ad? What is the setting to be specified, and why? How are the models or actors to be posed, and why?

9. Taking these items one at a time, what are some of the *meanings* an item would have for members of the intended audi-ence? What does each signal regarding status, leisure/work, gender, disposition, attractiveness, responsibility, domesticity, age, vitality, personality, mood, and so on? Ask, "What might this item, this feature, mean to the targeted consumer?" (It helps to begin with those items that occupy the largest amount of time and space and then work down to the smaller details.) To look at the allocation of meanings another way, what would someone from Outer Mon-golia have to know to make sense of a particular item?

10. What can be inferred about the *states of mind* of the humans in the ad? What might the relationship be between this attitude and members of the intended audience?

11. Establish a locale for this scene. Situate the symbolic appeal in *space*. Where does this happen? Does this locale have any significance for the intended audience?

12. Locate this scene in *time*. Past, present, or future? What is the temporal location suggesting?

13. Consider the ad now *as narrative*, playing out in time. If a print ad, can we supply a story, and what would that story mean to the intended audience? Is there a story in the television commercial, and how might the intended audience interpret it?

14. Sometimes, it is not what is in an ad that pulls people in but *what is missing*. Is there anything missing in this imagery that consumers would feel moved to supply and thus to be engaged?

15. Is the symbolic appeal in this ad *idealizing* anything, and if so, what is it?

16. By way of summary, imagine some people who are perfectly in the beam for this ad. What state of mind might they bring to the ad, and what does the ad supply them with?

17. Is there anything that we should know about the *earlier use* of these symbolic materials in either advertising or popular culture? Are there *intertextual referents* here to be acknowledged? Items extracted from popular culture?

18. As a creative construction, an ad will frame some things in and will exclude the rest of the world. What are some things that are logically related to the themes of the symbolic appeal that the creative personnel have *framed out*? Why?

Implications of the Ad

19. What might this ad be inferring about the nature of *relationships* between people? Describe the nonverbal communication within the frame of the ad. Who dominates?

20. What might this ad be saying about what it is to be a man? A woman? About *self-identity*? About attractiveness?

21. Is the ad conveying anything about *social status* or class?

22. What kinds of other *cultural beliefs* (or ideological tenets) are promoted in this ad? Again, it helps in responding to a question like this to imagine oneself as an Outer Mongolian or an alien.

Viewed from outside, what seems to be the values of the senders and receivers of this message?

23. From a Marxist perspective, advertising is seen as the instigator of a "commodification" of human life, in that purchasable commodities are equated with noncommercial human needs and capabilities and made to substitute for them. Let's bring the product back into the discussion now, and ask if the advertisement, by linking the product to a symbolic appeal, is attempting to *commodify* a particular area of human experience. Is Taster's Choice trying to substitute instant coffee for romance?

Jordache Deciphered

This advertisement for Jordache jeans is so strongly American that it could not be used in many other cultures. Only the initiated will know what is being sold (see Figure 8.1).

1. *Product category.* The market for jeans is a hotly competitive one, with new firms entering and exiting annually. Under these conditions, it will not do simply to display the garment; each manufacturer has to try hard to link its brand with a created set of meanings. Competitors include Bon Jour, Levis, Guess, Chic—all formidable advertisers.

2. *Placement.* This advertisement ran in the September 1994 issue of *Cosmopolitan.* The issue was available in August when the readership was leaving summer behind and preparing for fall, for school, perhaps for new relationships.

3. *Intended consumers.* The readers of *Cosmopolitan* are middle-class women in their 20s and 30s, frequently unmarried and working. For them, the editorial content of the publication supports successful lifestyles both at work and in relationships. Some of the editorial content emphasizes female sensuality. The ad would seem to be appropriately directed at readers who are attracted to this content.

4. *Aesthetics of the composition.* The ad is very carefully, even classically composed. Considering the composition as two-dimensional, the large figure of the female, slightly off center to the right, is balanced by the smaller figure of the male plus an ambiguous

Figure 8.1. Jordache jeans. From *Cosmopolitan*. (Courtesy of Jordache Enterprises Inc.)

rectangle of light on the left. Considered in three dimensions, the view recedes from the foregrounded female figure, to the male, and then to background ambiguities. The classicism of the composition is reinforced by the Roman typeface of the Jordache brand name. It is against these formalities that the emotionality of the ad plays.

In the original ad, the word "Jordache" is bright red; the rest of the ad appears colored in a light blue wash. The ad is a duotone, shot in black and also in blue, then recombined to give it a luminous quality. The duotone contributes a strong moodiness to the ad—a pensive, reflective memorability.

5. *The photograph.* Photography is the chosen artistic mode for advertising because of its deceptive ability to present fictions as if they were realities. We may know this photograph is a fabrication, but we choose to believe that it is a real-life possibility. Once we see it as an artifice, we realize that the models have been carefully lighted and that a strong beam illuminates the female's face, singling her out. The shot is tight around the models because they are the whole story; what they are symbolizing is meant to transfer to the commodity.

6. *Foreground.* What is most important, situated closest to the viewer, is the female model, in particular her face (from which we take meanings about her personality and her feelings) and her derriere (which suggests her sensuality as it displays the product, and is twice emblazoned with the brand name—sewn onto the product and printed onto the ad). Brand name, product, derriere, sensuality, femaleness, and back to brand—these are meant to constitute a circle of signification.

7. *The commodity.* Now is the time to mentally subtract the red-lettered Jordache from the composition and concentrate on the two figures.

8. *Elements.* Besides denim clothing, what is needed for this picture are two young and attractive models. The female must not be overstated—no blond locks or a butch haircut, but wholesome good looks, expressive (perhaps blue) eyes, and trim behind. The male should be a conventional hunk.

The pose they are to adopt is somewhat unconventional in advertising: She is the superior of the two, her head is higher than his, and she seems to be comforting him.

9. *Possible meanings.* What might a young working woman see in this advertisement? The scene offers a welcome respite from the world of work, for it appears to be a setting for leisure and romance, for pleasures. The female figure's outward gaze breaks the dyadic structure of the scene, makes contact with the reader's view, and offers a path for entrance into the picture. Although she is attractive, the female figure is not so beautiful as to solicit envy and deflect identification. The reader may momentarily and vicariously occupy the female's place; certainly, the composition invites this act of the imagination.

If the reader is to briefly be the featured female, who is that person? She is young and attractive, someone many men may want to associate with. She is open to life; her eyes are alert, her lips slightly pursed. She is in command of the situation, is the more dominant, the less dependent of the two figures. Her gaze is strong and away from him; his eyes are downcast. He clutches her; she consoles him. Yet she is not totally dominating, for her forearm is inside his shoulder, receiving a modicum of protection. Her shirt front is presumably open; is her breast exposed? Is this a sexual act, a nurturing act? His averted face suggests the latter.

And how might the reader see the supplicating male? He is attractive, someone many women may pursue, and so is a catch. Caught, he clings. He is weaker than she is. There are suggestions that he is of a lower class: the grease on the back of his hands, the rolled-up sleeves. Imputations of inferiority outweight those of superiority.

The reader finds here, then, a nominal reversal of conventional gender roles, with the female being the stronger, the protector. Yet the female loses none of her femininity in the process. Nor does she lose the relationship. Inferences might be that attractiveness counts; romances and the leisure to enjoy them are important; it is good to be outgoing; it is still all right to be a nurturer; it is all right for women to be emotionally stronger than men.

To understand the ad, an Outer Mongolian would have to know that denim denotes the blue-collar working class but confusingly connotes middle-class leisure and informality. A female Mongolian might conclude about the ad that "in America women are not demure," whereas her consort might think that "in America, it is all right for men to be babies."

10. *States of mind.* She is giving, doubt-free, open; he is introverted, crestfallen, perhaps contrite.

11. *Locale.* Their clothes situate them outside the workplace. Of a group of 27 adults examining this ad, 4 situated the scene in a stable. Does the denim explain this? Is a stable the site where classes intersect? In a similar vein, 2 others said, "Out West."

12. *Time.* Time would seem to be as unspecified as space, as there is an ageless quality to denim.

13. *The story.* The most common narrative among 27 adults had him seeking forgiveness for a transgression, and her granting it.

14. *The missing links.* It is a comment on the decontextualized imagery that so little is known, so much is missing. We can be certain of virtually nothing about the couple except their age and togetherness. Yet the emotional essence of the scene is blatant.

15. *Idealizations.* Ideals of male and female attractiveness are central to this advertisement. Also being idealized is a concept of an emotionally stronger woman, one who can dominate the male in her life and not risk losing him.

16. *The ideal consumer.* The perfect reader for this *Cosmopolitan* ad is a woman interested in male companionship. She is aware of the emotional weaknesses of males but not undone by that awareness. She herself feels emotionally strong but is not sure whether to display those strengths. The ad would encourage her sentiments.

17. *Intertextuality.* To appreciate this ad, it helps to know that in most American advertising featuring males and females, the male's head is higher than the female's.

18. *Framed out.* Everything is framed out except this emotional moment and its implications. Beyond their age, we know nothing about their paths in life.

19. *Relationships.* Relations between the genders, as idealized in advertising, are changing. Males do not always dominate; females are not always dependent on them.

20. *Self-identity.* Women can be stronger, men weaker. Women still need men but do not need them to always be in charge. And as always in advertising, appearances are important in defining us.

21. *Social status.* Class markers are muted in this advertisement, as in most American advertising, but they are not absent. In that the female is clean and the male is not, the male would appear to be of a lower social class. In this case, there may be an imputation of inferiority associated with lower classes.

22. *Cultural beliefs.* The advertisement would appear to be confirming changing public definitions of femaleness and maleness. One message is that women need not be dependent on men.

23. *Commodification.* The attempt is made to connect a brand of jeans to an ascendant definition of femaleness. Wear these jeans, the implication is, and you will be both independent and beloved. It is the condition of the modern woman that is being commodified.

Diet Sprite Deciphered

This advertisement for Diet Sprite is somewhat more complex. The single, independent figure—the predominant image in American advertising—makes its reappearance here (see Figure 8.2). However, this ad depends not on a straightforward message but on playful, mocking reversals along several dimensions: The abundant space given to text reverses the aesthetic convention of imagery dominating; the messy typography contradicts standard advertising practice (although messy type is on its way to becoming a cliché) and also contradicts the clean images at the top and bottom corners; the message that seems to be one thing turns out to be another. In several regards, this is a devious anti-ad.

1. *Product category.* Another higher competitive market, this time for diet soft drinks. This product is Coca-Cola's offering to young, weight-conscious, "with it" people. Competitors include Diet 7-Up and Fresca.

2. *Placement.* Its placement in the July 1994 issue of *Mademoiselle* suggests the advertiser was advancing it as a summertime beverage for fashionable young adults.

You're a woman

of the **90's**

B**o**ld, self-assured and empowered.

Climbing the ladder of success at work

and the StairMaster" at the gym.

You're socially aware and politically correct.

But you probably know all this already

because every **ad** and magazine

has told you a zilli**o**n times.

NO wonder you're **thirsty.**

Cool, Crisp, Clear.
OBey Your Thirst.

Figure 8.2. Diet Sprite. From *Mademoiselle.* (Courtesy of the Coca-Cola Company.)

3. *Intended audience.* The ad's placement implies that the targeted consumer is a young, fashion-conscious female. After all, the text begins "You're a woman of the 90's."

4. *Aesthetics.* The font is problematic, with at least two conceivable interpretations. One is that it is designed to invoke early, hand-set type, with an attendant unevenness; the other read is that it is a gritty, typewriterlike font of the sort used by revolutionaries or kidnappers to convey urgent messages. A group of 39 adults deciphering this ad settled on the second and saw in the type an insolent, insurgent quality. (This is going to work on two levels: the insurgent new woman as opposed to older gender stereotypes, and then a stridency in the backlash against the new stereotype.)

The composition of the ad is unconventional, in that the four corners stand out. The art director intends that a reader's attention will transverse the corners before being drawn into the smaller type in the middle, where the second, contrary message lies.

5. *Mode of artwork.* The product has been photographed and the model photographed before being superimposed on computer-generated artwork. But the artwork that stands out is the rough typeface of the text. It states, in a near parodistic way, that the communication contains an urgent advocacy "message" (and, as it turns out, a countermessage).

6. *Foreground.* The content of the corners would seem to occupy the foreground. But given the satirical nature of the advertisement, the punch is not in what is foregrounded but what lurks behind: the spoof that is waiting to be discovered.

7. *Commodity.* Now is the time to mentally subtract all Diet Sprite references from the ad and concentrate on the rest.

8. *Elements.* Needed for the ad are a young female model, neither too slim nor too voluptuous, a green gown (green because it is environmentally correct, a gown because the ad will play on the goddess image), combat boots (because the ad will *really* play with the goddess image), and a lot of computer-generated artwork—a globe, sunbeams, and a typewriterlike font.

9. *Meanings.* A young, urbane woman who attends to the ad might have two partially contradictory sets of meanings invoked. Initially, an idealized young female is seen, radiant and conquering. The shafts of light, the upraised arm, the flowing gown, the world at her feet—all speak to a high and allegorical stature. Next, the larger words are absorbed ("You're a woman of the 90's" and

"No wonder you're thirsty"), plus the image of the soda and glass, perhaps along with the injunction "Obey Your Thirst." The ad would seem to be a not-uncommon depiction of the new, affirmative gender definition for women. On second glance, however, the center text deprecates the initial message, first by inflating it to hyperbolic levels and then by tagging it as oversold. A glance back at the figure on top confirms the lampooning intent of the advertisement: The excesses of the plethora of sunbeams, the thorough greenness, the celestial pose, the "top of the world" image, juxtaposed with the combat boots, render this conception of the "woman of the 90's" ridiculous.

To make sense of the ad, someone alien to Western culture would have to know that gender definitions are in transition and that the uneasiness surrounding the transition can lead to the new definition being either affirmed or ridiculed, or both.

10. *State of mind.* For the one figure in the ad, her state of mind at first looks like the stuff of legends but is later seen to be out of touch and foolish.

Items 11 through 14 do not seem to apply to this ad.

15. *Idealization.* It appears that modern womanhood is being idealized, but what is really being idealized is a reaction to that categorization.

16. *The ideal consumer.* The perfect reader of this ad, someone the advertiser hopes for, is a young woman who holds ambivalent feelings about new gender definitions. On the one hand, she appreciates the affirmative, prideful description of the modern woman, and, on the other, she is resistant to the stridency of the new ideology. Reading this ad she finds both positions articulated and is able to confirm as well as mock the new definition.

17. *Intertextuality.* The ad refers explicitly to "every ad and magazine" that has provided the new gender description "a *zillion* times," so the informed reader would have to be familiar with these descriptions if this ad is going to successfully play off them.

Items 18 and 19 do not apply.

20. *Self-identity.* The ad makes dual statements: that it is all right to be glorious, independent, and self-affirming and that it is all right to be other than that.

21. *Status.* The ad seems free of class implications.

22. *Cultural beliefs.* This advertisement both confirms and rejects an avant-garde notion of womanhood. Whether the less conservative (which are foregrounded) or more conservative (which have the last say) beliefs are accepted would depend on the reader.

23. *Commodification.* The advertiser is attempting to situate its product at the very core of modern female gender definition and to commodify that complex cultural territory. It is a plan perhaps more grandiose than the advertiser recognizes.

Go Forth

With the guidelines in hand, and on the basis of the Jordache and Diet Sprite examples, one can now proceed to decipher the cultural content in other ads and commercials.

Note

1. Those interested in the development of advertising decipherment would do well to consult Leymore (1975), Goffman (1976), and Williamson (1978). For a deeply Marxist application of Barthes' approach, see Wernick (1983). His is a masterful treatment of an ad for Eve cigarettes.

9

Mixed Receptions

The singularity that one advertisement enjoys in the eyes of its sponsoring advertiser, or in the eyes of the agency personnel that created it, or in the eyes of those deciphering its cultural messages, is a singularity that does not exist in the normal course of events. Likewise, although the symbol domain of advertising serves one broad purpose (providing paragons of the individual's exterior) and the symbol domain of popular culture serves another (addressing and alleviating interior feelings), this distinction is not rigorously maintained during a person's session with the media. Under typical conditions of reception, the viewer permits the two symbol fields to mix together and specific instances of the two fields to blend. Experiencing the media is an experience of flow, of the sent material all blurring together and rolling on with the passage of time. British cultural studies scholar Raymond Williams (1974), visiting the United States in the 1960s, reacted uncertainly to the flow of American television; he was used to British broadcasting, where the separation of all the units is assiduously marked. Here, trying to watch a network movie, he became disoriented amid segments of the film, promotions for upcoming movies, regular commercials, and news breaks: "I can still not be sure what I took from the whole flow" (p. 92). But for the practiced American viewer, the mix is hardly unnerving. In fact, there are certain minor pleasures to be had as the meanings that one makes glide from one order of content to the next.

The reception of media content is mixed in another way also. The advertising/popular culture composite is not accepted in a wholesale fashion, but rather is received only partially, and those portions are sure to undergo contortions and reinterpretations according to the interests of the individual spectator. It has been demonstrated time and again that viewers have widely divergent understandings of any given media content. To select just one proof of the universal existence of polysemous readings, when Madonna's music videos were shown to 476 students under controlled conditions there was strikingly little agreement on the "meanings" of the performances (Brown & Schulze, 1990).[1] The reception of advertising and popular culture is a discerning one —not in a cerebral sense but with regard to a person's traits and purposes.

To illustrate how advertising content and popular culture content can become mixed upon reception, a representative *Roseanne* episode is analyzed. Even though the following reading of this advertising/popular culture mixture is only one of many conceivable interpretations, a sense of the possibilities for the interpenetration of the two orders of content can still be conveyed.

Receiving *Roseanne*

There is no denying the popularity of the *Roseanne* television series, which rose to the fore during the 1988-1989 television season and was for years among the very highest rated situation comedies, yet some observers admit to being mystified about the reasons for the show's success. Perhaps a portion of its initial triumph can be accounted for intertextually, in that for several seasons its chief competitor was the pleasant *The Cosby Show.* Like thesis and antithesis, *The Cosby Show*—upper middle class, paternalistic, gentile, harmonious, black—and *Roseanne*—working class, feminist, unruly, frictive, white—stood braced against each other. Yet when the prop of *The Cosby Show* was removed, *Roseanne* fared well on its own; the singular internal strength of the show would remain to be explained.

At bottom, there are two fictive elements that sustain *Roseanne*— the first often commented on, the second not. It is the remarkable character of Roseanne that has received the greater portion of critical attention. Corpulent and brash, Roseanne is anything but the usual prime-time homemaker. Asked to define her television character, the actress and comedienne Roseanne alluded to Jackie Gleason's Ralph Kramden and Carroll O'Conner's Archie Bunker (Mayerle, 1994, p. 112)—both sharing class, personality, and bodily features with her but differing conspicuously in gender. Roseanne's accomplishment has been to transfer a stock character in American situation comedy into the fenced-off territory of femaleness, and to do so insistently and confidently. It is this daring, flanking maneuver that has imbued the character with an electric charge.

Besides the traditional comedic rebuttals to status pretensions and body shape pretensions, Roseanne offers a rebuttal to the construction of the decorous female in modern life (Rowe, 1994). These multiple resistances that the character depicts resonate with the resistance to societal impositions that lurks to some degree within everyone, since what it is to be human is to negotiate constantly between internally generated demands and externally imposed ones. Roseanne speaks for the person within, and so the audience regards her fondly, if guardedly (how far can she go, and how far should we go with her?).

The second buoyant aspect of the *Roseanne* show is such a staple of situation comedy that it can go undiscussed in its current manifestation: the primacy of the family. For all of Roseanne's tartness and verbal aggression, much (if not most) of her attention and effort goes into the caretaking of the Conner household: the provision of food, the control of sibling energies, the fundamentally affectionate relationship with her husband Dan. The viewer enters a household that may be as conflicted as one the viewer knows, but, contrary to real life, is never in jeopardy. Not only does the immediate family cluster around the central character of Roseanne, but her sister is ever present, and her mother and other friends are never far off. Here there is no specter of loneliness, no specter of the wrenching loss of another. The value that undergirds the entire show, one that is missing or imperiled in the lives of millions of viewers, is the value of close and steadfast affection between people.

The episode scrutinized here is the 1993-1994 season opener, which aired nationally on September 14, 1993. The program concerns daughter Darlene's departure for college and Roseanne's handling of the event. (Viewers in the know would recognize the parallel between Darlene going off to college and Sara Gilbert, the actress who plays her, attending Yale.) In outline, the episode opens, as so many do, in the Conner's living room. Not only is Darlene leaving home, she wants to drive to college not with Dan and Roseanne but with her boyfriend David. A block of three commercials follows: for Sprint, All detergent, and a new movie.[2] The second segment, taking place in various rooms in the Conner home, concludes as David withdraws from the scene and Roseanne affirms that *she* will accompany Darlene to college. A string of six commercials follows: for L'Oreal, Toyota, AT&T, another movie in release, another ABC situation comedy, and an ABC documentary. In the third segment, Roseanne, Dan, and her sister Jackie settle Darlene into her apartment. The next commercials are for Friskies, yet another new movie, and yet another prime-time show. In the final, brief act, Dan and Roseanne are home in bed. The last commercials promote the upcoming Emmy Awards ceremony and a new Carnation product.

Roseanne is a sterling example of the most appreciated popular culture genre, that of televised situation comedy. The terms "situation" and "comedy" as they apply to this episode require investigation if the possible ties of the spectator and the show are to be understood. The ongoing situation of the Conner family is fully familiar to the viewership: the economic marginality of the family, the contesting of the children, the central position of the mother, Roseanne. There also exists an extratextual ongoing situation that the audience is aware of: the less stable persona of the actress, Roseanne, whose marriages, vicissitudes, mood swings, episodes of "creative differences," and confessions are public knowledge.

The particular episodic (as opposed to ongoing) situation here, of an offspring leaving for college, brings viewers deeply into the emotional territory of the family and of human affiliation, since those bonds are being tested. The themes of familial connection and disconnection are highlighted from the outset of the episode. Not only does this episode give narrative form to the fundamental affiliative concerns of situation comedy, but it is able to exploit a timely point in the maturation of the daughter's character as well as a timely moment in the American annual calendar (September is the month when students leave for college, the month when a proportion of the viewers will be dealing with the departure of their own children). All these impinge upon the emotional poignancy of the situation. Viewers are invited to offer up their own matching interpersonal longings and to do so in the knowledge that just as the show's emotional themes will be happily resolved by the end of the program, so too might their longings be mollified.

The emotions invoked in the viewer will be allowed to find their resolution not only through the machinations of the plot but also through the comedic outbursts occasioned by jokes and signaled by the laugh track. During the 22 minutes of the show, there were, by count, 98 instances of recorded laughter, or approximately 4.5 per program minute, so the viewer drawn to the program by the desire to laugh and to vent emotional pressures of all sorts, including those associated with affiliative needs, is provided with an abundance of opportunities.[3] The majority of the 98 jokes touch on the relationships between husband and wife and between parents and children, and depend for their effects on mild sarcasm, incongruous turns of expression, and adept pacing. So much credence does the program have with steady viewers that even when a few of the jokes are mumbled unintelligibly by Roseanne, their delivery alone seems funny.

The brief opening act sees Darlene attempting to persuade her mother to allow David to drive her to college, Roseanne turning the decision over to Dan, Dan blithely granting permission, and Roseanne growing mad at Dan for doing so. Roseanne unconvincingly asserts that Dan's feelings are hurt, when it is clear that she's the one with the hurt feelings. Against the emotional background of a poorly handled separation and resultant grief appears the first commercial—for a long-distance telephone service ("Sprint will split the bill on the person you call most"). It may be only coincidental that the program poses the difficulty of separation and the commercial offers a connective solution, but many viewers touched by the show will sense an equation at some level.

Another flow of meanings helps bind the popular culture material to the advertising message: The spokesperson for Sprint is Candice Bergen, a situation comedy star in her own right as news anchor Murphy Brown. Although hardly identical with Roseanne, Murphy shares several qualities—being female, funny, and in possession of a strident attitude. Murphy occupies a declamatory role in her world similar to that of Roseanne's in the Conners'; Murphy is the source of information for the anonymous male in the commercial. When the man responds to the suggestion of Sprint service, "I'll bet everybody's going to start doing it," Candice delivers the mildly wry tag line, "Maybe not everybody" (hinting at Murphy's flap with Dan Quayle and implying an exclusiveness to the service). In sum, the emotional tonality of the situation comedy rolls over into the subject matter of the commercial; the commercial's central figure parallels the program's central figure; the commercial connotes the entire domain of popular culture by its choice of spokesperson. Back and forth the allusions fly.

Similar layering of associations occurs in the next two commercials, coming on the heels of the Sprint announcement. The themes of mother and home appear in the detergent ad. "Mama's All got small," runs the jingle, which some older viewers might hear as resonating with Roseanne's shrinking household as well as theirs. Those younger viewers branching out on their own, searching for their own sort of housekeeping supplies, might see the products as contemporarily efficient ("half the liquid") and effective ("new double power").

Abruptly, there then appears a commercial for a new movie release, *For Love or Money*, starring Michael J. Fox. The voice-over states, "Michael J. Fox is a bellhop who thought there was nothing as seductive as money." Fox, in character, says, "Am I wrong?" Voice-over: "He was wrong." Instead of money, it is love, per the title. Affiliation again comes into the foreground. Fox is to be playing a role he has previously excelled at in television (*Family Ties*) and film (*Risky Business*), that of the young, single-minded entrepreneurial sort who proves strongly susceptible to affairs of the heart (again, the triumph of affiliation). The appearance of Fox within the context of the program provides a personality that straddles many symbol domains—the popular culture fields of both film and television, comedy and situation comedy, advertising in general and in particular—and causes them to run together. In all, the three commercials have restated, amplified, and extended the experience of viewing the episode.

Back to the show. David and Darlene have an argument, whose undercurrents would seem to be David's difficulty with Darlene's impending departure. Darlene, Dan, and Roseanne then plan the day and personnel for the trip, a discussion that concludes with Roseanne saying (to audience laughter and applause), "We're going to take you up there on Saturday and I don't give a flying crap if you like it or not." Next unreels the longest stretch of commercials during the program—six 30-second advertisements, one right after the other.

The first would seem to fit in with the show's exploration of the passage of years and the maturation of the next generation, and would seem to suit the demographic characteristics of those audience members who delighted in Roseanne's parental assertion (which received the only applause heard during the entire program). Viewers who feel a kinship with Roseanne's plight, as the character experiences the departure of her daughter, may also feel a kinship with Plenitude Advanced Wrinkle Defense Cream from L'Oreal. For those who are feeling deplenished, there is Plentitude; for those who feel themselves aging, there is Wrinkle Defense Cream. All this is gender specific; there is a loud cultural message here about femaleness in modern life.

To viewers whose family and life span are diminishing, whose self-worth may be in question, the second commercial is going to forego the idealized individual and rely on crowd psychology. In the background, a number of nicely dressed people are seen talking to each other. To establish the word-of-mouth motif, it is popular culture items that are inserted as the nominal subject: "If a movie got great reviews, you'd go see it, wouldn't you? If everyone kept talking about a book, you'd probably read it." The crowd treatment stays the same as the subject is switched to the commodity in question: "The 1993 Toyota Camry—everything you've heard is true." The unsure consumer is provided an acceptable solution. In the third commercial, the connection/disconnection theme reappears, for the advertiser is once again a long-distance service—not Sprint this time but AT&T's 1-800-COLLECT. Did these advertisers know in advance the precise content of this evening's program?

Next, the emotionality of the *Roseanne* episode is writ large in the emotionality of a new movie release: "Experience the desire, the suspicion, the betrayal, the lies, the rage, the passion at the heart of *The Age of Innocence*!" The season premiere of the situation comedy *Coach* is then advertised; this trailer's subject (which, as it turns out, will flow back into the *Roseanne* episode) concerns a debate over having a baby (Hayden does not want one). To the female viewer who is now defined as getting on in life, ABC promotes a documentary airing later that evening on breast cancer.

The viewer of this set of angst-ridden commercials is going to need some hearty laughs to restore emotional balance. We are now back with Roseanne, Dan, Jackie, and Darlene in Darlene's newly rented rooms, which draw close to squalor and provide an ample target for Roseanne's tart tongue. Unable to give up her daughter easily, Roseanne becomes contentious. Jackie privately reproves her sister: "You can say good-bye the right way—or you can say good-bye your way. But you're not going to get a second chance." Dan and his sister-in-law leave to drive home, and Roseanne says she will follow after she finishes moving Darlene in. With bogus nonchalance, Darlene asks her mother to sleep over, and Roseanne agrees to. In bed beside each other, mother and daughter have a long, personal, satisfying conversation about sex, men, and life. Darlene says, "This is the first time we ever talked, you know, like friends," and Roseanne replies, "Yeah, well, we could be friends. Definitely." The transition has been effected, and the family remains intact.

The warmth of familial bonds slides over into the dog food commercial that follows. "Riley, I'm home," an actress calls to a dog, establishing a relationship between human, animal, and habitat that will be completed with "new Friskies Prime Steaks and Strips." The condition of hominess is retold through its horrifying opposite in the next commercial for the movie *A Good Son* starring Macaulay Culkin; in a reversal of his *Home Alone* character, Macaulay's Henry has "been doing things, terrible things." Affiliation is breached, and so reinvoked by its denial, as Henry dangles another child from a great height and says, "If I let you go, do you think you could fly?" In the sixth and concluding commercial, domestic affiliation is moved back to the middle of the register as a romantic duo edge into what is intended as cute name-calling. The promotion is for a new series that, as the season progressed, viewers would not take to.

Back to the show for the last act. The affiliative dilemma raised in the episode has been amiably responded to by the transition of Darlene from child to child/friend but has not been thoroughly solved. Dan and Roseanne are in bed, and sex is in the air as Dan asks, "Do you want to be ribbed or tickled tonight?" Roseanne announces to an astonished Dan that she would like another child, and after some verbal fencing Dan seems to agree. On this procreative note the episode concludes—but not the half hour, which contains two more commercials. A supreme instance of the intermeshing of popular culture and advertising occurs with a commercial for the upcoming 45th Annual Emmy Awards. Television actors (more specifically, stand-up comedians who are in their own situation comedies, like Roseanne) tout the televised affair that will celebrate the largest fiefdom within the domain of popular culture. It is a resounding conflation of the two symbol domains.

And finally, to bring it all back to the emotional denouement of the show (the baby) and to couch that in appropriately commercial terms is the announcement of a new product named "Carnation Kids," which must be superior beyond conception because even though this product is hardly on the market it is already labeled "Kids' favorite food." There is one final gesture of the advertising domain toward the domain of popular culture: "Carnation Kids" come in the shape of Mickey and Minnie Mouse.

For a committed female viewer, the half hour has conceivably moved her from feelings of adequacy to discontentment to affirmation as the meanings she has taken reverberated between the advertising minutes and the show. The episode's cluster of closely connected emotional themes—of affiliation as played out in family life—have rolled into the commercial seconds, lost or gained facets, and rolled on into the next act. The commercials may have given the viewer idealizations of how to be—Candice Bergen, the L'Oreal woman, the Friskies dog owner—and possible products connected with those ideals, whereas the entertainment, like all popular culture, has performed the maintenance activity of shifting feelings into norms and norms into feelings. Thus, the viewer has seen (if the viewer cared to) how separation and hurt can be translated into child-parent friendship and, moreover, new life. Although these meaning flows have occurred within the borders of the half hour, other connections are built through intertextual references: Many advertising messages pointed directly at popular culture material, as in the promotion of other programs and movies, or less patently, as with the use of Candice Bergen or Mickey and Minnie. The sight of Roseanne can kindle awareness of the clothing line she promotes or of her performances in other venues. Around and around the references have flown.

Meanings From the Mix

The mixing of symbol domains, which is done easily, even pleasurably, in the activity of reception, is believed by some observers to be accelerated by the way the content is composed and sequenced at the sending end. In his thought-provoking book *Promotional Culture*, Andrew Wernick (1992) refers to a recurrent "promotional reflexivity" in the media, whereby everything seems to be promoting everything else (p. 101). Thinking of both advertising and the programming, Wernick states that "the mutual entanglement of promotional signs in one domain with those in another has become a pervasive feature of our whole produced symbolic world" (p. 12). The commercial for the Emmy Awards that ran during a break in the just-examined *Roseanne* episode is an excellent example. The program showcases the promotional message; the message promotes the ceremony as it also promotes the various shows of the featured performers; the televised ceremony will promote the entirety of the medium; the advertising during the telecast will promote other products and other programs; and on and on.

There is one genre that would seem to ideally illustrate Wernick's (1992) thesis. Music videos, which have run since 1981 on MTV (Music Television), are a composite artistic form—marrying a pop, rap, or rock song to a visual track of poetic and evocative imagery—that has rapidly evolved into a genre of substance. Videos synthesize popular music and pop stars with visual aesthetics and staging whose origins lie in the high art of avant-garde film and in fast-paced television commercials, all of which is often played out in a narrative framework; to this modal potpourri is occasionally added a dash of antic, nuanced humor. The whole is intended as a contribution to popular culture and is received as such by its audience, but it can also be understood as an advertisement for the album containing the song, a point often emphasized by commentators.

Music video would then appear to be a vigorous fusion of the domain of popular culture and the domain of advertising. Yet Joe Gow (1992), reviewing the literature on music videos, argues against overstressing the commercial aspects: "Anyone who has ever spent a significant amount of time watching a service such as MTV would most likely scoff at the notion that music video is nothing more than a new type of advertising" (p. 35). Viewers do not see the televised videos as aggressive sales pitches, do not get weary of them as they do of advertising, and do not see MTV as a venue for sales. Gow's review of the small academic literature concludes with an endorsement of the spectatorship: "In sum, these studies indicate that music video is a complex media form attended to by a heterogeneous audience capable of creating a multiplicity of interpretations" (p. 39).

What an individual viewer selects from the congenial advertising/popular culture mix that comprises broadcasting will depend on the particular meanings the individual is in need of at a given point in time. All of the televised material attended to is immaterial and symbolic, and yet all of it is of rock-solid significance to a functioning human being, who by definition is a furious wholesaler of meanings, taking them up here and giving them off over there. So the spectator, a speculator in meanings, is on the prowl not for any and all meanings but for those that are, or will be, of personal value. The spectator looks at the popular culture/advertising mix, where (experience has taught) useful meanings are to be found, more so than in any other pastime. (However, not all needed meanings exist here, as Chapters 10 and 11 show.) The spectator seeks out the particular imagery that invokes and draws out the spectator's own harbored and snarled feelings. The spectator looks for depictions of faded social norms—loyalty, love, steadfastness—to see them manifested in behaviors and episodes. For the creation and maintenance of self-identity, the spectator looks for those special personalities that can be imaginatively emulated or interacted with. The spectator is also looking for those products whose symbolic overtones suit the meanings the spectator wishes to elicit in oneself or in others.

Notes

1. For other, large-scale demonstrations of the polysemous readings of media content, see Dorothy Hobson's (1982) *Crossroads: The Drama of a Soap Opera*; David Morley's (1980) *The "Nationwide" Audience*; Ien Ang's (1985) *Watching "Dallas": Soap Opera and the Melodramatic Imagination*; Janice Radway's (1984) *Reading the Romance: Women, Patriarchy and Popular Literature*; David Buckingham's (1987) *Public Secrets: "EastEnders" and Its Audience*; John Tulloch and Manuel Alvarado's (1983) *"Doctor Who": The Unfolding Text*; Bob Hodge and David Tripp's (1986) *Children and Television: A Semiotic Approach*; and Henry Jenkins's (1990) *Textual Poachers: Television Fans and Participatory Culture*.

2. During the 1993-1994 season, one 30-second spot on *Roseanne* cost an advertiser $300,000 (Mandese, 1993), 85% of which went to the medium (ABC) and the remaining 15% to the advertising agency that designed and placed the message.

3. One person I watched this program with—or better put, whom I watched watching the program—expressed a laughlike response, ranging from a chuckle to a guffaw, to all 98 moments.

10

The Project of the Self

Orrin Klapp (1969) begins *The Collective Search for Identity* by describing the central dilemma of modern times in a manner that would be less likely to occur to an early-20th-century observer but is immediately comprehended by a late-20th-century person. That is, Klapp presents this major issue not in macroscopic and societal terms (even though he is a sociologist) but in microscopic and personalized ones. He shrinks the general problematic down to the individual when he relates that

> my father lacked many things, but one thing he did not lack was a definite conception of himself. I am sure it never occurred to him . . . to ask "who he was"; and he would have thought it odd, to say the least, that anyone should be concerned with such a problem. His problems—of which he had his share—were with external affairs; he had no time for introspection. (p. 3)

And so the wise Klapp, in both his concept and his manner of conveying that concept, specifies the personal conundrum of the age: the universally emergent question of "Who am I?"

Recent history has witnessed a shift in the locus of social control from society to the individual, from external constraints to internal ones (Elias, 1982; Elias & Dunning, 1986). The ordering structures that once took the form of institutions (religion, marriage, family), of social strata, of ethnicities, of lineages, or of professions have been weakened or rejected, and been replaced in whole or part by individuated and internalized coda (Leiss et al., 1990, p. 52). The socially engraved categories for personal definition that would have fully served Klapp's father and all those who lived around him and before him—categories such as Methodist or Presbyterian?, Scotch or German?, from Boston or Savannah?, banker or barber?, orphan or not?, "her people?"—now seem quaint and inadequate, and have been succeeded by the answers to questions on the order of "What is he like?," "What kind of personality does she have?," and, more introspectively, "What kind of person am I?" Precisely why this basal shift should be occurring is open to speculation,[1] but the fact that it is in progress is indisputable. The transition receives impetus from extant values, both older (freedom, individualism) and newer (against racism, elitist, regionalism, sexism). But the removal of these now reproved, oppressive grids necessitates compensatory controls for social order, controls which have taken the form of internalized constraints. What had previously been impressed from outside must increasingly be generated from within.

The signal repercussion of this transition is that self-identity, which used to be handed to the individual through the impositions of societal schema (as it had been for Klapp's father), now must be formulated in lieu of those eroding schema, and must be maintained without the sureties and precepts they provided, but via self-stabilization. Consequently, the creation and maintenance of the self becomes not just a leading personal concern of these times but the paramount one. This rising problematic of self-identity has been accompanied by the rising prominence of the twin symbol domains of advertising and popular culture. This concurrence leads logically to a query: What is the role of the advertising/popular culture mix in the formation of personal identity? The linkage of these times' unique maturation challenge and unique symbol domains requires investigation, in the interest of shedding light on both.

That the matter of the formation of self-identity has risen from relative obscurity to dominate the cultural foreground is indicated by the novel appearance in the 20th century of a prolonged stage in human development: the insertion before adulthood of a decade-long adolescent period, one added on to the traditional stage of childhood. During this extended time for maturation, the individual is left relatively free of economic responsibilities so that the formation of the self can occur without impediment. The inconsistencies, the turbulence, the hardships of this period are obvious to all, not the least of whom are those suffering through it. So important and so difficult is the development of self-identity that much forebearance and support are extended to it. Modern life would be unlikely to allocate such extensive resources to childhood and adolescence if the survival of the culture did not depend on the outcome. This prolonged stage is also marked by its participants' devotion to media content—popular culture of high salience and of limited appeal to those older. Youngsters fold themselves into particular orders of movies, television, magazines, and especially popular music on recordings, on radio, and in concert. The embrace of this content at the same time when the cultivation of personality is in progress would seem to weld the two preoccupations together (see Figure 10.1). But in what ways, and to what ends?

Gender in the Media

The development of selfhood and the relationship of the symbol domains of advertising and popular culture to that process can become more of an addressable topic if the entirety is momentarily limited to the matter of gender construction, gender being the keel of self-identity. It is common to think of gender constitution as distinct from sexual constitution, in that male or female sex is biologically given whereas the masculinity or femininity of gender is culturally determined; that distinction is preserved here. The cultural genesis of gender becomes apparent when different cultures' understandings of gender are contrasted—the Western female versus the Islamic female, for instance, or the 18th-century dandy versus today's man. Whether they want to or not, maturing individuals must take onto themselves some version of gender identity.

Figure 10.1. From *Seventeen*. The solitary human is the most prevalent image in American advertising, one that addresses these times' most insistent personal concern: the development of a sure self-identity. This ad, aimed at young women, captures this prevailing theme by depicting a commanding, doubt-free person and, through its exhortation, "Try to be like your self." But who is that self that one should try to be like? Where is that strong self to be found? In advertising? (Courtesy of the Hartwell Company.)

The prominence of gender concerns in the maturation process is matched by the prominence of gender portrayals in advertising and popular culture. Maleness and femaleness are strident features of the mediated content available to the young (see Figures 10.2 and 10.3). Sut Jhally (1990) reports, "In modern advertising, gender is probably the social resource that is used most by advertisers" (p. 135). The importance of gender concerns in both the world of the adolescent and the world of the media may be part of the reason why the two have received enough scholarly attention that ruminations on their relationship do not have to be conducted in the dark.[2]

As soon as their media participation begins, children are exposed to a vast assemblage of starkly bimodal gender depictions. In a study of males and females featured on programs aimed directly at youngsters, it was learned that female characters were much more likely to have their marital status and family role established, were less often shown as employed, and were typically younger than the male characters—all suggestive of a dependent and diminished status (Barcus, 1983, p. 64). Possibly the most significant finding in this study, however, was that only 22% of the characters shown in children's television were female (p. 63). The predominance of males could be taken by young viewers to mean that males are more important than females. In a later study limited to network Saturday morning commercials, it was determined that males figures continued to predominate throughout the 1980s (Kolbe, 1991).

Youngsters may come across highly gendered depictions of children throughout the media (see Figure 10.4). One research project established the gender attributes of all characters under the age of 20 telecast by the three major networks during a week of prime-time broadcasts (Peirce, 1989). Of 13 personality traits categorized by naive coders, 4 turned out to be significant: Young male characters were more active, aggressive, rational, and unhappy than their female counterparts. Particularly striking were the kinds of activities the characters were undertaking: Girls played with dolls, played "dress up," helped in the kitchen, and talked on the phone, whereas boys participated in sports, played roughhouse,

Figure 10.2. The project of the self, of the establishment and maintenance of self-definition, is in considerable part the project of the *gendered* self. Here is the female ideal featured in profile—attractive, young, committed to working on her own well-being. (Courtesy of Evian Natural Spring Water.)

Figure 10.3. The ideal male version of the self—young, well-muscled, solitary. The project of the self never ends; it must be worked on daily. (Courtesy of Evian Natural Spring Water.)

and behaved mischievously. Peirce (1989) believes prime-time television teaches that "the girl's place is in the home, and the boy's place is wherever he wants to be" (p. 327).

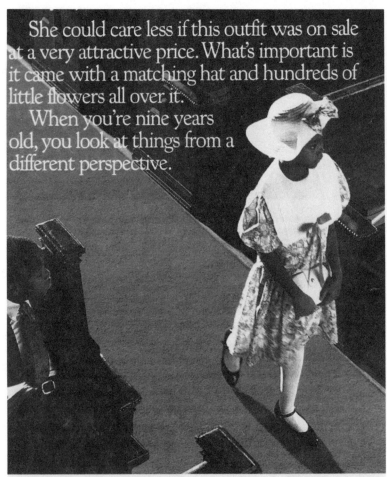

Figure 10.4. In advertising, the gendered depiction of the sexes begins early. Males gaze, and females are gazed at. (Courtesy of Sears, Roebuck and Co.)

An earlier, nonquantitative study by Jean Umiker-Sebeok (1979) of the depictions of children in American print advertising reported similar gender stereotyping: "Female children are often displayed in ads as almost an organic part of the domestic setting, whose colors, contours, and textures they mimic" (p. 205). They are more likely than their brothers to be shown alone and asleep (in a vulnerable state), and are often in the company of dolls (whereby the doll and the girl symbolically flow into each other; see Figure 10.5). Boys, however, are frequently featured outside the home, and although they still exhibit some babylike signs, they also exhibit signs of control and power (p. 206).

The maturing child finds similarly gendered depictions in media renditions of adolescent males and females. Umiker-Sebeok's (1986) study of print advertisements found that by adolescence males are no longer pictured in domestic or family settings; rather, they appear in athletic activities or in automobiles (girls are on foot or on bicycles) (p. 548). When an adolescent male is in the company of other males, he is aggressive, and when he is in the company of females, he is appeasing; in both situations, though, the adolescent male is a person in control. "Unlike males, females in magazine advertisements experience a kind of second infancy during adolescence," Umiker-Sebeok (1981) observes (p. 218). Girls are frequently depicted with infantile traits: soft, wide-eyed, emotional, vulnerable, sucking or licking, with a canting posture (see Figure 10.6).

The circumscribed and subordinate rendition of women-in-training is detailed in a study of the changing editorial content of *Seventeen*, a magazine for young women (Peirce, 1990). Comparing content from 1961, 1972, and 1985, this study found that 60% of the copy consistently dealt with beauty, fashion, cooking, and decorating. In 1972, the number of articles treating relations between the genders declined, whereas the number devoted to self-development rose, inferring greater emphasis on the independence and integrity of the female adolescent, but these changes were reversed by 1985, and the prior 1961 proportions were reinstated.

In being targeted directly and unambiguously at adolescent viewers, MTV videos convey particularly poignant renditions of

Fisher-Price Puffalump Kids
Little softies for big hugs.

Here come the sweetest dolls your little doll
will ever cuddle. Irresistibly soft Puffalump Kids are
light as a feather and dressed for snuggling.
And because they're machine-washable and
dryer-safe, Fisher-Price Puffalump Kids stay soft
and sweet for years of happy hugs.

Figure 10.5. Young girls in advertising are often situated in proximity to dolls, promoting a meaning flow between the two. Here, because of the model chosen, the equivalency is striking. (Used by permission of Fisher-Price, Inc.)

Figure 10.6. Adolescent girls are usually depicted quite differently from the opposite gender. This scene renders them happy, convivial, conversant, open. They are indoors and protected, whereas boys are usually outside the home. (Courtesy of Plano Molding Co.)

gender. One content analysis disclosed that central female characters were noticeably lacking: 83% of the music videos featured white males as the lead figures (Brown & Campbell, 1986, p. 98). Perhaps contrary to feminist hypotheses, however, when females did appear in the videos they were just as likely as male figures to be aggressors and no more or less likely to be victims (p. 102).[3] Females also *never* appeared in domestic settings, although 2% of male leads did (p. 100).

To the extent that adolescents look beyond media content designed expressly for them, they find there adult versions that further confirm delimited gender definitions (see Figures 10.7 and 10.8). Julia Wood (1994) summarizes these media depictions as follows:

> Typically men are portrayed as active, adventurous, powerful, sexually aggressive, and largely uninvolved in human relationships. Just as consistent with cultural views of gender are depictions of women as sex objects who are usually young, thin, beautiful, passive, dependent, and often incompetent and dumb. Female characters devote their primary energies to improving their appearances and taking care of homes and people. (p. 235)

Wood's generalizations are supported by empirical research (e.g., Busby, 1985). In one content analysis of prime-time network characters, the predominance of male figures (65% vs. 35% for females) was once again demonstrated (Davis, 1990, p. 329). Those female characters who did appear were about 10 years younger than the males, were disproportionately blonde or auburn, were more likely to be identified as single (50% vs. 29% for males), and were four times more likely to be provocatively dressed: "The portrait developed here is of the young, attractive, and sexy female who is more ornamental in many shows than functional" (Davis, 1990, p. 331). Throughout the mass media, women are slimmer than men, a slimness that has become more pervasive over time (Silverstein, Perdue, Petersen, & Kelly, 1986).

These gender depictions in popular culture are further stipulated in the advertising messages that adolescents may be exposed to. Several studies have documented that the voice-overs in television commercials are about 90% male (Bretl & Cantor, 1988; Lovdal, 1989), inflecting this gender with an aura of authority and

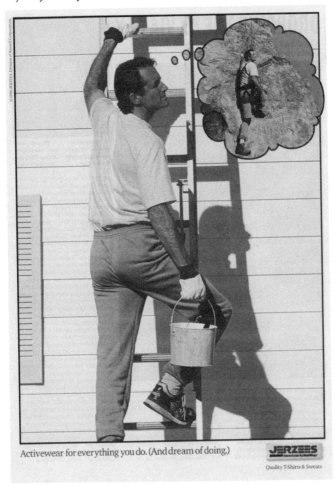

Activewear for everything you do. (And dream of doing.)

JERZEES
American Activewear
Quality T-Shirts & Sweats

Figure 10.7. Men in advertising are often active—here doubly so, since he ascends also in his fantasy. Another solitary figure. (Courtesy of the Russell Corporation.)

omniscience. As portrayed in beer commercials targeted at men, males are devoted to "challenge, risk, and mastery—mastery over nature, over technology, over others in good-natured 'combat,' and over oneself" (Strate, 1992, p. 82). Women in network television

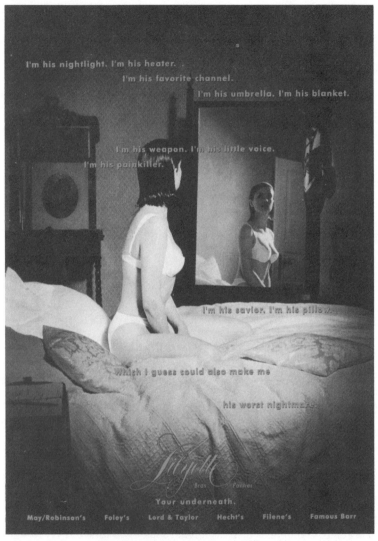

Figure 10.8. If men in advertising are active, women are more often passive. Women are less likely to be on their feet and more likely to be indoors. In this ad, the solitary female figure is still, posing not so much for her own view as for the contemplated gaze of a lover. The reveries here, unlike the dream of scaling cliffs solo (see Figure 10.7) are those of a relationship, of romantic complexities. (Courtesy of Lilyette Co.)

commercials, according to one content analysis, "are not seen outside the home as often as males, do not represent products for nondomestic items, and are not viewed in wider professional contexts" (Lovdal, 1989, p. 722).

Similar stereotypes are captured in research on print advertisements.[4] Masse and Rosenblum's (1988) study of gender imagery in six American magazines confirmed that females are more likely to be in a subordinate position (27% vs. 4% of the males) and depicted in partial views: "The ready dismemberment and multiplication of female bodies presumes the absence of any coherent, integrated, substantive self" (p. 132; see Figure 10.9). Masculine codes exhibited in *Esquire*'s advertisements in the 1980s centered on the same two themes focused on in the 1930s: success ("The Big Wheel") and self-reliance ("The Sturdy Oak") (Kervin, 1990; see Figures 10.10 and 10.11).

To complete the picture of the mediated gender depictions that are available to the young, it should be pointed out that these portrayals, while firm over time, have been evolving—although not always in ways that everyone finds agreeable. Over the 1970s and 1980s, in Saturday morning commercials, female presence in major roles increased from 6% to 33%, and female voice-overs increased from 6% to 19% (Kolbe, 1991). There is evidence from one study that males and females now appear in equal numbers in prime-time commercials (Bretl & Cantor, 1988). It seems safe to say that the ranking problem of the occluded female gender in the media is in the process of being remedied. However, females in prime-time commercials are still more often depicted as not employed, in domestic settings, and using products (although males are increasingly shown in the roles of spouses and parents) (Bretl & Cantor, 1988).

As for print advertisements, from 1959 to 1989 women were featured decreasingly as homemakers, increasingly without a male present, and increasingly in a decorative pose (see Figure 10.12). "Based on the images in these advertisements, the American woman has diverted energy from the family to herself and has increased her role as decorative object" (Busby & Leichty, 1993, p. 259). The major change in the representation of men in print ads, according

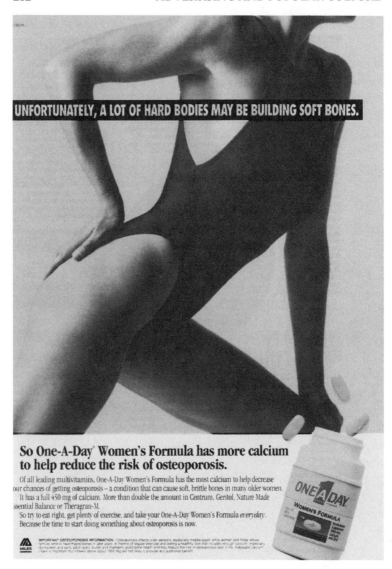

Figure 10.9. Critics might see this as a decapitated figure, a derisive comment on the feminine gender. But many women interested in toning their bodies or in familiarizing themselves with the ideals of the toned body would not find the ad offensive. (© 1993, Miles Inc., a Bayer Company.)

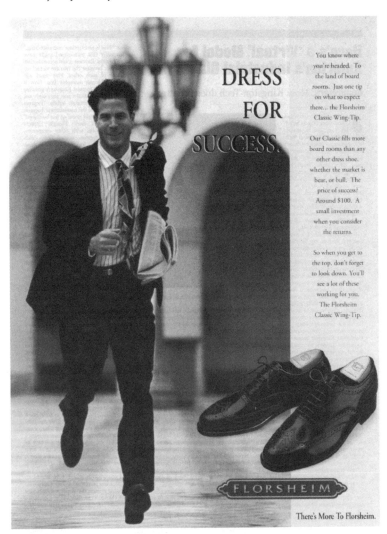

DRESS FOR SUCCESS.

You know where you're headed. To the land of board rooms. Just one tip on what to expect there... the Florsheim Classic Wing-Tip.

Our Classic fills more board rooms than any other dress shoe, whether the market is bear, or bull. The price of success? Around $100. A small investment when you consider the returns.

So when you get to the top, don't forget to look down. You'll see a lot of these working for you. The Florsheim Classic Wing-Tip.

FLORSHEIM

There's More To Florsheim.

Figure 10.10. The successful, on-the-go male in advertising. In keeping with the conventional portrayal, he is outdoors, on his feet, solitary. (Courtesy of the Florsheim Shoe Company.)

to Denise Kervin (1990), is the recent arrival of "the male as erotic spectacle" (p. 63); she is thinking primarily of the Calvin Klein campaigns.

Figure 10.11. The self-reliant male in advertising. Again, outdoors, on his feet, solitary. (Used with permission of Newport Harbor® Division of Whaling Industries.)

The simple availability of mediated gender imagery, however, is not informative about the uses the young make of it, because what is sent is never identical to what is received. To understand youths' purposeful exploitation of the imagery requires a change in emphasis from the content that is transmitted to the practices of reception.

Using Gender Portrayals

Advertising and popular culture are heavily imbued with highly delineated images of masculinity and femininity not because the culture industries are committed to foisting particular gender depictions on their spectators but because the audience, and especially the young, are captivated by gender imagery and seek out those models, performers, and performances that best exemplify cultural concepts of maleness and femaleness. Younger audience members, particularly adolescents, demand that the media transmit highly sculpted instances of masculinity and femininity, with gender traits flaring. To develop their own version of gender definition, the young are compelled to be on the outlook for exemplars in their most succinct and epitomized forms. The media excel at polished representations, so the representation of gender will be found perfected here as nowhere else.

Historically, attention to gender paragons results from the fact that, while almost all other social categories have shed some of their definitional and proscriptive force over the course of the 20th century, the category of gender endures, robust as ever. This remains the category that the individual must negotiate if that person is to successfully find intimate companions in life; its attributes must be comprehended, selected, and wielded. Important as these concerns are for the individual, they are hardly less important for societies, or indeed for the entire species, because they underlie propagation.

Yet, steadfast as the category of gender has proved to be, its very survival brings it into conflict with the central vector of 20th-century cultural change: the erosion of traditional social demarcations. Many of the same people who are becoming restive within stereotyped categories of race, religion, region, occupation, class,

Figure 10.12. This ad is representative of recent trends in the portrayal of women: less as homemakers, less in the company of males, and more as decoration. (By permission of Toyota Motor Sales U.S.A.)

and the rest are also growing restive within traditional gender definitions. Thus, gender definitions increasingly carry within them their own amendments and reversals: It is all right for a male to be sensitive (at moments); it is all right for a female to be independent and decisive (to a point). Gender is increasingly contested territory, with definitions and traits in some degree of flux; this is especially the case for femaleness, as feminist counterpressures wax and wane, feint and shift. As gender constructions become more flexible, they become more worthy of careful scrutiny by young people.

The young, then, turn to media depictions of gender for help with a doubly difficult transition—first, into adult genders, and second, into adult genders whose definitions may turn out to be mutable (see Figures 10.13 and 10.14). Given this arduous task, how do they make use of the gender portrayals they see? The first thing to be said, and said emphatically, is that the young do not adopt in a wholesale fashion the media depictions of maleness and femaleness to serve as their operating templates of gender. The British and American scientific literature on the topic of the influence of television portrayals on children's conceptualizations of gender and gender development has been surveyed by Kevin Durkin (1985). If television directly shaped gender beliefs and behaviors, he said, then those who viewed the most television would be the most affected in this regard; the existing body of studies, however, does not substantiate such an effect. "It turns out to be very difficult to measure satisfactorily the relationship between amount of viewing and as complex an aspect of personal development as sex roles" (p. 71). Durkin postulates that children are active, not passive, viewers and that "what children bring with them to their viewing will influence substantially what they extract from it" (p. 72).[5]

Testimony to resistance and selectivity regarding gender portrayals comes in the form of a study that compared high school students' estimates of gender-related social statistics to television representations and to census facts (McCauley, Thangavelu, & Rozin, 1988). Asked to guess the proportion of females in the U.S. population, the teenagers' average came within 1 percentage point of the actuality (52% vs. the census count's 51%) and so was apparently uninfluenced by the lower figure on television. When the students were asked about gender proportions for certain occupational groups, their average estimates often varied from

Figure 10.13. Part of the reason why advertising's idealizations of people are wanted and are studied is that gender definitions are often in flux. This recent ad suggests that a transition is under way; it bears watching. (With permission of Chesebrough-Ponds USA Co.)

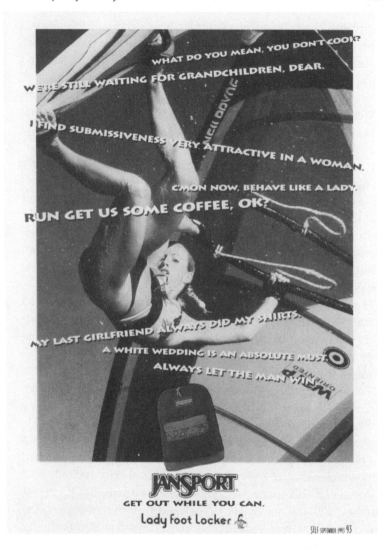

Figure 10.14. Just as masculine gender definitions are in flux, so are feminine ones. Here is a young woman refusing to "behave like a lady," as the copy puts it. She is smashing the conventions of womanhood. Yet she presents a conventional picture of youthful attractiveness. In this striking photograph, the reader gets to know her first through her anatomy, from the bottom up. Gender definitions can be highly complex creations. (Jansport®. Used with permission of VF Corporation.)

reality, but their distortions were always *contrary* to television's depictions. That is, even though television underrepresents the proportion of doctors, lawyers, and police who are female, the students overestimated it. McCauley et al. conclude, "It is worth noting the TV and respondent distortions do not match for any of the occupational categories, which indicates that TV distortion is not contributing to viewer distortion of sex-occupational stereotypes" (p. 203).

In another study, adolescents' amount of television viewing (taken to suggest the amount of exposure to gender stereotypes) was compared to their sex-role behaviors (gauged by the extent that they did such gendered chores as taking out the household trash or washing dishes): "The data show no relationship at all between amount of television viewing and sex-role behavior" (Morgan, 1987, p. 279). Just as for gender perceptions, gender behaviors do not correlate readily with exposure to television.

That the media should prove poor at imposing pronounced gender stereotypes and behaviors is not surprising upon reflection. The content is only symbolic, after all, and has little of the force of real-world interaction among living human beings. Although the audience for mediated symbolic content is active, this activity is characterized by attention, selection, and interpretation, and not by the thrusts and checks, the immediacy and interactivity of face-to-face communication.

Real-world instruction about gender begins early in life within the family setting; in a meta-analysis of 172 studies on parents' differential rearing of boys and girls, the sole uncontroverted effect was parental encouragement of gender-typed activities (Lytton & Romney, 1991). Sex-role stereotypes and preferences for gender-specific toys are observable in children as young as 26 months; by 31 months of age, most children can place themselves in a gender category and will mark their gender with appropriate clothes, toys, attitudes, and behaviors (McCoy, 1990, p. 32). As children age, they concentrate on same-sex models, observing and interacting with those of their gender who are their age or older, confirming their own gender and adopting ever more consistent gendered behaviors. Their same-sex peer groups become important sources of gender information; into the conversational interactions among peers there may enter, as ancillary material, renditions of males and females observed in the media, but this content is rarely accepted at face value and is necessarily refashioned within the peer group (Peterson & Peters, 1983, p. 71). Gender concepts are firm by the time children enter adolescence (Moschis & Moore, 1979, p. 110). Attention now turns to the opposite gender, who are observed and interacted with until their gender definitions are revealed and made approachable. Confirmation of opposite-gender definitions is aided somewhat by attention to the media; adolescents find opposite-gender celebrities more attractive and interesting (Greene & Adams-Price, 1990).

If media depictions of gender play a removed role in gender formations, the fact remains that they do play some role, however minor. What is the nature of the contribution from the advertising/popular culture mix? Or to reverse and improve the question, what use do young people make of mediated gender depictions in the formation of their own gender identities? To begin at the surface of things, the young take appearance features from mediated males and females (particularly from advertising and other highly polished content) and use them in the construction of ideals of attractiveness. These idealizations are needed to establish an orientation, a direction for change (if desired), and to establish a gradient for attractiveness so that a young person can rank one's own surface as well as those of others. The need for acmes of attractiveness, never extinguished in life, is especially important for the young as one ingredient in the determination of self-identity and self-esteem. Studies disclose that, for adolescents, ratings of self-esteem are closely correlated with one's rating of one's physical appearance (Harter, 1990, p. 367), a rating that obviously cannot be done without a sense of the operant cultural standards. These standards are modeled in the domains of advertising and popular culture and realized to a lesser extent in the real world, where they are worked on by the forces of everyday life.

Moving now below the surface, the media also provide idealizations of gendered personality, whereby male traits are clustered at one place and female traits at another. The service offered by the advertising/popular culture mix in this respect is no different from the service provided regarding appearance. When the youthful viewer sees that males are typified as rational, ambitious, smart, competitive, powerful, stable, dominant, and tolerant and that females are typified as sensitive, warm, romantic, sociable, peaceful, fair, and submissive (Peterson & Peters, 1983, p. 79), they are being exposed to definitions of personalities that lend some form to gender but are still nonbinding, offering greater or lesser fixity depending on the needs of the viewer. These gendered stereotypes of personality can become fixed only after they have been brokered in the real world of the young person.

For the adolescent, equally important as the media's presentation of ideals for the appearance and personality of one's own gender, is the presentation of ideals of the opposite gender. "In effect to construct an identity, to know who you are, you need to know who you are not," writes Mike Featherstone (1991, p. 82). The attributes that the media associate with the opposite gender are ones to be wary of in the composition of one's own gender identity. Viewed in a more positive light, concentration on portrayals of the other gender, instead of on one's own, may broaden one's range of developmental possibilities. Such study leaves available a widened unclaimed territory that one may inhabit as one wishes. Stereotypes of the other gender can also provide hints on how to approach that gender, how to ingratiate oneself with those who are defined otherwise. None of this other-gender information is preclusive; all of it is provisional to be used or not as the adolescent sees fit.

Additionally, to the extent that gender depictions are accepted, part of the reason for their acceptance may have nothing to do with gender formation but, rather, with the need among teenagers for a shared culture and the generational solidarity that it provides. Operating with a common definition of what a "fox" is, of what a "hunk" is, is part of what unites a cohort and allows for a sense of group identity and common mission. Judith Williamson (1978) calls attention to this communal feature for teenagers but, because she objects to the discrepancy between advertising's depiction of females and females in the real world, decries it: "So it is in fact a positive instinct, the desire to share in a social reality, which deprives us of a true knowledge of social realities" (p. 170).

If the emphasis is shifted away from advertising and onto popular culture, from the provision of idealizations to the provision of emotional redress, then the depictions of gender may take on different and contrasting functions for the young. Because popular culture operates between two poorly reconciled fronts, navigating between psychological emotions and social norms, popular culture content is rife with contradictions and often serves contradictory purposes. In this regard, part of what popular culture can do is set up gender silhouettes to serve as contemptible targets for the other gender, who can vent some of their inter-gender spleen on the cutouts. Thus, in some music videos women are presented as bitches or bimbos. Feminists have been quick to detect these caricatures but may forget that males are also rendered as brutish or doltish at times, to serve as whipping boys for the female viewership. These portrayals have almost nothing to offer by way of gender construction but much to offer for the vicarious retribution that popular culture elicits and specializes in.

Although the gender depictions forwarded by the media are narrowed representations of what it is to be a male and what it is to be a female, that definitiveness could be advantageous to audience members. As viewer response varies according to the needs of the individual, some individuals, for reasons of their own, may partake deeply of the stereotype, and so for them the sharp circumscription of the depicted gender may be helpful in that it is seen to remove ambiguity. Other individuals may encounter the gender portrayals only slightly or not at all, or in an oppositional manner. The variability of the reception and interpretation of mediated gender must always be acknowledged. "If media effects research is any guide," states Fred Fejes (1992), "one would expect to find that members of the audience 'read' media messages about masculinity in a highly individualistic fashion, supporting the notion that there are many masculinities" (p. 22). Discussing the images of females in magazine advertisements, Ellen McCracken (1993) admits that such imagery is engaged in "a semiotic battle against the everyday world which, by its mere presence, often fights back as an existential correction to the magazine's ideal images" (p. 3). Both Fejes and McCracken are conceding that mediated gender images are not slavishly accepted but are involved in very complex, although ultimately purposeful, negotiations with people. These negotiations are testimony to the willfulness of the viewers and their determination to be selective and self-appeasing in their consumption of gender imagery.

The gender images that appear in the advertising/popular culture mix are, in the final analysis, creations not of the culture industries but of the spectatorship. A sense of the power of audience members comes from a study by R. Steven Craig (1992) of gender portrayals as they vary among television time periods. To the largely housebound female daytime viewers, women in commercials are shown linked to home and family life; to male weekend sports fans, women are depicted as subservient; to the mixed prime-time audience, women are most likely to be portrayed in positions of authority and in settings away from the home. Craig writes, "Advertisers wish to make commercials a pleasurable experience for the intended audience. They construct the ads in ways that reinforce the image of gender most familiar to and comfortable for their target audience" (p. 208). The preferences of the audience in shaping gender depictions may be extended down to the most subtle features represented, for workers in the culture industries strive to create images that best capture the preferences of the public and will be most favorably received. Mediated gender images give visible, symbolic form to preexisting cultural inclinations.

From this position it is now possible to respond to an opposing argument: that mediated gender imagery is hegemonic and coercive. Such criticisms emanate from those who either do not understand that the portrayals are fictive idealizations, or do understand they are idealizations but reject these particular ideals. In point of fact, gender imagery has little power at all, as any observation of the real world demonstrates. In everyday life, masculinity and femininity are multiform, occasionally rife with internal contradictions, variably in evidence, and variable over time. Very few individuals conform well or always. People situate themselves close to the stereotypes or far away or in opposition or in ways heedless of their biologically assigned sex. Any one individual is likely to possess a greater conflux of characteristics, some at odds, than any simplified gender portrayal will possess. This nonconformity to mediated gender depictions reveals the integrity, the intransigence of the individual.

In sum, the process of formulating gender, a prime ingredient in the creation of self-identity, draws on several sources. The true hammer and anvil of gender formation is the real world, where the maturing individual comes in contact with flesh-and-blood others who personify or instruct regarding maleness and femaleness. Specifically, the young's working definitions of masculinity and femininity are forged through interactions with family, peers, and school personnel—all contexts described by vital, physically present, nonmediated interpersonal contact. The symbolic material in the advertising/popular culture mix has only a secondary role, supplying distant and tentative navigational aids.

The Symbol Domains and Self-Identity

The relationship of the advertising/popular culture mix to gender formation is indicative of the relationship of the mix to the entirety of self-identity. The two symbol domains offer up idealizations of appearance, personality, and behavior, but they are ideals alone and can never be fully actualized in everyday life, at least not for long. If there is any leeway in a person's development of self-identity, the person is invited to steer nearer to the ideal, but when interior reluctance or resistance is encountered, as it must be sooner or later, or when reality obstructs, then movement toward the ideal is halted. It is the real person, existing in the real world, that has primacy; it could hardly be otherwise.

Advertising and popular culture are overestimated as agents in the development of self-identity, an overestimation that stems in part from the ubiquity of these expressive domains. They have spread into our domiciles, into hour after hour of our days. Occupying private time and space with us, they might seem to be a looming presence, one capable of pronounced effects. While their visibility makes them conspicuous in the here and now, they are also conspicuous in a longer temporal framework, enjoying a prominence they did not have a century ago. The comparative novelty of mediated advertising and popular culture renders them suspicious and invites misperceptions of their circumscribed social roles.

When children are young, they sometimes confuse the mediated world and the real world, but in time they learn to discriminate. The boy who wants to fly off the shed roof like Superman seldom needs to learn his lesson a second time. An adult version of the same sort of discrimination is needed to comprehend the limited impact of the advertising/popular mix on such real-world challenges as the development of self-identity. Although visible, the content of the media is only symbolic; it is never alive, never palpable. As such, it has little coercive power and can be accepted or rejected, in whole or in part, according to the needs or whims of the spectator. The content of the two symbol domains is far-fetched, and so is the notion of its might.

Notes

1. The shift in social control from societal to individual constraints could be accounted for by the shift of the highly arranged life out of the social sphere and into the world of work—specifically, into business organizations. Within the past 150 years, the appearance and proliferation of highly regulated organizations (as opposed to prior conditions, when people had been self-employed or worked in small groups) could mean that the protocols adequate for general social order would be lodged in the workplace. The strictures applicable to society became redundant and ultimately vestigial. Outside of work hours, individuals would be left on their own.

The decline in traditional social constraints could also result from what is ostensibly so simple a matter as the increase in human population density. In one version of this particular analysis, more people leads to more strangers; more strangers entails more autonomy and more anonymity; individuation weakens broader social controls; and exteriorly imposed social checks such as shame have to be replaced by interior social controls such as guilt (Nock, 1993, p. 7).

2. Although some research has been done on adolescents and media, this cannot be taken to mean that the question is completely or even adequately

studied. In fact, Fine, Mortimer, and Roberts (1990) assert that "existing research tells us remarkably little about the role of the mass media in adolescence" (p. 245).

3. Fantsay violence between genders (apparently on equal terms) is a feature of music videos that is analyzed later in this chapter.

4. The classic work on gender depictions in print advertising is Erving Goffman's. Goffman (1976) identified six representational markers of gender:

- Females are likely to be pictured as shorter than males and so less authoritative.
- Females are likely to be touching or caressing objects; men grasp them.
- The functions that females are performing are likely to be less important to them and to society.
- Females are likely to be physically subordinated.
- Females are less likely to be well oriented to the depicted scene.
- Female roles are revealed in family portrayals.

An attempt to quantify Goffman's conjectures with a sample of 1,000 print ads found that only feminine touch and physical subordination were prevalent images (Belknap & Leonard, 1991). A quantitative study solely of Goffman's superior/subordinate dimension suggests that, while males still dominate about 70% of the time, poses with females in charge or with an equality between the genders are on the increase (Klassen, Jasper, & Schwartz, 1993).

5. For a similar literature review, one reconfirming that children are active, not passive, viewers, see Anne Wadsworth (1989), who writes, "Contrary to very early beliefs about television and media, children are far from being passive respondents to media. Research clearly shows that children actively select media for particular purposes" (p. 110).

11

In Perspective

The courtroom trial of O. J. Simpson left the nation feeling exhausted, dulled. This fatigue in the aftermath told of an earlier, heightened fascination, one nearly boundless. An analysis of the popular obsession with the case would point to the issues manifested there, all of them festering within the body of American culture: white versus black, male versus female, the control of anger, rich versus nonrich, the egoistic hedonism associated with Los Angeles versus the proper values of middle America. And other more enduring themes: justice versus injustice, life versus death. Other trials might have exemplified similar matters, so what made this one so very remarkable? The answer, of course, is the celebrity of the defendant. O. J. Simpson is famous, doubly so: Not only was he a hero within the domain of popular culture (having been a leading running back on televised football for 10 years before becoming a network commentator and an occasional movie actor), he also was a hero within the domain of advertising (hurtling through airports in a long-running Hertz rental car campaign, modeling a line of boots). The presence that he had established in both symbol domains lent him a dual iconic status and created a personage that, although known only through the media, was so immense that numerous social issues would attach themselves to it, to glimmer in the public consciousness and to amplify public fixation.

If mediated popular culture and advertising were the venues of O. J. Simpson's enormous fame, lending him a stature as symbol so towering that it elicited an unprecedented and ultimately enervating spasm of public attention, then this phenomenon can precipitate, once again, questions about the power and scope of the two mediated symbol domains. French philosopher Jean Baudrillard (1983) has offered a daring and all-encompassing reply: that in modern times, reality has capitulated and been obliterated by the hyperreality of the imagery conveyed through the mass media. It is a theme that runs through much of postmodernist critical thinking regarding the current media environment. Fredric Jameson (1984) deplores the culture industries' "aestheticization" of everyday life, and Stuart Ewen (1988) refers scathingly to an "utter triumph of abstract value" and the "valorization of thin air" (p. 159). A sense of the actualities of the matter, of the relative weight of the domains of advertising and popular culture within the conduct of contemporary affairs, must be teased out of such absolutist assertions.

From internal evidence it is clear that popular culture and advertising are highly ambitious symbol domains, striving to bring all of human time and space under their wings. Movies stretch the cinematic aesthetic over the distant past and distant future, from the prehistoric rendering in *Quest for Fire* to the futuristic spacescapes of *Star Wars,* and television makes a similar effort, if in triter fashion, in the span from *The Flintstones* to *Star Trek.* The far corners of the world are supposedly captured on film (*Sand Pebbles, The Gods Must Be Crazy, Nanook of the North*) and video (*M.A.S.H., Hogan's Heroes, Northern Exposure*). Advertising likewise reaches out to colonize space (O'Barr, 1994) and time (see Figures 11.1 and 11.2).[1] In Andren's (1978) sample of American print advertisements, about 7% invited readers into the past and about 3% into the future (p. 147). A study of network television commercials documented that 10% of them nostalgically invoke the past through image, word, or music (Unger, McConocha, & Faier, 1991). How successful are the efforts to subsume the sum of human experience under these two symbol fields? How powerful and totalizing are these domains?

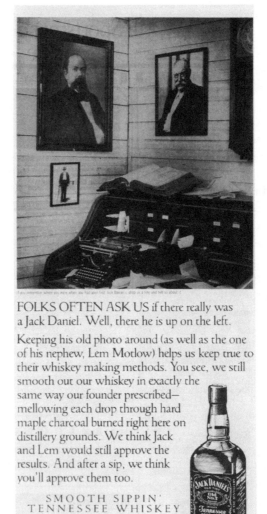

Figure 11.1. Advertising is an ambitious symbol domain, attempting to claim all of human time. Here the symbols refer to the recent past. Jack Daniel's may be the leading advertiser at invoking rural, bygone ways of life. (Jack Daniel's and design are registered trademarks of Jack Daniel Distillery, Lem Motlow, Prop., Inc.)

Figure 11.2. Colonizing time—but in the opposite direction. This campaign attempts to construct a self-fulfilling prophecy, a commodified future that awaits the consumer. (Courtesy of AT&T.)

Untouched by
Advertising and Popular Culture

The argument made here regarding the force of the advertising/ popular culture mix upon the entirety of the human experience is an extension of the argument made in Chapter 10, where the severe shortcomings of the two symbol domains in the forging of people's self-identities were stressed. Mediated advertising and popular culture, late arrivals in human history, have not taken over consciousness, have not obliterated reality, and do not hold humanity captive.[2]

It takes only a moment's reflection to recognize how large a portion of American life is untouched, or virtually untouched, by the two fields. For example, the activity of education is little mentioned in popular culture and rarely depicted in advertising, yet almost everyone is exposed to 12 years of it, and about half of every generation will attempt to get 4 more years of it in college, with 10% continuing on after that until they are well into their 20s. They do this, day after day from the age of 5, absorbing what they can, with little to no guidance, no gloss, from the advertising/ popular culture mix. Here is a large section of everyone's life that is conducted apart from, and is largely uninformed by, the two dominant symbol fields. The purported hegemony of advertising and popular culture begins to look less than total.

Even more striking, typical employment—at which most people will spend most of their lives—is only occasionally featured in popular culture and almost never appears in advertising. Because the focus in advertising and popular culture is on the individual, close viewers of the symbol domains learn little of what they will have to exhibit when in the workplace. Young men and women going to work for the first time are often amazed at the extent of the adjustment, an amazement equal to that of entering a foreign culture, an amazement that is revealing about what goes untaught and unlearned during their extensive hours with the media. What clothes to wear, how to function cooperatively with others, patterns of deference—all the lessons of the workplace that the advertising/popular culture mix did not impart and will not reinforce must be absorbed quickly by the new hire. The hegemony of advertising and popular culture clearly does not extend to the all-important world of work.

Although advertising and popular culture are steeped in images of worldly goods and worldly behaviors, of all industrialized countries the United States remains the most religious and the most spiritual. This entire dimension of American life—an ample, vigorous dimension—operates not just with disregard for the two symbol domains but in straightforward opposition to them, espousing communal and otherworldly orientations that fly in the face of the orientations broached in advertising and popular culture. The evidence is that, even though these two profane symbol domains have prospered in the last half of the 20th century, devotion to the sacred remains an undiminished preoccupation of Americans. Andrew Greeley (1989), in examining the relevant social statistics, found no support for the widely assumed secularization of national life: 95% of the population continues to affirm a belief in the existence of God, and consistently about 75% are convinced that there is life after death (p. 14). The eternal rewards to be found in heaven are believed in by over 70% of adults, and 50% believe that hell is a real place (p. 14). According to Gallup poll findings, 58% of Americans affirm that religion is very important in their lives (Newport & Saad, 1992). Of the Gallup sample, 75% are formal members of an organized religion; 44% state that they attended a church service the previous week. Moreover, 78% of Americans pray at least once weekly, and 57% pray every day (Woodward, 1992, p. 39)—a practice they would be unlikely to derive from mediated popular culture or advertising.

Education, work, religion—they are not heavily promoted in the symbol mix, nor are other institutional pillars of national life, such as financial systems or government. Nor, indeed, is ordinary life itself, as it is in the nature of the media that their content must strive to be extraordinary. Part of ordinary life for most Americans is the willingness to contribute to charitable causes, a behavior that contradicts the apparently rampant narcissism at the core of

advertising and popular culture. Of the $123 billion given to
charitable causes in 1990, 83% came from individuals, with the re-
mainder coming from foundations and corporations (Weber, 1991,
p. 20). Americans gave away more money that year than they
spent on gasoline and oil. For a population of supposedly self-
fixated people, the amount spent on clothing in 1990—$150 billion
(U.S. Bureau of the Census, 1993, p. 106)—was in the same order
of magnitude as the amount donated to charity. During the same
period when the culture has become ever more saturated with
advertising and popular culture, Americans' generosity has also
been on the rise, climbing in constant dollars from $30 billion in
1955 to $83 billion in 1990 (Weber, 1991, p. 11).

Advertising and popular culture cannot even overwhelm leisure
hours. Much of the humbler outdoor activity of Americans is
completely uninfluenced by these symbol domains. Gardening,
for example, is an avocation of some 61 million people (Waldorp,
1993, p. 44), or about one quarter of the total population, but
not 1 of those 61 million learned to garden or to appreciate the
pleasures of gardening by looking at popular culture or general
advertising. Their interest in gardening and the execution of that
interest derived from other sources, from internal desires and personal observations. There were some 23 million hikers in America
in 1994, pursuing an activity that went virtually unseen in popular
culture and (with the exception of some shoe ads) in advertising
(McEvoy, 1994). Camping, a family activity perhaps too prosaic to
find representation in the highly charged image domains, is a $1
billion annual business, a figure roughly equal to the annual sales
of bicycles or of fishing equipment—two other missing activities
(U.S. Bureau of the Census, 1993, p. 255).

The touted hegemony of advertising and popular culture lies in
shambles. There are great swatches of national life that proceed
with vigor and purpose and do so uninspired, uninterpreted, and
untouched by the imagery of the two symbol domains. Advertising and popular culture may command the circulation of symbolic
material, but they do not command the sum of national life.

The Future of Advertising Imagery

Yet care must be taken not to commit the opposite intellectual error of undervaluing the growing symbol domains of advertising and popular culture. The rise of these expressive art forms since the Civil War and their expansion to their present dimensions and saliency are predictive of their robust health in times to come. Conceivably, mass communications (the systems minus the content) could have come into being for technological or financial reasons, obliging some sort of corporate imperative, but the imagistic content that was developed to occupy these communications systems consists of material designed solely to satisfy spectators. The mode of conveyance may have belonged to corporations, but the content belonged to the users. The specific content demanded was content that spoke to the increasingly insistent and increasingly troublesome dictum of the age: create and maintain thyself. In the wake of subsiding social categories—whose declines are witnessed either enthusiastically or nostalgically but, irrespective of the values placed on them, occur nonetheless—the individual has often been left bobbing alone, to survive as best as possible.[3] On all sides, societal firmness has surrendered: Families become smaller and smaller, caste erodes, religions lose some of their determination, group identities weaken, occupations turn impermanent, allegiances are short.[4] Americans sought out that pictorial content, in preference to all other, that would, in an easeful and pleasurable a manner as possible, help with this new and strenuous responsibility for the self.

As the culture industries attempted to respond to these needs, a division of symbolic labor transpired. Advertising, in part because its time and space are costly and its periods of presentation are consequently briefer, has concentrated on succinct idealizations of the self. Presenting model selves as polished objects addresses the spectator's duty for the creation of the surface of the self. Although the figures that are offered in popular culture may serve as idealizations of the self, they more generally serve with their comparatively protracted performances as vehicles for the working out of tangled emotions and unwanted feelings, and so provide for the maintenance of the self.

This broad system—involving the culture industries, members of the audience, and preferred orders of content—is here projected to continue strongly in the future, a projection based on conjectures that social categories and social precepts will continue to dwindle, that the creation and maintenance of the self will become an ever more prominent fixture of American life, and that the culture industries, energized by competition, will consequently offer symbolic content in greater volume and with greater applicability.

To better forecast the future, the two symbol domains must be considered. Can it be expected that the semiotic services which advertising renders will be in greater or lesser demand in years to come? Advertising is a way station in a hypothesized flow of meanings: The symbols chosen for an ad are extracted by the advertising agency from the all-encompassing culture that is realized through individuals; this symbolic material can infuse the product, if individual consumers permit it to; should the consumer buy the advertised product, the consumer is also buying the meanings found in the advertising. Thus, meanings can flow from the consumer's abstract cultural world to the advertisement, to the product, and back to the consumer in physical form (see Figure 11.3).

The need for products infused with the meanings that advertising symbols can lend them is likely to rise in the decades ahead. Keeping in mind Lévi-Strauss's (1963) maxim that goods are good for thinking, that goods convert the abstract into the observable, it would appear that as the horizons of awareness are enlarged, the demand for meaning-conveying goods would increase as well. Horizons of awareness are indeed widening, due not only to scientific and technological advances, but also to greater access to populations around the globe and to those previously invisible within the nation, as well as to greater exposure to and appreciation of the natural world. Vistas to the rear are also opening up, as history and archaeology impart form upon a vague past. The sphere of culture in its own right seems to be swelling both in size and complexity. All this would imply more goods and more need for advertising's investment of possible meanings into goods.

Figure 11.3. Advertising's intended flow of meanings—from the cultural world at large to an ad's reconfigured imagery and then onto the product and finally to the consumer—is here a carefully and tightly regulated one. The essential problematic of the self is invoked with that advertising mainstay, the solitary figure, and through the reference in the headline to loneliness. The tastefulness symbolized by the selected furnishings is meant to flow onto the Waterford bowl. If purchased, the bowl's psychological and social meanings are then to flow on and assuage the consumer. (With permission of Waterford Wedgwood USA, Inc.)

Moreover, to return to the central theme, the definition of the self portends to be a yet greater task in the future. One of the chief ways the self is defined to oneself and to others is through the adoption and display of symbol-offering (and in intent, meaning-invoking) goods. People will be shopping for more and newer symbols to help locate themselves within an ever more socially amorphous world. The broader search for symbol-conveying items, to articulate meanings for an expanding semantic territory that extends from deep inside to far outside, can only imply greater need for the meaning-suggesting services of advertising.

The incrementally increasing need to situate oneself by means of meaningful products is vastly complicated by the fluidity of the symbolic lexicon, further heightening the need for advertising's definitional services. A symbol can offer a particular set of possible meanings today and a different (and perhaps unwanted) set tomorrow; new symbols replace old symbols in a wink. Fluctuation in symbols underlies the principle of fashion change, by which waves of new styles are offered and occasionally adopted to mark where one is situated along the vector of change—as either avant-garde, au courant, or passé. Fashion change is often credited to the heartless manipulation of fashion industries, but such an interpretation grotesquely overestimates the power of those industries and denigrates the control and purposefulness of the consumer. Mark Poster (1990) notes, "Fashion must sustain itself as a code and must be analyzed at the semiotic level. If fashion is understood as manipulation to increase sales, one misses its semiotic power" (p. 60). A fast-changing, rapidly evolving society, one whose axis is no longer solely that of vertically stacked social strata but also that of a horizontal push through time, is going to add the gradient of fashionableness to the gradient of social rank (Fowles, 1974). The choice of stylistic symbols from among the novelties offered, influenced but not determined by advertising, states how voguish a person is. One selects one's clothing, one's automobile, one's housing, one's appliances, one's accoutrements so as to say, "Here is where I stand along the dimension of time."

The stylistic symbols that one adopts, however, do not only say how modish one is or is not, how close or not close one is to the vanguard. Styles, layered with possible meanings, also contain within themselves references to things past and to differing versions of things past. Advertisements for new items often offer allusions to a history either actual or imaginary. Daniel Czitrom (1987) argues that exhortations to consume "created the need for products in large part through an appeal to a mythical past—lost community, lost intimacy, lost self-assurance. Consumer goods promised to make one happy by returning what had vanished" (p. 14). Advertising, by offering both symbols of the cutting edge and symbols of a sustaining past, tries to steady the consumer in the currents of time.

Besides alignment in time, there are other yet more confounding dimensions along which personal symbols flow and for which advertising offers partial instruction. Advertising operates like a guide who attaches oneself to a wary tourist in a foreign country, a guide who does not speak the tourist's language very well and may misrepresent some of the sights, but still is good for something provisional. Modern individuals, shorn of much traditional, exterior categorization, need to locate themselves in spatial dimensions as well as along the temporal one. They must find and take to themselves the symbols that satisfactorily define place. This occurs in two ways: First, there are the geographically foreign symbols that say, "I am familiar with that distant place and find it of definitional value for me here." Thus, Oriental rugs, Chinese vases, African masks, and English prints make their appearance. There are, of course, stylistic concerns reflected in these selections, as different foreign cultures rise and sink in fashion, just as there are stylistic elements in the second way that symbols define place—the accumulation of furnishings, whether geographically referential or not, that establish one's household. Here advertising plays an important role, presenting views of interiors that one may be unlikely to ever actually enter. In the words of Robert Sack (1992), "Advertising provides a publicly shared understanding of the power of a commodity to create context and place and an idealized picture of what the context or place could or ought to be like" (p. 107).

While the provision of those symbols that help to locate the individual in time and space comes ever more to the fore, the more venerable symbol systems regarding social status have not yet disappeared, and advertising attempts to be of service in this regard also. As with other symbol lexicons, this one too is in flux and merits watching; advertising wants to do the watching for the consumer—and occasionally does. "The constant supply of new, fashionably desirable goods, or the usurpation of existing marker goods by lower groups, produces a paperchase effect in which those above will have to invest in new (informational) goods in order to reestablish the original social distance," observes Mike Featherstone (1991, p. 19).

However, in the 20th century, to make matters all the more complex and interesting, the cycling of status markers turns in both directions; not only are the lower dominated classes appropriating the symbols of the dominant, but the dominant in turn steal from the dominated.[5] In mid-century, blue jeans, the clothing of the working class, were adopted by the young and then the elders of the higher classes, signaling their resistance to the very elite and to highly formalized life. More recently, torn blue jeans and backward-worn caps, appearing higher and higher in the social hierarchy as symbols of rebelliousness, are adopted by increasing numbers for the fun of it and so are drained of their original oppositional meanings (Fiske, 1989b, p. 15). The turnover in symbols means that the symbolic chase ensues not only at the upper end but also at the lower end and from the margins as well. It is a whirling maelstrom of symbols, but to the initiated (whose knowledge comes in part from advertising) it is easily readable. Because it is comprehensible, society coheres.

What is not new in all this is that people have always looked everywhere for meanings and have imparted them everywhere— and they have selected certain objects to encapsulate those meanings. What has changed is the scope of the "everywhere"— now it reaches further inside and further outside, a widening that promises to continue. More objects and newer products will be needed, and so will the services of the advertising symbols that proffer possible meanings for those commodities.

The Future of Popular Culture

Personal identity in the new era is reflected in one's possessions, possessions that have symbolic force, possessions whose taken meanings may have been touched up by the advertising that accompanied those commodities. But the self-identity externally displayed in this manner has to be internally groomed on almost a daily basis, in the interest of its ongoing well-being. Here is where popular culture enters. Are the services that popular culture provides going to be in greater or lesser demand in the future? These services, it will be recalled, consist in the pro-vision of symbolic content that can be used primarily for purposes of emotional management, and secondarily in the navigation toward social norms. With the exception of a massively conservative swing in the nation's course, one that is the equal of Iran's rejection of Westernization and establishment of a medieval theocracy, there is no foreseeable path that would entail a reduction in the need for popular culture. Quite the opposite: The most likely evolution of national life would involve greater attention to, and greater reliance upon, the beguiling invocations in the many genres of popular culture. The social norms often promoted in this symbol domain—of right and wrong, justice, nationalism, love, friendship, tolerance—are seen here but decreasingly elsewhere, as other social institutions are eclipsed; this display of norms is appreciated by viewers and is bound to be appreciated more and more. The depicted norms may, on average, be steadfastly mainstream, but they are capable of change over time and indeed can respond quickly to any shifts in the channel that the stream of culture cuts.

As discussed in Chapter 5, of all the problematic emotions that popular culture content is called upon to rectify, it is anger and hostility that stand out for Americans, and that correspondingly occupy the greater share of popular culture's content. In their study of the centuries-long history of anger in the United States, Carol Stearns and Peter Stearns (1986) state that aggressive feelings are not more prevalent now than in the past; what has changed is that their display is less tolerated. "Thus has the prolonged battle to control anger borne fruit, not only in the goal of seeking internal restraint over anger and disapproving those who lack this restraint, but also in the intensity with which this goal is held" (p. 211). People used to vent their anger unreflectingly on others— servants, spouses, children, social inferiors, and certain ethnic groups—but with the passage of time these "others" have been redefined as off bounds, as unsuitable as scapegoats, and as meritorious individuals in their own right.

In the workplace, standards of deportment have moved steadily away from cruelty and surliness, and toward friendliness, cooperation, and obeisance at whatever personal cost. Those who can effect a smile during the entire workday will hold their jobs, and those who cannot may have to look elsewhere for employment. According to the Stearns (1986), "Expressions of anger have been blocked or reduced without a corresponding reduction of angry sentiment. Dammed in key channels, anger seeks outlet elsewhere" (p. 227). What other alternatives are there once the superiority/ inferiority scale has been collapsed so that all are of nominally equal worth and none are fit targets? What other alternatives are there once it is incumbent upon the individual to practice strenuous selfcontrol over hostile impulses? The Stearns (1986) offer an analysis also found in the work of Norbert Elias (1982) when they write,

> In using sports to divert anger, and in developing new opportunities for spectatorship that may have vented angers as well through intense partisanship, the later nineteenth century developed a durable outlet for expressing anger and enthusiasm that could not be safely displayed in ordinary life. (p. 228)

Examining next the 20th century, they entertain the idea that the recent rise in crime rates stems from inadequate social outlets for aggression before they turn to the subject of popular culture:

> [The need to vent anger] may also help explain the popularity of media violence and our willingness, however reluctant, to tolerate its availability for young viewers. In various aspects of popular culture, we may implicitly recognize the need for some safe targets or symbols of violence since we seek to deny anger in so many daily interactions. (p. 230)

Their proposal, gingerly phrased and left unelaborated, indicates and summarizes the argument here: that the management of hostile impulses is a gnawing problem in 20th-century life and that much of popular culture has been called into being just to address this problem. Considering only television's portion of popular culture, invocations to aggress are not only a conspicuous portion of the action/adventure shows and similar programs that critics deplore, but also are the more tolerated essence of televised sports and, in disguised form, the gist of the jokes and barbs on situation comedies. There is nothing to suggest that the need for such content will diminish. As living targets for invective grow ever more protected and scarce, and as the individual becomes ever more responsible for controlling one's own behavior, a logical consequence will be the search for the symbolic material with symbolic targets that permits the harmless discharge of aggressive feelings.

That popular culture plays a restorative role in human affairs (rather than being, as some wrongly insist, an instigator) and absorbs disapproved impulses is additionally suggested by its devotion to sexual material. Like anger and aggression, sexual urges have to be managed in the interest of social order, and like anger and aggression, the expression of sexuality has become more a matter of personal management. The social institution of prostitution, once a staple if obscured presence in every community, has receded. It has not disappeared, any more than anger toward others has disappeared, but it operates within a more constrained cultural territory. Meanwhile, the symbolic expression of sexuality in the form of pornography has grown into a multi-billion-dollar film and video industry. Television too figures into the symbolic figuration of sexual activity, although more modestly, limited for the most part to bodily displays short of nudity, to flirtation, and to embraces short of copulation. Sex in the media, however, arguably absorbs rather than instigates rampant sexuality in real life, for Americans on the whole appear to lead extremely restrained sexual lives. A substantive national report published in 1994 disclosed that 83% of adults have no more than one sexual partner per year (Michael, Gagnon, Laumann, & Kolata, 1994). Over a lifetime, the typical American male has six partners, the typical female two—this in spite of the fact that 54% of men and 19% of women think about sex daily. There is little reason to suspect that the compensatory services of popular culture in this regard will be less in demand in the future when the management of impulses becomes ever more the responsibility of the individual.

The True Meaning of Christmas

In American life, the calendrical year concludes resoundingly with the festival of Christmas, and it is in this massive celebration that all the topics discussed in this book are both encapsulated and magnified.[6] More advertising is displayed in December than in any other month (see Figure 11.4); more popular culture—in the forms of recordings, videocassettes, works of fiction, video games, ticket sales—is purchased than in any other season; in fact, more consumer goods of all sorts are bought than at any in any other time of the year. The primacy of the individual is also central to the occasion, although, as will be seen, inversely, conspicuous by its putative absence.

Although the modern Christmas celebration has a curiously brief social history, the portion of the year surrounding the winter solstice, the one day in 365 when the period of sunlight is briefest, has always been sacred in the Northern Hemisphere. It is the moment when one annual cycle ends and another is about to begin, the moment in-between, the opportunity to take leave of normal activities. In pagan Europe, the day was the occasion of the Winter Feast—Saturnalia in the south, Yuletide in the north—characterized by excesses of eating and drinking, revelry, and debauchery (Golby & Purdue, 1986, chap. 2). Gifts of food and clothing flowed from superiors to inferiors, from lords to vassals, to bind and ameliorate hierarchical ties. Customary conduct was frequently reversed during the festival: Masters waited on servants, men and women cross-dressed, gambling was permitted where it

Figure 11.4. Christmas—the season for advertising and consumption as well as the season of interpersonal harmony. Here the commodity (signaled by the configuration of the choir in the shape of the vodka bottle) is meant to flow into the celebration and the spirit of the season to flow into the commodity. (Used with permission of TBWA Advertising.)

was usually forbidden, and so forth. The festivities provided compensatory relief for the rigors of normal existence during the year; one could trace backwards from the behaviors of that riotous day to the more hurtful and resisted aspects of everyday life.

When the holiday was Christianized after the 5th century, new trappings overlaid but could not submerge much of the customary carousing. At British festivals, Lords of Misrule were elected—usually those of lower status who were temporarily empowered to lead and incite the immoderate merrymaking. It was against such boisterous activity that Protestant reformists were able to mount a censorious offensive in the 17th and 18th centuries, an offensive that was in large part successful, for in England and in the Puritan portions of the New World the celebration of Christmas fell out of favor. Its repudiation was codified in the colony of Massachusetts, where Christmas was illegal between 1659 and 1681 (Waits, 1993, p. xv); the ostensible cause was the lack of any biblical directive to celebrate the day, but the true reason was a disapproval of the frivolities and insolence associated with the festival.

It is against the backdrop of the near disappearance of the holiday that its reinvention over the course of the 19th century must be understood, for as it slowly emerged in the first decades of that century and crystallized in the 1880s, the celebration found itself largely unencumbered by its bacchanal traditions and able to evolve to serve new and pressing social purposes. With the exception of a few incidental ingredients, such as Rudolph the Red-Nosed Reindeer, the makeup of the festival has remained the same from the 1880s to the present, even as the scope of it has immensely widened. This time frame, also that of this book, is the period in which mediated advertising and popular culture arose and in which the production/consumption economy bloomed. Needless to say, it is also the period that registered the steepest decline in the force of traditional social structures and the sharpest rise in the realization of the concept of the individual. All of these developments enter into an interlocking composite.

The modern holiday does not primarily offer compensation for the impositions of social life as the Winter Feast did, for social life is no longer so imposing. The modern solstice celebration offers compensations that are mostly the reverse of the earlier festival's; it offers compensation for the relative *lack* of social life. What

Americans have come to commemorate at the winter solstice is the human connectedness that has become ever more precious as it has become ever more scarce. The individualism and competitiveness that increasingly describe normal conduct during the regular year and that strain or dissolve communal ties are momentarily set aside in favor of an inflated, counterbalancing affectation of fellow feeling and goodwill (see Figure 11.5).

Gifts (commonplace material objects signified as having special properties through a wrapping of special paper) are widely distributed, marking lines of connection that have lost their immediacy, that fully exist only in nostalgia. Some of the stream of gifts mark traditional superior/inferior arrangements, as from parents to children, employers to employees, and as beneficence to the unknown poor, but much of it is a great lateral circulation among near equals, a national swap of items that are inexpensive, of limited utility, and essential for the marking of faint social connections. Gifts are no longer given; they are *exchanged*. In concentric circles with an increasingly wistful quality about the exchanging, gifts go to spouses, to relatives near and far, to friends and their families, to office mates, to neighbors—all of it an attempt to reestablish a feeling of social membership, which before 1880 was omnipresent and did not need to be specially or intensely invoked. Layered on top of the gift-exchanging networks and extending beyond them is the circulation of symbolic messages in the form of Christmas cards—a more extenuated marking system but one dedicated to the same end, to redress the same deficiencies.

It is not just that this activity—the giving of gifts in the attempt to revive receding sets of relationships—goes on but that it goes on with such ferocity. The dollars spent at it continue to mount, as does the time allocated: Christmastime was only a day or two in duration 100 years ago, but now it has expanded to incorporate the surrounding holidays. The season opens explosively with Thanksgiving dinner and day-after Thanksgiving shopping, and terminates exhaustedly following New Year's Day—two holidays that for most of the 19th century in the United States had overshadowed Christmas. This expansion has occurred at such a headlong pace, without time for culturewide adjustments, that it has incited a chorus of complaints about the expense involved or

Figure 11.5. This imagery cleverly blends the icon of the Christmas star with various types of people. The symbols of Christmas plus fellowship are then intended to flow over to the charity, which has waited all year for this season of giving. (With permission of the Salvation Army, National Communications.)

the extension of the season into November and earlier. The charge of "commercialism"[7] is brandished to show displeasure with the widening practice of giving and getting gifts. But such resistance is feeble in the face of the gathering forces of the Christmas festival, whose celebratory fervor reveals the dimensions of what is being commemorated.

There are two closing ceremonies to this remedial holiday season. Following an immoderate celebration on New Year's Eve, in which

Before

There's something you should do before life hits you in the knees with ten bags

the spouse,

of groceries and the need for a garden hose. You should know how it feels to have

the house,

the sun on your head and a growl at your back as you flick through five gears

the kids,

with no more baggage than a friend. This has been known since the beginning of cars.

you get

Which is why roadsters were invented. The Mazda Miata. The roadster returned.

one chance.

mazda
IT JUST FEELS RIGHT

The Mazda MX-5 Miata is backed by a 36-month/50,000-mile, no-deductible, bumper-to-bumper limited warranty. See dealer for details. For a free brochure 1-800-639-1000. © 1993 Mazda Motor of America, Inc.

Figure 11.6. The project of the self regains centrality. (© 1993, Mazda Motor of America, Inc. Used by permission.)

the self is allowed vulgar indulgence in compensation for the unrelenting exercise of interpersonal pleasantries over the previous month, the individual engages in the ritualistic activity of New Year's resolutions. These resolutions, done by oneself for oneself, signal that the self has returned to its previous high station and that the year is about to commence on its regular course with the project of the self in the forefront (see Figure 11.6).

The second and final closing ceremony occurs in the form of Super Bowl Sunday, which is in effect an elaborate homage paid by the domains of advertising and popular culture to themselves. Both domains are puffed up far beyond the cultural value of the nominal content. The advertising is excessive, hyperbolic, overinflated—unconnected to any realistic marketing plans, comprising an excessive exhibition of advertising qua advertising. The televised football game is more often than not a poor specimen of the sport, yet it is represented as the annual apex of popular culture and is viewed by a large enough number of Americans as if it were. After this exorbitant, self-congratulating display, advertising and popular culture will settle back down to their jobs of providing the personal services that modern individuals demand of them year round.

Notes

1. Judith Williamson (1978) argues that advertising appropriates time and space (nature) successfully, and deceitfully. Advertising, she says, misplaces the consumer in its own construction of time and space: "Advertisements refer to this misplacement as an inevitable and 'natural' fact" (p. 102).

2. Those who think in monetary terms may grasp the relative weight of advertising and popular culture through the observations that advertising as a business expenditure is only about 2.5% of Gross Domestic Product, and that Americans' spending on entertainment (which includes but is not limited to mediated popular culture) is about 3% of all personal expenditures. Advertising and popular culture do not represent major outlays in American life.

3. Besides the diminishment of traditional social categories and precepts, the sureties that defined human existence are under attack in another sense. Due to scientific advances, the lid on what is known and what can be known has been lifted off, and awareness is expanding with great rapidity in both microscopic and macroscopic directions. For these expanding territories to be comprehended in everyday life, symbols must be exported into them so that meanings can be taken. Advertising, essentially conservative, has done little duty in this regard, but popular culture, bold as brass and ever hungry for new material, has rushed into the newly exposed terrain with a slew of medical and space stories. Apprehensions regarding newness are laid to rest, and curiosities are satisfied. New scientific territory becomes converted into narratives, narratives to be mined by the spectatorship for meanings.

4. That social categories are eroding may be more recognizable to European visitors (who can compare the Europe of now to the United States of now and make temporal inferences) than to American observers (who must compare a hazy past to a challenging, seemingly multiform present). Jean Baudrillard (1988) writes, on the basis of his tour of North America, "We in Europe are stuck in the old rut of worshipping difference; this leaves us with a great handicap when it comes to radical modernity [as in the United States], which is founded on the absence of difference" (p. 97).

5. Kirk Yarnadoe and Adam Gopnik (1990), in their study of the flow of aesthetic styles, note the same sort of dual cycling, as popular culture rises into elite art at the same time that high culture is absorbed into popular culture and advertising art.

6. For all of the massiveness of the Christmastime celebration and its pre-eminent position within the annual cycle of holidays, it is curious that the season has received little scrutiny by scholars. William Waits (1993) comments on "the general lack of scholarly effort analyzing the Christmas celebration" (p. xviii). Does the holiday rear so large that it overwhelms students of American society and culture just as it does others? Could there be some reluctance to see what is displayed there?

7. The charge of "commercialism," with the implication that Christmas used to be less so and now is more, is not profound. The holiday was not much celebrated in the English-speaking world for the two centuries before the arrival of the production/consumption economy in the 19th century. As the holiday reemerged, it used as gifts the goods that were at hand—in this case, manufactured ones. Pre-17th-century Christmases had employed as gifts the goods available then—items produced by hand.

Bibliography

Aaker, D. A., & Bruzzone, D. E. (1981). Viewer perceptions of prime-time television advertising. *Journal of Advertising Research, 21*(5), 15-23.

Alperstein, N. M. (1991). Imaginary social relationships with celebrities appearing in television commercials. *Journal of Broadcasting and Electronic Media, 35*(2), 43-58.

Andren, G. (1978). *Rhetoric and ideology in advertising: A content analytical study of American advertising.* Stockholm: Liberforlag.

Ang, I. (1985). *Watching "Dallas": Soap opera and the melodramatic imagination.* London: Methuen.

Another Pepsi star fades. (1993, September 6). *Advertising Age,* p. 22.

Arnold, M. (1971). *Culture and anarchy: An essay in political and social criticism* (3rd ed.). Indianapolis: Bobbs-Merrill. (Original work published 1869)

Aronowitz, S. (1993). *Roll over Beethoven: The return of cultural strife.* Hanover, NH: Westleyan University Press.

Atwan, R., McQuade, D., & Wright, J. W. (1979). *Edsels, Luckies, and Frigidaires: Advertising the American way.* New York: Delta.

Banner, L. W. (1983). *American beauty.* New York: Knopf.

Barcus, F. E. (1983). *Images of life on children's television: Sex roles, minorities, and families.* New York: Praeger.

Barnett, J. H. (1954). *The American Christmas: A study in national culture.* New York: Macmillan.

Barthel, D. (1988). *Putting on appearances: Gender and advertisers.* Philadelphia: Temple University Press.

Barthes, R. (1977). The rhetoric of the image. In R. Barthes, *Image, music, text* (pp. 32-51). New York: Hill & Wang. (Original work published 1964)

Barthes, R. (1990). *Mythologies.* New York: Noonday Press. (Original work published 1957)

Baudrillard, J. (1983). *Simulations.* New York: Semiotext(e).

Baudrillard, J. (1988). *America.* London: Verso.

Beatty, S. E., & Hawkins, D. (1989). Subliminal stimulation: Some new data and interpretation. *Journal of Advertising, 18*(3), 4-8.

Belk, R., & Pollay, R. W. (1985). Images of ourselves: The good life in twentieth century advertising. *Journal of Advertising Research, 11,* 887-897.

Belk, R., & Pollay, R. W. (1987). The good life in twentieth century U.S. advertising. *Media Information Australia, 46,* 51-57.

Belknap, P., & Leonard, W. N., II. (1991). A conceptual replication and extension of Erving Goffman's study of gender advertisements. *Sex Roles, 25*(3/4), 103-118.

Beninger, J. R. (1986). *The control revolution: Technological and economic origins of the information society.* Cambridge, MA: Harvard University Press.

Bennett, T. (1986). The politics of the "popular" and popular culture. In T. Bennett, C. Mercer, & J. Wollacott (Eds.), *Popular culture and social relations* (pp. 6-21). Milton Keynes, England: Open University Press.

Berger, J. (1972). *Ways of seeing.* London: British Broadcasting Corporation and Penguin.

Berger, J., & Mohr, J. (1982). *Another way of telling.* New York: Pantheon.

Berger, W. (1991, May 4). Dis me deadly. *Advertising Age,* pp. 23-30.

Betterton, R. (Ed.). (1987). *Looking on: Images of femininity in the visual arts and media.* London: Pandora.

Blair, M. E. (1993). Commercialization of the rap music subculture. *Journal of Popular Culture, 27*(3), 21-33.

Blonsky, M. (1992). *American mythologies.* New York: Oxford University Press.

Bloom, A. (1987). *The closing of the American mind.* New York: Simon & Schuster.

Bourdieu, P. (1984). *Distinction: A social critique of the judgement of taste.* Cambridge, MA: Harvard University Press.

Brantlinger, P. (1983). *Bread and circuses: Theories of mass culture as social decay.* Ithaca, NY: Cornell University Press.

Brantlinger, P. (1990). *Crusoe's footprints: Cultural studies in Britain and America.* New York: Routledge.

Bretl, D. J., & Cantor, J. (1988). The portrayal of men and women in U.S. television commercials: A recent content analysis and trends over 15 years. *Sex Roles, 18*(9/10), 595-609.

Brown, B. W. (1981). *Images of family life in magazine advertising, 1920-1978.* New York: Praeger.

Brown, J. D., & Campbell, K. (1986). Race and gender in music videos: The same beat but a different drummer. *Journal of Communication, 36*(1), 94-106.

Brown, J. D., & Schulze, L. (1990). The effects of race, gender, and fandom on audience interpretations of Madonna's music videos. *Journal of Communication, 40*(2), 88-102.

Bruner, G. C., II. (1990, October). Music, mood, and marketing. *Journal of Marketing,* pp. 94-104.

Buckingham, D. (1987). *Public secrets: "Eastenders" and its audience.* London: British Film Institute.

Busby, L. J. (1985). The mass media and sex-role socialization. In J. R. Dominick & J. E. Fletcher (Eds.), *Broadcasting research methods* (pp. 267-295). Boston: Allyn & Bacon.

Busby, L. J., & Leichty, G. (1993). Feminism and advertising in traditional and nontraditional women's magazines, 1950s-1980s. *Journalism Quarterly, 70*(2), 247-264.

Buzz on bra ads. (1994, October 24). *Advertising Age*, p. 17.

Carey, J. W. (1989). *Communication as culture*. Boston: Unwin Hyman.

Caughey, J. L. (1984). *Imaginary social worlds*. Lincoln: University of Nebraska Press.

Certeau, M. de. (1984). *The practice of everyday life*. Berkeley: University of California Press.

Charged-up foes for Bunny. (1993, October 11). *Advertising Age*, p. 3.

Choe, J.-H., Wilcox, G. B., & Hardy, A. P. (1986). Facial expressions in magazine ads: A cross-cultural comparison. *Journalism Quarterly, 63*(1), 122-126.

Cleveland, C. E. (1986). Semiotics: Determining what the advertising message means to the medium. In J. Olson & K. Sentis (Eds.), *Advertising and consumer psychology* (pp. 227-241). New York: Praeger.

Collins, J. (1989). *Uncommon cultures: Popular culture and postmodernism*. New York: Routledge.

Couch potato. (1994, April 21). *Houston Post*, p. A26.

Coulling, S. (1961). Matthew Arnold and the *Daily Telegraph*. *Review of English Studies, 12*, 173-184.

Courtney, A. E., & Whipple, T. W. (1983). *Sex stereotyping in advertising*. Lexington, MA: Lexington Books.

Coward, R. (1985). *Female desires: How they are sought, bought, and packaged*. New York: Grove.

Craig, R. S. (1992). The effects of television day part on gender portrayal in television commercials. *Sex Roles, 26*(5/6), 197-211.

Craig, S. (Ed.). (1992). *Men, masculinity, and the media*. Newbury Park, CA: Sage.

Crane, D. (1992). *The production of culture: Media and the urban arts*. Newbury Park, CA: Sage.

Csikszentmihalyi, M., & Rochberg-Halton, E. (1981). *The meaning of things: Domestic symbols and the self*. New York: Cambridge University Press.

Cutler, B. (1990, November). Where does the free time go? *American Demographics*, pp. 36-38.

Czitrom, D. (1987). Dialectical tensions in the American media. In P. Buhle (Ed.), *Popular culture in America* (pp. 7-18). Minneapolis: University of Minnesota Press.

Danna, S. R. (Ed.). (1992). *Advertising and popular culture: Studies in variety and versatility*. Bowling Green, OH: Popular Press.

Davis, D. M. (1990). Portrayals of women in prime-time network television: Some demographic characteristics. *Sex Roles, 23*, 325-332.

Day, G. (1990). Introduction: Popular culture—the conditions of control? In G. Day (Ed.), *Reading in popular culture: Trivial pursuits?* (pp. 1-12). New York: St. Martin's.

Douglas, M., & Isherwood, B. (1979). *The world of goods: Toward an anthropology of consumption*. New York: W. W. Norton.

Dowling, W. J., & Harwood, D. L. (1986). *Music cognition*. New York: Academic Press.

Dunbar, D. S. (1990). Music and advertising. *International Journal of Marketing, 9*(3), 197-203.

Durkin, K. (1985). *Television, sex roles, and children.* Milton Keynes, England: Open University Press.

Dylan goes commercial in ad for accounting firm. (1994, January 12). *Houston Post,* p. 36.

Elias, N. (1982). *Power and civility: Vol. 2. The civilizing process* (E. Jephcott, Trans.). New York: Pantheon.

Elias, N. (1987). On human beings and their emotions: A process-sociological essay. *Theory, Culture and Society, 4,* 339-361.

Elias, N., & Dunning, E. (1986). *Quest for excitement: Sport and leisure in the civilizing process.* London: Basil Blackwell.

Eliot, T. S. (1949). *Notes towards the definition of culture.* New York: Harcourt Brace.

England, P., Kuhn, A., & Gardner, T. (1981). The ages of men and women in magazine advertisements. *Journalism Quarterly, 58*(3), 468-471.

Esslin, M. (1982). Aristotle and the advertisers: The television commercials considered as a form of drama. In H. Newcomb (Ed.), *Television: The critical view* (pp. 260-276). New York: Oxford University Press.

Ewen, S. (1976). *Captains of consciousness: Advertising and the social roots of the consumer culture.* New York: McGraw-Hill.

Ewen, S. (1988). *All consuming images: The politics of style in contemporary culture.* New York: Basic Books.

Featherstone, M. (1991). *Consumer culture and postmodernism.* London: Sage.

Fejes, F. (1989). Images of men in media research. *Critical Studies in Mass Communication, 6*(2), 215-221.

Fejes, F. (1992). Masculinity as fact: A review of empirical mass communication research on masculinity. In S. Craig (Ed.), *Men, masculinity, and the media* (pp. 9-22). Newbury Park, CA: Sage.

Ferrante, C. L., Haynes, A. M., & Kingsley, S. M. (1988). Images of women in television advertising. *Journal of Broadcasting and Electronic Media, 32*(2), 231-237.

Fine, G. A., Mortimer, J. T., & Roberts, D. F. (1990). Leisure, work, and the mass media. In S. Feldman & G. R. Elliott (Eds.), *At the threshold: The developing adolescent* (pp. 225-252). Cambridge, MA: Harvard University Press.

Fiske, J. (1987a). *Television culture.* London: Methuen.

Fiske, J. (1987b). British cultural studies and television. In R. C. Allen (Ed.), *Channels of discourse* (pp. 254-289). Chapel Hill: University of North Carolina Press.

Fiske, J. (1989a). *Reading the popular.* Boston: Unwin Hyman.

Fiske, J. (1989b). *Understanding popular culture.* Boston: Unwin Hyman.

Fitzgerald, K. (1993, May 3). Star presenter. *Advertising Age,* p. S12.

Foster, M. L., & Botscharow, L. J. (Eds.) (1990). *The life of symbols.* Boulder, CO: Westview.

Fowles, J. (1974). Why we wear clothes. *Et Cetera: The Review of General Semantics, 31*(4), 343-351.

Fowles, J. (1976). *Mass advertising as social forecast.* Westport, CT: Greenwood.

Fowles, J. (1983, October 10). What I learned at the agency. *Advertising Age,* pp. 54-58.

Fowles, J. (1984). The craniology of the 20th century: Research on television's effects. *Television Quarterly, 20*(4), 61-68.

Fowles, J. (1985). Advertising's fifteen basic appeals. In R. Atwan, B. Orton, & W. Vesterman (Eds.), *American mass media: Industries and issues* (pp. 43-54). New York: Random House.

Fowles, J. (1992a). *Why viewers watch: A reappraisal of television's effects.* Newbury Park, CA: Sage.

Fowles, J. (1992b). *Starstruck: Celebrity performers and the American public.* Washington, DC: Smithsonian Institution Press.

Fowles, J. (1994). Stereography and the standardization of vision. *Journal of American Culture, 17*(2), 83-87.

Fox, S. (1984). *The mirror makers.* New York: William Morrow.

Freedman, J. L. (1988). Television violence and aggression: What the research shows. In S. Oskamp (Ed.), *Television as a social issue* (pp. 144-162). Newbury Park, CA: Sage.

Freud, S. (1959). The economic problem in masochism. In E. Jones (Ed.), *Collected papers* (Vol. 2, pp. 255-268). New York: Basic Books. (Original work published 1924)

Freud, S. (1960). *Jokes and their relation to the unconscious* (J. Strachey, Trans.). New York: W. W. Norton. (Original work published 1905)

Frith, K. T., & Wesson, D. (1991). A comparison of cultural values in British and American print advertising: A study of magazines. *Journalism Quarterly, 68*(1/2), 216-223.

Fromm, E. (1941). *Escape from freedom.* New York: Holt, Rinehart & Winston.

Fulford, D. G. (1993, November 14). A star is born—at 88 years old. *Houston Chronicle*, p. 15G.

Gabor, A. (1987, December 7). Star turns that can turn star-crossed. *U.S. News & World Report*, p. 57.

Gagnard, A. (1986). From feast to famine: Depictions of ideal body type in magazine advertising. In E. F. Larkin (Ed.), *Proceedings of the 1986 Conference of the American Academy of Advertising* (pp. R46-R50). Norman: University of Oklahoma Press.

Galbraith, J. K. (1971). *The affluent society* (2nd ed.). Boston: Houghton Mifflin. (Original work published 1958)

Gans, H. J. (1974). *Popular culture and high culture: An analysis and evaluation of taste.* New York: Basic Books.

Geertz, C. (1975). *The interpretation of cultures.* New York: Basic Books.

Gleick, E. (1993, November 29). Michael Jackson cracks up. *People*, pp. 42-47.

Goffman, E. (1976). *Gender advertisements.* New York: Harper & Row.

Golby, J. M., & Purdue, A. W. (1986). *The making of the modern Christmas.* Athens: University of Georgia Press.

Goldman, R. (1992). *Reading ads socially.* London: Routledge.

Gombrich, E. H. (1981). Image and code: Scope and limits of conventionalism in pictorial representation. In W. Steiner (Ed.), *Image and code* (pp. 11-42). Ann Arbor: University of Michigan Press.

Gossage, H. L. (1967). The gilded bough: Magic and advertising. In F. W. Matson & A. Montague (Eds.), *The human dialogue* (pp. 363-370). New York: Free Press.

Gow, J. (1992). Making sense of music videos: Research during the inaugural decade. *Journal of American Culture, 15*(3), 35-43.

Gramsci, A. (1971). *Selections from the prison notebooks*. New York: International Publishers.

Greeley, A. (1989). *Religious change in America*. Cambridge, MA: Harvard University Press.

Greene, A. C., & Adams-Price, C. (1990). Adolescents' secondary attachments to celebrity figures. *Sex Roles, 23*(7/8), 335-348.

Grossberg, L. (1986). Teaching the popular. In C. Nelson (Ed.), *Theory in the classroom* (pp. 177-200). Urbana: University of Illinois Press.

Grossberg, L. (1992). *We gotta get out of this place: Popular conservatism and postmodern culture*. New York: Routledge.

Gunter, B. (1986). *Television and sex role stereotyping*. London: John Libbey.

Hall, S. (1980). Encoding/decoding. In S. Hall (Ed.), *Culture, media, language* (pp. 128-138). London: Hutchinson.

Hall, S. (1981). Notes on deconstructing "the popular." In R. Samuel (Ed.), *People's history and socialist history* (pp. 227-240). London: Routledge.

Harter, S. (1990). Self and identity development. In S. Feldman & G. R. Elliott (Eds.), *At the threshold: The developing adolescent* (pp. 352-387). Cambridge, MA: Harvard University Press.

Hartley, J. (1987). Invisible fictions: Television audiences, paedocracy, pleasure. *Textual Practice, 1*(2), 121-138.

Hartley, J. (1988). The real world of audiences. *Critical Studies in Mass Communication, 5*, 234-238.

Hecker, S., & Stewart, D. (Eds.). (1989). *Nonverbal communication in advertising*. Lexington, MA: Lexington Books.

Hirsch, E. D., Jr. (1987). *Cultural literacy: What every American needs to know*. Boston: Houghton Mifflin.

Hobson, D. (1982). *Crossroads: The drama of a soap opera*. London: Methuen.

Hodge, B., & Tripp, D. (1986). *Children and television: A semiotic approach*. London: Polity.

Hodge, R., & Kress, G. (1988). *Social semiotics*. Ithaca, NY: Cornell University Press.

Horkheimer, M., & Adorno, T. (1972). The culture industry: Enlightenment as mass deception. In M. Horkheimer & T. Adorno, *Dialectic of entertainment* (pp. 120-167). New York: Herder & Herder. (Original work published 1944)

Hume, S. (1992, May 25). Best ads don't rely on celebrities. *Advertising Age*, p. 20.

Huyssen, A. (1986). Mass culture as woman: Modernism's other. In T. Modleski (Ed.), *Studies in entertainment: Critical approaches to mass culture* (pp. 188-207). Bloomington: Indiana University Press.

Inge, M. T. (Ed.). (1989). *Handbook of American popular culture* (2nd ed.). Westport, CT: Greenwood.

Jacobson, M. F. (1988, December 23). The bull in "Bull Durham." *New York Times*, Sec. 1, p. 39.

Jacoby, J., & Hoyer, W. D. (1989). The comprehension/miscomprehension of print communication: Selected findings. *Journal of Consumer Research, 15*(4), 434-443.

Jacoby, J., Hoyer, W. B., & Sheluga, D. A. (1980). *Miscomprehension of televised communications*. New York: Educational Foundation of the American Association of Advertising Agencies.

Jameson, F. (1984). Postmodernism, or the cultural logic of late capitalism. *New Left Review, 146,* 53-92.

Jenkins, H. (1992). *Textual poachers: Television fans and participatory culture.* New York: Routledge.

Jensen, J. (1994, April 25). Jordan still king of ad presenter game. *Advertising Age,* pp. 3, 59.

Jhally, S. (1989). Advertising as religion: The dialectic of technology and magic. In I. Angus & S. Jhally (Eds.), *Cultural politics in contemporary America* (pp. 217-229). New York: Routledge.

Jhally, S. (1990). *The codes of advertising: Fetishism and the political economy of meaning in the consumer society.* New York: Routledge.

Jhally, S., & Lewis, J. (1992). *Enlightened racism:* The Cosby Show, *audiences, and the myth of the American dream.* Boulder, CO: Westview.

Jones, S. (1993, November 1). Overpaid, overhyped, over here. *The London Times,* p. 26.

Joseph, W. B. (1982). The credibility of physically attractive communicators: A review. *Journal of Advertising, 11*(3), 15-24.

Jowett, G. (in press). *The mass society/mass culture debate.* Thousand Oaks, CA: Sage.

Just in case you hadn't heard—the '60s are over. (1994, January 31). *Time,* p. 23.

Kahle, L. R. (1984). The values of Americans: Implications for consumer adoption. In R. E. Pitts & A. G. Woodside (Eds.), *Personal values and consumer behavior* (pp. 77-86). Lexington, MA: Lexington Press.

Kanner, B. (1993, September 27). Country style. *New York,* pp. 25-26.

Kervin, D. (1990). Advertising masculinity: The representation of males in *Esquire* advertisements. *Journal of Communication Inquiry, 14*(1), 51-70.

Key, W. B. (1972). *Subliminal seduction.* New York: Signet.

King, T. (1985, August 19). Credibility gap: More consumers find celebrity ads unpersuasive. *Wall Street Journal,* p. 27.

King, T. (1993, December 2). "Demolition Man" trades tacos for pizzas abroad. *Wall Street Journal,* pp. B1, B6.

Klapp, O. (1969). *The collective search for identity.* New York: Holt.

Klassen, M. L., Jasper, C. R., & Schwartz, A. M. (1993). Men and women: Images of their relationships in magazine advertisements. *Journal of Advertising Research, 33*(2), 30-39.

Kolbe, R. H. (1991). Gender roles in children's television advertising: A longitudinal content analysis. In J. H. Leigh & C. R. Martin, Jr. (Eds.), *Current issues and research in advertising* (pp. 197-206). Ann Arbor: University of Michigan Business School, Division of Research.

Lakoff, R. T., & Scherr, R. L. (1984). *Face value: The politics of beauty.* Boston: Routledge & Kegan Paul.

Lane, R. (1993, December 20). Prepackaged celebrity. *Forbes,* pp. 86-90.

Lasch, C. (1978). *The culture of narcissism: American life in an age of diminishing expectations.* New York: W. W. Norton.

Lears, J. (1995). *Fables of abundance: A cultural history of advertising in America.* New York: Basic Books.

Lears, T. J. J. (1983). From salvation to self-realization: Advertising and the therapeutic roots of the consumer culture, 1880-1930. In R. W. Fox & T. J. J. Lears (Eds.), *The culture of consumption* (pp. 1-38). New York: Pantheon.

Lears, T. J. J. (1984). *No place of grace: Antimodernism and the transformation of American culture, 1880-1920.* New York: Pantheon.

Lebergott, S. (1993). *Pursuing happiness: American consumers in the twentieth century.* Princeton, NJ: Princeton University Press.

Leeds-Hurwitz, W. (1993). *Semiotics and communication: Signs, codes, cultures.* Hillsdale, NJ: Lawrence Erlbaum.

Leiss, W., Kline, S., & Jhally, S. (1990). *Communication in advertising: Persons, products and images of well-being* (2nd ed.). Scarborough, Ontario: Nelson Canada.

Lévi-Strauss, C. (1963). *Totemism.* Boston: Beacon.

Lévi-Strauss, C. (1966). *The savage mind.* London: Weidenfeld & Nicholson.

Levy, S. J. (1969). Symbols by which we buy. In L. H. Stockman (Ed.), *Advancing marketing efficiency* (pp. 409-416). Chicago: American Marketing Association.

Levy, S. J. (1981). Interpreting consumer mythology: A structural approach to consumer behavior. *Journal of Marketing, 45*(3), 49-61.

Levy, S. J. (1986). Meanings in advertising stimuli. In J. Olson & K. Sentis (Eds.), *Advertising and consumer psychology* (pp. 214-226). New York: Praeger.

Lewis, J. (1991). *The ideological octopus: An exploration of television and its audience.* New York: Routledge.

Lewis, L. (Ed.). (1992). *The adoring audience: Fan culture and popular media.* New York: Routledge.

Leymore, V. L. (1975). *Hidden myth: Structure and symbolism in advertising.* New York: Basic Books.

Liesse, J. (1990, September 17). Bunny back to battle Duracell. *Advertising Age,* pp. 4, 78.

Liesse, J. (1991, April 8). How the bunny charged Eveready. *Advertising Age,* pp. 20, 55.

Liesse, J. (1992, April 6). Opening day, and the Bunny goes up to bat. *Advertising Age,* pp. 1, 37.

Liesse, J., & Jensen, J. (1993, October 11). Whole new game without Jordan. *Advertising Age,* pp. 1, 48.

Lovdal, L. T. (1989). Sex role messages in television commercials. *Sex Roles, 21* (11/12), 715-724.

Lowenthal, L., & Fiske, M. (1957). The debate over art and popular culture in eighteenth century England. In M. Komarovsky (Ed.), *Common frontiers of the social sciences* (pp. 33-112). Glencoe, IL: Free Press.

Lull, J. (1992). Popular music and communication: An introduction. In J. Lull (Ed.), *Popular music and communication* (pp. 1-32). Newbury Park, CA: Sage.

Lyotard, J.-F. (1984). *The postmodern condition: A report on knowledge.* Minneapolis: University of Minnesota Press.

Lytton, H., & Romney, D. M. (1991). Parents' differential socialization of boys and girls: A meta-analysis. *Psychological Bulletin, 109*(2), 267-296.

Macdonald, D. (1957). A theory of mass culture. In B. Rosenberg & D. M. White (Eds.), *Mass culture: The popular arts in America* (pp. 59-73). Glencoe, IL: Free Press.

Mandese, J. (1993, September 6). "Home Improvement" wins race. *Advertising Age,* p. 3.

Mandese, J. (1995, September 25). Star presenter of the year. *Advertising Age,* pp. 1, 6.

Marchand, R. (1985). *Advertising the American way: Making way for modernity, 1920-1940.* Berkeley: University of California Press.

Marcuse, H. (1964). *One-dimensional man: Studies in the ideology of advanced industrial society.* Boston: Beacon.

Marx, K. (1904). *Contribution to the critique of political economy.* Chicago: Kerr. (Original work published 1859)

Masse, M. A., & Rosenblum, K. (1988). Male and female created they them: The depiction of gender in the advertising of traditional women's and men's magazines. *Women's Studies International Forum, 11*(2), 127-144.

Mayerle, J. (1994). "Roseanne"—how did you get inside my house? A case study of a hit blue-collar situation comedy. In H. Newcomb (Ed.), *Television: The critical view* (pp. 101-116). New York: Oxford University Press.

McCauley, C., Thangavelu, K., & Rozin, P. (1988). Sex stereotyping of occupations in relation to television representations and census facts. *Basic and Applied Social Psychology, 9,* 197-212.

McCoy, D. B. (1990). *The impact of personality formation and gender role development.* Kent, OH: Kent State University.

McCracken, E. (1993). *Decoding women's magazines: From Mademoiselle to Ms.* New York: St. Martin's.

McCracken, G. (1986). Culture and consumption: A theoretical account of the structure and movement of the cultural meaning of consumer goods. *Journal of Consumer Research, 13,* 71-81.

McCracken, G. (1988). *Culture and consumption: New approaches to the symbolic character of consumer goods and activities.* Bloomington: Indiana University Press.

McCracken, G. (1989). Who is the celebrity endorser? *Journal of Consumer Research, 16*(3), 310-321.

McEvoy, C. (1994). Giant steps. *Sporting Goods Business, 27*(4), 35-36.

McIlwraith, R. D., & Schallow, J. R. (1983). Adult fantasy life and patterns of media use. *Journal of Communication, 33*(1), 73-87.

McLuhan, M. (1964). *Understanding media: The extensions of man.* New York: McGraw-Hill.

McNeal, J. U., & McDaniel, S. W. (1981). *An analysis of need-appeals in television advertising.* Unpublished manuscript, Texas A & M University, College Station.

McQuade, D. A., & Williamson, E. (1989). Advertising. In M. T. Inge (Ed.), *Handbook of American popular culture* (2nd ed., pp. 1-40). New York: Greenwood.

Michael, R. T., Gagnon, J. H., Laumann, E. O., & Kolata, G. (1994). *Sex in America: A definitive survey.* Boston: Little, Brown.

Mick, D. G. (1986). Consumer research and semiotics: Exploring the morphology of signs, symbols, and significance. *Journal of Consumer Research, 13*(2), 196-213.

Mintz, L. (1988). Broadcast humor. In L. Mintz (Ed.), *Humor in America: A research guide to genres and topics* (pp. 91-108). New York: Greenwood.

Misra, S., & Beatty, S. E. (1990). Celebrity spokesperson and brand congruence: An assessment of recall and affect. *Journal of Business Research, 21,* 159-173.

Modleski, T. (1986). Femininity as mas(s)querade: A feminist approach to mass culture. In C. MacCabe (Ed.), *High theory/low culture: Analysing popular tele-*

vision and film (pp. 37-52). Manchester, England: Manchester University Press.

Morgan, M. (1987). Television, sex-role attitudes, and sex-role behavior. *Journal of Early Adolescence, 7*(3), 269-282.

Morley, D. (1980). *The "nationwide" audience.* London: British Film Institute.

Morris, E., & Holley, D. (1992, October 17). Madison Ave. sees vehicle in country music explosion. *Billboard*, pp. 1, 80.

Moschis, G. P., & Moore, R. L. (1979). Decision making among the young: A socialization perspective. *Journal of Consumer Research, 6*, 101-112.

Mukerji, C., & Schudson, M. (1991). Introduction: Rethinking popular culture. In C. Mukerji & M. Schudson (Eds.), *Rethinking popular culture: Contemporary perspectives in cultural studies* (pp. 1-62). Berkeley: University of California Press.

Murray, H. A. (1938). *Explorations in personality.* New York: John Wiley.

Myers, K. (1986). *Understains: The sense and seduction of advertising.* London: Comedia.

Myers, P. N., Jr., & Biocca, F. A. (1992). The elastic body image: The effects of television advertising and programming on body image distortions in young women. *Journal of Communications, 42*(3), 108-133.

Nebenzahl, I. D., & Secunda, E. (1993). Consumers' attitudes toward product placement in movies. *International Journal of Advertising, 12*, 1-11.

Nelson, C., Treichler, P. A., & Grossberg, L. (1992). Cultural studies: An introduction. In L. Grossberg, C. Nelson, & P. A. Treichler (Eds.), *Cultural studies* (pp. 1-22). New York: Routledge.

Newcomb, P., & Chatzky, J. S. (1992, September 28). The top 40. *Forbes*, pp. 87-91.

Newport, F., & Saad, L. (1992, April 18). 23% of Americans have switched religions. *Houston Post*, p. A16.

Nichols, B. (1981). *Ideology and the image.* Bloomington: Indiana University Press.

Nock, S. L. (1993). *The costs of privacy: Surveillance and reputation in America.* New York: Aldine de Gruyter.

Norden, E. (1969, March). Playboy interview: Marshall McLuhan. *Playboy*, pp. 26-27, 45, 55-56, 61, 63.

Norris, J. D. (1990). *Advertising and the transformation of American society, 1865-1920.* Westport, CT: Greenwood.

Nye, R. (1970). *The unembarrassed muse: The popular arts in America.* New York: Dial.

O'Barr, W. (1994). *Culture and the ad: Exploring otherness in the world of advertising.* Boulder, CO: Westview.

Ogilvy, D. (1983). *Ogilvy on advertising.* New York: Crown Books.

Olson, J., & Sentis, K. (Eds.). (1986). *Advertising and consumer psychology* (Vol. 3). New York: Praeger.

O'Meara, M. A. (Ed.). (1994). *Brands and their companies.* Detroit: Gale Research.

O'Sullivan, T., Hartley, J., Saunders, D., Montgomery, M., & Fiske, J. (1994). *Key concepts in communication and cultural studies* (2nd ed.). London: Routledge.

Packard, V. (1957). *The hidden persuaders.* New York: David McKay.

Pease, O. A. (1958). *The responsibilities of American advertising: Private control and public influence.* New Haven, CT: Yale University Press.

Peirce, C. S. (1931-1958). *Collected papers* (8 vols.). Cambridge, MA: Harvard University Press.

Peirce, K. (1989). Sex-role stereotyping of children on television: A content analysis of the roles and attitudes of child characters. *Sociological Spectrum, 9,* 321-328.

Peirce, K. (1990). A feminist theoretical perspective on the socialization of teenage girls through *Seventeen* magazine. *Sex Roles, 23*(9/10), 491-500.

Peterson, G. W., & Peters, D. F. (1983). Adolescents' construction of social reality: The impact of television and peers. *Youth & Society, 15*(1), 67-85.

Pollay, R. W. (1984). Twentieth century magazine advertising: Determination of informativeness. *Written Communication, 1*(1), 56-77.

Pollay, R. W. (1985). The subsiding sizzle: A descriptive history of print advertising, 1900-1980. *Journal of Marketing, 49*(3), 24-37.

Pollay, R. W. (1986). The distorted mirror: Reflections on the unintended consequences of advertising. *Journal of Marketing, 50,* 18-36.

Pope, D. (1983). *The making of modern advertising.* New York: Basic Books.

Poster, M. (1990). *The mode of information: Poststructuralism and social context.* Chicago: University of Chicago Press.

Postman, N. (1985). *Amusing ourselves to death: Public discourse in the age of show business.* New York: Viking.

Press, A. (1991). *Women watching television: Gender, class, and generation in the American television experience.* Philadelphia: University of Pennsylvania Press.

Radway, J. A. (1984). *Reading the romance: Women, patriarchy, and popular literature.* Chapel Hill: University of North Carolina Press.

Reisman, D. (1950). *The lonely crowd: A study of the changing American character.* New Haven, CT: Yale University Press.

Richins, M. (1991). Social comparison and the idealized images of advertising. *Journal of Consumer Research, 18,* 71-83.

Rogers, M., & Seiler, C. (1994). The answer is no: A national survey of advertising industry practitioners and their clients about whether they use subliminal advertising. *Journal of Advertising Research, 34*(2), 36-45.

Rosen, D. L., & Singh, S. N. (1992). An investigation of subliminal embedded effect on multiple measures of advertising effectiveness. *Psychology & Marketing, 9*(2), 157-173.

Rosenberg, B., & White, D. M. (Eds.). (1957). *Mass culture: The popular arts in America.* New York: Free Press.

Rosenbluth, J. (1988, August 27). Singles click as Madison Ave. jingles. *Billboard,* pp. 1, 77.

Rosenthal, A. (1992, July 2). Focus is elusive for Bush. *New York Times,* pp. 1, 14.

Rossiter, J. R., & Percy, L. (1980). Attitude change through visual imagery in advertising. *Journal of Advertising, 9*(2), 10-16.

Rowe, K. K. (1994). Roseanne: Unruly woman as domestic goddess. In H. Newcomb (Ed.), *Television: The critical view* (pp. 202-211). New York: Oxford University Press.

Ryan, J. (1994, February 9). [Interview with Julie Liesse, *Advertising Age* reporter.] Unpublished interview.

Sack, R. D. (1992). *Place, modernity, and the consumer's world.* Baltimore: Johns Hopkins University Press.

Sahlins, M. (1976). *Culture and practical reason.* Chicago: University of Chicago Press.

Saussure, F. de. (1966). *Course in general linguistics*. New York: McGraw-Hill. (Original work published 1915)

Savage, J. (1988, March 25). Leave my history alone. *New Statesman*, p. 32.

Schiller, H. I. (1989). *Culture, Inc.: The corporate takeover of public expression*. New York: Oxford University Press.

Schudson, M. (1984). *Advertising, the uneasy persuasion: Its dubious impact on American society*. New York: Basic Books.

Schwartz, J. (1988, September 28). Wing-tip rock and roll. *Newsweek*, pp. 48-49.

Schwichtenberg, C. (Ed.). (1993). *The Madonna connection: Representational politics, subcultural identities, and cultural theory*. Boulder, CO: Westview.

Scott, L. (1990). Understanding jingles and needledrop: A rhetorical approach to music in advertising. *Journal of Consumer Research, 17*(2), 223-236.

Seldes, G. (1950). *The great audience*. New York: Viking.

Seldes, G. (1957). *The seven lively arts*. New York: A. S. Barnes. (Original work published 1924)

Sentis, K., & Markus, H. (1986). Brand personality and self. In J. Olson & K. Sentis (Eds.), *Advertising and consumer psychology* (Vol. 3, pp. 132-148). New York: Praeger.

Shani, D., & Sandler, D. (1991, August 5). Celebrity alone isn't a sure hit. *Marketing News*, p. 8.

Silverstein, B., Perdue, L., Petersen, B., & Kelly, E. (1986). The role of the mass media in promoting a thin standard of bodily attractiveness for women. *Sex Roles, 14*, 519-532.

Sinclair, J. (1987). *Images incorporated: Advertising as industry and ideology*. London: Croom Helm.

Soley, L., & Kurzbard, G. (1986). Sex in advertising: A comparison of 1964 and 1984. *Journal of Advertising, 15*(3), 46-55.

Solomon, M. R., & Greenberg, L. (1993). Setting the stage: Collective selection in the stylistic context of commercials. *Journal of Advertising, 22*(1), 11-24.

Sparing a dime. (1991, August 17). *The Economist*, pp. 24-25.

Stearns, C. Z., & Stearns, P. N. (1986). *Anger: The struggle for emotional control in America's history*. Chicago: University of Chicago Press.

Stewart, D. W., Farmer, K. M., & Stannard, C. I. (1990). Music as a recognition cue in advertising-tracking studies. *Journal of Advertising Research, 30*(4), 39-48.

Storey, J. (1993). *An introductory guide to cultural theory and popular culture*. Athens: University of Georgia Press.

Stout, P. A., & Leckenby, J. D. (1989). Let the music play: Music as a nonverbal element in television commercials. In S. Hecker & D. Stewart (Eds.), *Nonverbal communication in advertising* (pp. 207-223). Lexington, MA: Lexington Books.

Stout, P. A., Leckenby, J. D., & Hecker, S. (1990). Viewer reactions to music in television commercials. *Journalism Quarterly, 67*(4), 887-898.

Stout, P. A., & Moon, Y. S. (1990). The use of endorsers in magazine advertisements. *Journal Quarterly, 67*(3), 536-546.

Strasser, S. (1989). *Satisfaction guaranteed: The making of the American mass market*. New York: Pantheon.

Strate, L. (1992). Beer commercials: A manual on masculinity. In S. Craig (Ed.), *Men, masculinity, and the media* (pp. 78-92). Newbury Park, CA: Sage.

Sullivan, G. L., & O'Conner, P. J. (1988). Women's role portrayals in magazine advertising, 1958-1983. *Sex Roles, 18*(3/4), 181-188.

Swingewood, A. (1977). *The myth of mass culture.* Atlantic Highlands, NJ: Humanities Press.

Tedesco, N. J. (1974). Patterns of prime time. *Journal of Communication, 24,* 119-124.

Teinowitz, I., & Liesse, J. (1991, May 20). Coors "bunny" ad gets going. *Advertising Age,* p. 55.

Tulloch, J., & Alvarado, M. (1983). *"Doctor Who": The unfolding text.* London: Macmillan.

Turner, G. (1992). *British cultural studies: An introduction.* New York: Routledge.

Tylor, E. B. (1958). *The origins of culture.* New York: Harper & Row. (Original work published 1871 as *Primitive Culture*)

Umiker-Sebeok, J. (1979). Nature's way? Visual images of childhood in American culture. *Semiotica, 27*(1/3), 173-220.

Umiker-Sebeok, J. (1981). The seven ages of women: A view from American magazine advertisements. In C. Mayo & N. M. Henley (Eds.), *Gender and nonverbal behavior* (pp. 209-252). New York: Springer-Verlag.

Umiker-Sebeok, J. (1986). Growing signs: From firstness to thirdness in life and art. In P. Bouissac, M. Herzfeld, & R. Posner (Eds.), *Iconicity: Essays on the nature of culture* (pp. 527-573). Tubingen, Germany: Stauffenburg Verlag.

Unger, L. S., McConocha, D., & Faier, J. A. (1991). The use of nostalgia in television advertising: A content analysis. *Journalism Quarterly, 68*(3), 345-353.

U.S. Bureau of the Census. (1975). *Historical statistics of the United States: Colonial times to 1970.* Washington, DC: Government Printing Office.

U.S. Bureau of the Census. (1993). *Statistical abstract of the United States, 1993.* Washington, DC: Government Printing Office.

U.S. Bureau of the Census. (1994). *Statistical abstract of the United States, 1994.* Washington, DC: Government Printing Office.

Wadsworth, A. J. (1989). The uses and effects of mass communication during childhood. In J. F. Nussbaum (Ed.), *Life-span communication: Normative processes* (pp. 93-116). Hillsdale, NJ: Lawrence Erlbaum.

Waits, W. B. (1993). *The modern Christmas in America.* New York: New York University Press.

Waldrop, J. (1993, April). Garden variety customers. *American Demographics,* pp. 44-49.

Walker, M., Langmeyer, L., & Langmeyer, D. (1992). Celebrity endorsers: Do you get what you pay for? *Journal of Consumer Marketing, 9*(2), 69-76.

Weber, N. (Ed.). (1991). *Giving USA: The annual report on philanthropy for the year 1990.* New York: American Association of Fund-Raising Counsel.

Weinberger, M. G., & Gulas, C. S. (1992). The impact of humor in advertising: A review. *Journal of Advertising, 21*(4), 35-59.

Weinberger, M. G., & Spotts, H. E. (1989). Humor in U.S. versus U.K. TV commercials: A comparison. *Journal of Advertising, 18*(2), 39-44.

Weisz, P. (1994, December 12). 1994's new products winners and sinners, à la consumer panels. *Brandweek,* pp. 46-48.

Wells, A., & Hakanen, E. A. (1991). The emotional use of popular music by adolescents. *Journalism Quarterly, 68*(3), 445-454.

Wernick, A. (1983). Advertising and ideology: An interpretive framework. *Theory, Culture and Society, 2*(1), 16-33.

Wernick, A. (1992). *Promotional culture: Advertising, ideology, and symbolic expression.* Newbury Park, CA: Sage.

Williams, R. (1958). *Culture and society, 1780-1950.* New York: Columbia University Press.

Williams, R. (1974). *Television: Technology and cultural form.* New York: Schocken.

Williams, R. (1980). Advertising: The magic system. In R. Williams, *Problems in materialism and culture* (pp. 170-195). London: Verso. (Original work published 1960)

Williams, R. (1983). *Keywords: A vocabulary of culture and society.* New York: Oxford University Press.

Williamson, J. (1978). *Decoding advertisements.* London: Marion Bogar.

Willis, P. (1990). *Common culture.* Boulder, CO: Westview.

Wood, J. T. (1994). *Gendered lives: Communication, gender, and culture.* Belmont, CA: Wadsworth.

Woodward, K. L. (1992, January 6). Talking to God. *Newsweek,* pp. 39-44.

Wouters, C. (1986). Formalization and informalization: Changing tension balances in civilizing processes. *Theory, Culture and Society, 3*(2), 1-18.

Wouters, C. (1989). The sociology of emotions and flight attendants: Hochschild's *Managed Heart. Theory, Culture and Society, 6,* 95-123.

Yarnadoe, K., & Gopnik, A. (1990). *High and low: Modern art and popular culture.* New York: Museum of Modern Art.

Author Index

Aaker, D. A., 146
Adams-Price, C., 221
Adorno, T., 10, 56, 75, 164
Alperstein, N. M., 118, 131
Alvarado, M., 195
Andren, G., 151, 152, 153, 156, 166, 229
Ang, I., 195
Arnold, M., 54, 55, 56, 59, 60, 67, 75
Aronowitz, S., 59
Atwan, R., 35, 76

Banner, L. W., 140
Barcus, F. E., 201
Barthel, D., 166
Barthes, R., xv, 168, 169, 183
Baudrillard, J., 229, 251
Beatty, S. E., 76, 125
Belk, R., 151
Belknap, P., 227
Beninger, J. R., 32
Berger, J., 38
Berger, W., 147
Betterton, R., 142
Biocca, F. A., 15, 164
Blair, M. E., 135
Blonsky, M., 24
Bloom, A., 53, 60
Bourdieu, P., 67

Brantlinger, P., 54, 75
Bretl, D. J., 149, 208, 211
Brown, B. W., 157
Brown, J. D., 185, 208
Bruner, G. C., II, 132
Bruzzone, D. E., 146
Buckingham, D., 195
Busby, L. J., 142, 156, 208, 211

Campbell, K., 208
Cantor, J., 149, 208, 211
Carey, J. W., xv
Caughey, J. L., 119
Certeau, M. de, 104
Chatzky, J. S., 123
Choe, J.-H., 153
Collins, J., 75
Coulling, S., 75
Courtney, A. E., 152
Craig, R. S., 224
Cutler, B., 40
Czitrom, D., 239

Danna, S. R., 11
Davis, D. M., 208
Day, G., 96
Douglas, M., 28, 29, 161

Dunbar, D. S., 132, 146
Dunning, E., 106, 113, 122, 197
Durkin, K., 217

Elias, N., 106, 113, 122, 197, 242
Eliot, T. S., 56
England, P., 156
Esslin, M., 102
Ewen, S., 3, 14, 47, 63, 64, 157, 229

Faier, J. A., 231
Farmer, K. M., 131, 132
Featherstone, M., 59, 98, 222, 240
Fejes, F., 223, 224
Fine, G. A., 227
Fiske, J., xv, 11, 21, 51, 58, 76, 240
Fiske, M., 54
Fitzgerald, K., 129
Fowles, J., 43, 116, 118, 122, 151, 156, 238
Fox, S., 76, 126
Freud, S., 105, 112
Frith, K. T., 152, 156
Fromm, E., 61
Fulford, D. G., 137, 138, 147

Gabor, A., 125
Gagnard, A., 142, 153
Gagnon, J. H., 244
Galbraith, J. K., 61
Gans, H. J., 76
Gardner, T., 156
Geertz, C., 20
Gleick, E., 124
Goffman, E., 65, 101, 183, 227
Golby, J. M., 244
Goldman, R., 25, 48, 53, 64, 65, 102
Gombrich, E. G., 21, 84
Gopnik, A., 251
Gossage, H. L., 100, 166
Gow, J., 194
Greeley, A., 233
Greene, A. C., 221
Grossberg, L., 72, 75, 108, 120
Gulas, C. S., 139, 147

Hakanen, E. A., 120
Hall, S., xv, 122, 162
Hardy, A. P., 153
Harter, S., 221
Hartley, J., 21, 22, 109
Hawkins, D., 76
Hirsch, E. D., Jr., 60
Hobson, D., 195
Hodge, B., 195
Holley, D., 135
Horkheimer, M., 10, 56, 75, 164
Hoyer, W. B., 162
Hoyer, W. D., 162, 166
Hume, S., 125
Huyssen, A., 71, 162

Inge, M. T., 111
Isherwood, B., 28, 29, 161

Jacobson, M. F., 144
Jacoby, J., 162, 166
Jameson, F., 229
Jasper, C. R., 227
Jenkins, H., 195
Jhally, S., 25, 64, 98, 122, 156, 165, 166, 198, 201

Kahle, L. R., 160
Kanner, B., 136
Kelly, E., 208
Kervin, D., 211, 213
Key, W. B., 62
King, T., 125, 147
Klapp, O., 197, 198
Klassen, M. L., 227
Kline, S., 156, 165, 166, 198
Kolata, G., 244
Kolbe, R. H., 201, 211
Kuhn, A., 156
Kurzbard, G., 151, 153

Lakoff, R. T., 140
Lane, R., 103
Langmeyer, D., 127

Langmeyer, L., 127
Lasch, C., 62
Laumann, E. O., 244
Lears, T. J. J., 33
Lebergott, S., 164
Leeds-Hurwitz, W., xvi
Leichty, G., 142, 156, 211
Leiss, W., 156, 165, 166, 198
Leonard, W. N., II, 227
Lévi-Strauss, C., xv, 5, 51, 236
Lewis, J., 122
Leymore, V. L., 90, 183
Liesse, J., 3, 8, 24
Lovdal, L. T., 208, 211
Lowenthal, L., 54, 56
Lull, J., 120
Lytton, H., 220

Macdonald, D., 53, 57, 58, 75
Mandese, J., 196
Marchand, R., 44, 47, 76, 98, 101
Marcuse, H., 56, 57, 75
Markus, H., 165
Marx, K., 26, 27, 64, 68
Masse, M. A., 149, 156, 211
Mayerle, J., 186
McCauley, C., 217, 220
McConocha, D., 229
McCoy, D. B., 220
McCracken, E., 223, 224
McCracken, G., 30, 49, 50, 118, 127
McEvoy, C., 234
McIlwraith, R. D., 121
McLuhan, M., 65
McQuade, D., 35, 76
McQuade, D. A., 11
Michael, R. T., 244
Mick, D. G., 161
Misra, S., 125
Modleski, T., 71
Montgomery, M., 21
Moon, Y. S., 125, 146
Moore, R. L., 221
Morgan, M., 220
Morley, D., 195
Morris, E., 135
Mortimer, J. T., 227

Moschis, G. P., 221
Mukerji, C., 10, 59, 111
Myers, K., 162
Myers, P. N., Jr., 15, 164

Nebenzahl, I. D., 145
Nelson, C., 75
Newcomb, P., 123
Newport, F., 233
Nichols, B., 86, 107
Nock, S. L., 226
Norris, J. D., 37, 38, 76
Nye, R., 76

O'Barr, W., 229
Ogilvy, D., 16, 102
O'Sullivan, T., 21

Packard, Y., 53, 62
Pease, O. A., 34, 76
Peirce, C. S., xvi
Peirce, K., 201, 203, 205
Perdue, L., 208
Peters, D. F., 221, 222
Petersen, B., 208
Peterson, G. W., 221, 222
Pollay, R. W., 61, 62, 65, 76, 84, 151, 161
Pope, D., 34, 46, 76
Poster, M., 238
Postman, N., 59
Purdue, A. W., 244

Radway, J. A., 195
Reisman, D., 50
Richins, M., 166
Roberts, D. F., 227
Rogers, M., 76
Romney, D. M., 220
Rosen, D. L., 76
Rosenblum, K., 149, 156, 211
Rosenbluth, J., 132
Rosenthal, A., 1
Rowe, K. K., 186
Rozin, P., 217, 220

Ryan, J., 3

Saad, L., 233
Sack, R. D., 239
Sahlins, M., 26, 27, 28, 29
Sandler, D., 125
Saunders, D., 21
Saussure, F. de, xv, xvi, 24
Savage, J., 133
Schallow, J. R., 121
Scherr, R. L., 140
Schiller, H. I., 3
Schudson, M., 10, 32, 59, 66, 67, 101, 111, 162, 163
Schulze, L., 185
Schwartz, A. M., 227
Schwartz, J., 135
Secunda, E., 145
Seiler, C., 76
Seldes, G., 75
Sentis, K., 165
Shani, D., 125
Sheluga, D. A., 162
Silverstein, B., 208
Singh, S. N., 76
Soley, L., 151, 153
Stannard, C. I., 131, 132
Stearns, C. Z., 241, 242
Stearns, P. N., 241, 242
Stewart, D. W., 131, 132
Storey, J., 10, 58, 67
Stout, P. A., 125, 146
Strasser, S., 35
Strate, L., 209

Teinowitz, I., 8
Thangavelu, K., 217, 220
Treichler, P. A., 75
Tripp, D., 195
Tulloch, J., 195

U.S. Bureau of the Census, 17, 31, 41, 43, 49, 234
Umiker-Sebeok, J., 205
Unger, L. S., 229

Wadsworth, A. J., 227
Waits, W. B., 246, 251
Waldrop, J., 234
Walker, M., 127
Weber, N., 234
Weinberger, M. G., 139, 147
Weisz, P., 19
Wells, A., 120
Wernick, A., 90, 149, 183, 193, 194
Wesson, D., 152, 156
Whipple, T. W., 152
Wilcox, G. B., 153
Williams, R., xv, 21, 102, 104, 184
Williamson, E., 11
Williamson, J., 11, 63, 64, 98, 183, 222, 250
Wood, J. T., 208
Woodward, K. L., 233
Wouters, C., 117
Wright, J. W., 35, 76

Yarnadoe, K., 251

Subject Index

Ace Hardware, Suzanne Somers and, 129
Adidas shoes, Eddie Rabbitt and, 136
Adolph Coors Company:
    Artic ice beer, 14
Advertisements:
    as cultural documents, 167
    as professional products, 77
    historical, 68, 69
    simple, 11
    See also Advertisements, compound; Advertisements, deciphering
Advertisements, compound, 11, 45, 46, 169
    audience and, 169
    commodity material in, 80-81, 169
    connotative level of, 169
    contested frame in, 87-90
    denoted image level of, 169
    individual consumer versus masses and, 94-96
    intertextual strains in, 90-93
    linguistic message level of, 169
    product shots in, 87, 88
    product versus appeal in, 80-83
    sender and, 169
    symbol appeal in, 169
    versus consumer, 93-94
    words versus images in, 83-87

    See also Advertising, compound
Advertisements, deciphering, 168-170
    composition, 170, 171-173
    context, 170, 171
    for Diet Sprite, 179-183
    for Jordache jeans, 174-179, 183
    guidelines for, 170-174
    implications, 171, 173-174
Advertisers, 17
    definition of, 78
    versus advertising agencies, 78-79
Advertising:
    advertisers and, 17
    aesthetic presentation of, 14
    appearance as success in, 14
    as ambitious symbol domain, 229, 230
    as artistic product, 17
    as communication, 13
    as culture industry product, 17
    as economic entity, 27-28
    as narrative, 18
    as proselytizing, 96-102
    as public symbol system, 70
    as symbol domain, xiv, xv, 27
    brevity of, 13-14
    by-products, 40
    commonalities of with popular culture, 17-20

270

communication style of, 14
consumer exploitation of, xvi,
    161-165
consumer reception of, 18-19
cycle of attractiveness refined in,
    140
definition of, 13, 48
direct, 38
evolution of modern, 34-42
focus of, 14
form in, 9
gender portrayals in, 201
goals of, 13
humor in, 136-139
indirect, 38
intrusiveness of, 68
journal, 37
magazine, 37, 39, 46
mass media and, 18
material in, 9
models in, 14
music in, 18, 131-136
newspaper, 37, 39
personal identity and, 19
production sites of, 17
radio, 38, 39
style in, 17-18
symbolic content of, 11
television, 38-39
to change behavior, 13, 149
versus popular culture, 11-17
Advertising, compound, 11-12, 41-42,
    168. *See also* Advertisements,
    compound
Advertising, criticism of, 20, 60-66
benefits of, 73
feminist, 70-71, 161-162
functional aspect of, 73
Marxist, 63-65
non-Marxist, 62
Advertising, simple, 41
Advertising agencies, 40-41, 168
versus advertisers, 78-79
Advertising content:
    mixed with popular culture
        content, 185-195
Advertising creators, 40, 77, 168
anonymity of, 16

Advertising imagery, 47, 83
appearance of self, 49, 94
classlessness, 152
emotionality in, 95
females, 153
future of, 235-240
gender, 152-153, 157
idealized human beings, 149,
    156-157, 158
meaningful, 149
of people, 149, 151
omissions from, 159
pleasant, 149
pleasures, 151, 157
sexuality, 151
social values and, 157-161
solitary figure, 156, 200, 237
stereotypes and, 160
themes, 149-157
youthfulness, 153, 156, 157
Advertising industry:
    artistic professionalism in, 18
    financial stature of, 19
Advertising messages, ulterior
        motives of, xiii
Advertising profession, 40
Advertising research:
    versus creative execution,
        79-80
Advertising symbols, failed, 9
Advertising tableaux pictorial
        parables, 44, 46
    Captivated Child, 44, 46
    Civilization Redeemed, 46
    Democracy of Goods, 44
    First Impression, 44
American Cereal Company, 35
Anheuser-Busch, failed product of,
    19
Attractiveness:
    advertising and, 139-143
    of females in ads, 142-143
    popular culture and, 139-143
Audience:
    condescension toward, 67
    definition of, 22-23
    distinguishing feature of, 48-49

Barkley, Charles:
    Nike and, 131
Bergen, Candice:
    Sprint and, 127, 129, 162, 189
Bird, Larry:
    Nike and, 127, 129
Birmingham Center for Contem-
    porary Cultural Studies, 58
Black, Clint:
    Miller Lite Beer and, 135
Black Velvet Canadian Whiskey:
    Tanya Tucker and, 136
Bow, Clara:
    as product endorser, 126
Brando, Marlon, 24
Braun, 145
Bricolage, 5
Brinkley, Christie, 127
Budweiser beer, 165
    Bud Man and, 9
Bush, George (President), 1

Calvin Klein campaigns, males in, 213
Campbell Soup, failed product of,
    19
Capitalist realism, 101
Charitable giving:
    advertising and, 233-234
    popular culture and, 233-234
Charles, Ray:
    Pepsico and, 129
Cher:
    in infomercials, xiv, 145
Chiat/Day, 1
Christmas:
    advertising glut during, 244, 245
    as interpersonal harmony season,
        245
    commercialism and, 248, 251
    consumer purchasing during, 244,
        247
    gift exchanges during, 247
    greeting cards, 247
    popular culture purchasing
        during, 244
Client studies, British, xv
Coca-Cola, 68

Comic books:
    as popular culture, 10
Commercial realism, 101
Commodification, 42
    of diversion, 42-43
    of human life, 174
    successful, 42
Commodities, fetishism of, 64
Commodity:
    exchange value of, 64
    use value of, 64
Commodity self, 47
Consumerist belief system, 96-102
    magic and, 97, 101
    religion and, 97-98
    tribal fetishes and, 98, 101
Consumer product failures, 19
Consumption of goods:
    need for, 28-30
    to articulate cultural meanings, 29
    to communicate social meanings, 28
    to establish self-identities, 30
    to strengthen interpersonal
        relationships, 30
Coors Beer commercials, 8
"Coors Light Channel," xiv
Cosby, Bill, 116, 118
    E. F. Hutton and, 129
    Ford and, 129
    Jello and, 129
Crawford, Joan, 145
    as product endorser, 126
Culture, definition of, 21-22
Culture corporations, 17
Culture industries, xiii, 10, 17, 43, 56,
    229, 236
Curtis, Cyrus H. K. Curtis, 37
Curtis Olives, 47

Dalai Lama, 122
Datril, John Wayne and, 129
DDB Needham, 1, 3, 23, 24
Decoding, definition of, 162
Del Monte vegetables, 46
DeLuise, Dom:
    NCR and, 129
Domino's Pizza, Noid and, 9

Duracell, 3, 6, 9, 24
   commercials, 7
Dylan, Bob:
   music in commercial, 133

E. F. Hutton, Bill Cosby and, 129
Eastman, George, 36
Eastman Kodak Company, 36
Economic perspective:
   on advertising, 27
   on popular culture, 27
Economy, production/consumption,
   30-34
   evolution of, 31-33
Education:
   advertising and, 232
   popular culture and, 232
Emery Shirts, 46-47
Employment:
   advertising and, 232-233
   popular culture and, 232-233
Energizer bunny, 1-9, 21, 83
   as breakthrough into popular
     culture, 7-8
   as commercial symbol, 3
   as endurance symbol, 4, 7
   as parody, 7
   as playful symbol, 5
   as potency symbol, 4
   as rebirth symbol, 4
   as social symbol, 3
   as trickster, 4
   Brer Rabbit and, 5
   parodies of, 8
   Peter Rabbit and, 4-5
   representative qualities of, 5-6
Eveready Battery Company, 7, 8, 24
   advertising campaign of, 1-9
   See also Energizer bunny

Federal Communication Commission
   (FCC), 73, 144
Federal Trade Commission (FTC), 73
Films:
   as popular culture, 10

Fiske Tires, 46
Ford, 37
   Bill Cosby and, 129
Frankfurt School, 56, 58, 67

Gaynor, Janet:
   as product endorser, 126
Gender:
   and self-identity, 199
   cultural genesis of, 199
   in media, 199-214
   See also Gender portrayals
Gendered self, 202-203
Gender markers, 227
Gender portrayals:
   audience use of, 215-225
   evolving, 211
   in children's television, 201
   in music videos, 206-208
   in primetime television, 203, 208
   in print advertising, 204-205, 206,
     211-214
   in television voice-overs, 208
   of adolescent females, 205, 207
   of adolescent males, 205
   of men in beer commercials, 209
   of women, 210-211
   prominence of in advertising, 201
   prominence of in popular culture,
     201
General Mills, failed product of, 19

Heraclitus, 53
Hertz Corporation, O.J. Simpson and,
   124, 228
Hopper, Dennis, 81
Houseman, John:
   McDonald's and, 125
   Smith Barney and, 125
Humor:
   in advertising, 136-139
   in print ads, 147
   in radio advertising, 139
   in television advertising, 139
   See also Little Caesar's Pizza

Hupmobiles, 46

Infomercials, 144-145
Informalization, 117
Ivory Soap, 37, 46, 68

Jackson, Michael, 119
    fall of, 123
    Pepsico and, 124, 135, 146
Jello, Bill Cosby and, 129
Joe Isuzu, 80
Johnson, Magic:
    Pepsico and, 124
Jordan, Michael:
    Nike and, 129
Jose Cuervo, Willie Nelson and, 135
Juvenal, 54

Kenwood, Tiny Tim and, 130
Kimberly-Clark, failed product of, 19
Kitsch, 57
Klugman, Jack:
    endorsing copiers, 131
Kodak, 36

Lee, Spike:
    Nike and, 143
Leisure:
    advertising and, 234
    popular culture and, 234
Listerine commercial, 90
Little Caesar's Pizza, 147
    humor in advertising of, 136-139

Macpherson, Elle:
    as model turned actress, 143
Madonna, 24, 127
    music videos of, 185
    Pepsico and, 124
Mass communication, 40
Mass Culture, 57, 58, 71
McDonalds, 83
    John Houseman and, 125

McMahon, Ed:
    as insurance endorser, 131
Mandrell, Barbara:
    Sunsweet prunes and, 136
Meaning, definition of, 21
Media:
    gender in, 199-214
    using gender portrayals in, 215-225
Media content, reception of, 185
Miller Lite Beer:
    Bob Uecker and, 143
    Clint Black and, 135
Models, advertising:
    in popular culture realm, 143-146
Montana, Joe:
    Diet Pepsi and, 125
MTV, 194
Music, popular, 60
    adolescents' use of, 120-121
    as pleasurable experience, 121
    as popular culture, 10, 119-121
    Beatles' in Nike commercial, 132
    Crosby, Stills, Nash, and Young's in
        commercial, 135
    Dylan's in commercial, 133
    emotion management and, 120
    excitement and, 120
    feelings invoked by, 120
    group ties and, 121
    happiness and, 120-121
    in advertising, 131-136
    in television commercials, 131
    love and, 120, 121
Music videos, 194-195, 205, 208

NCR, Dom DeLuise and, 129
Nelson, Willie, 24
    Jose Cuervo and, 135
Nike, 81
    ads and Reebok ads, 91
    Beatles' music in commercial for, 132
    Charles Barkley and, 131
    Michael Jordan and, 129
    Spike Lee and, 143

Oil of Olay commercial, 90

Old Milwaukee beer, Swedish Bikini
    Team and, 9
Oliver, Louis:
    Vuarnet Optical and, 128
O'Neal, Shaquille, 103

Pepsico, 126
    ads and Coke ads, 91
    Crystal Pepsi as failed product of,
        19
    Lionel Richie and, 129
    Madonna and, 124
    Magic Johnson and, 124
    Michael Jackson and, 124, 125, 146
    Mike Tyson and, 124
    Ray Charles and, 129
Pillsbury Doughboy, 135, 147
Popular culture:
    adolescents' preoccupation with,
        199
    art of using, 104-105
    as ambitious symbol domain, 229
    as artistic product, 17
    as culture industry product, 17
    as economic entity, 27-28
    as narrative, 10, 18, 106-107
    as performance, 10
    as public symbol system, 70
    as symbol domain, xiv, xv, 27
    audience members and, 17
    censorious disdain of, 11
    commonalities of with advertising,
        17-20
    consumer reception of, 18-19
    cycle of attractiveness defined in,
        140
    definitions of, 10-11, 48
    double movement of, 122
    examples of, 10
    form in, 9
    future of, 241-244
    gender portrayals in, 201
    genres, 112
    goal of, 13
    gratification from, xiii
    intrusiveness of, 68
    mass media and, 18

material in, 9
music as, 18
performers, 18
personal identity and, 19
pleasure-giving aspect of, 10
popularity of, 104-112
production sites of, 17
role of in human affairs, 243
style in, 17
symbols and, 10-11
versus advertising, 11-17
visual component of, 10
See also Situation comedies;
    Popular music
Popular culture, criticism of, 20,
    53-60, 106
    benefits of, 73
    feminist, 70-71
    functional aspect of, 73
Popular culture, reception of, 104-112
    audience investment and, 110
    augmentation of feelings and, 106
    emotional management and,
        106-108
    feedback and, 110-111
    pleasure and, 105
    psychic tension release and, 106
Popular culture content:
    mixed with advertising content,
        185-195
Popular culture creators, 109
    lack of anonymity of, 16
Popular culture imagery, 47
    emotional self and, 49, 94, 95, 112
Popular culture industry, 109
    artistic professionalism in, 18
    financial stature of, 19
Popular culture stars, 116-119
    as commercial spokespeople, 18,
        103, 119, 124-131
    as failed endorsers, 129, 131
    individual spectator and, 117-118,
        119
Proctor and Gamble advertising,
    unimaginativeness of, 80
Product labeling, 35
Product naming, 34-37
    brand names, 35, 36

Product placements:
    in films, 143, 144, 145-146, 147
Promotional reflexivity, 193

Quaker Oats, 35

R. J. Reynolds, failed product of, 19
Rabbit, Eddie:
    Adidas shoes and, 136
Religion:
    advertising and, 233
    popular culture and, 233
Renault, George C. Scott and, 129
Richie, Lionel:
    Pepsico and, 129
Rold Gold, 81
Romance novels:
    as popular culture, 10
Roseanne, infomercials by, 145
Roseanne show:
    advertising rates for, 196
    as example of advertising/popular
        culture mix, 185-193
    popularity of, 185-186

Scott, George C.:
    Renault and, 129
Seagram's, Bruce Willis and, 129
Self:
    advertising and idealizations of,
        235
    popular culture and idealizations
        of, 235
    See also Self-identity
Self-identity:
    advertising/popular culture mix
        and, 225-226
    advertising's role in, 198
    creation of, 198
    gender in media and, 199-214
    maintenance of, 198
    popular culture's role in, 198-199
    symbol-offering and, 238-240
Semiotics, French, xv
Shepherd, Cybill:

L'Oreal Cosmetics and, 125
    National Live Stock and Meat
        Board and, 125
Simpson, O. J.:
    Hertz Corporation and, 124, 228
    social issues and image of, 228
Simpson trial, O.J.:
    popular obsession with, 228
Situation comedies, 112-116
    Cosby Show episode as example of,
        114-116, 122
    human relationships in, 113, 187
    joke creation in, 112
    joke delivery in, 112
    laugh track in, 112
    restorative jokes in, 113
    Roseanne show, 185-193
    secondhand sociability and, 114
Smith Barney, John Houseman and,
    125
Social change, threat of:
    advertising and, 66
    popular culture and, 66
Somers, Suzanne:
    Ace Hardware and, 129
Sprint, Candice Bergen and, 127, 129,
    162, 189, 193
Stanley tools, 37
Starr, Ringo:
    and Sun Country Classic wine
        coolers, 129
Strait, George:
    Wrangler jeans and, 135
Subliminal advertising messages, 74,
    75
Sun Country Classic, Ringo Starr and,
    129
Sunsweet prunes, Barbara Mandrell
    and, 136
Symbol, definition of, 21
Symbol transfer:
    from popular culture to advertising,
        126
    See also Music, popular; Popular
        culture stars; Situation comedies

Taster's Choice commercial, 90, 174

Television series:
    as popular culture, 10
Thick description, 20
Tiny Tim, Kenwood and, 130
Tucker, Tanya:
    Black Velvet Canadian Whiskey
      and, 136
Tyson, Mike:
    Pepsico and, 124

Uecker, Bob:
    Miller Lite Beer and, 143

Vampire creative, 81
Varney, Jim:
    as commercial character turned
      actor, 143

Viewer, definition of, 23
Virginia Slims, 83
Volvo, 145

Ward, Artemas, 35
Wayne, John:
    Datril and, 129
Welles, Orson:
    as wine endorser, 131
Weyerhaeuser, failed product of, 19
White, Vanna:
    infomercials by, 145
Willis, Bruce:
    Seagram's and, 129
Wrangler jeans, George Strait and, 135

About the Author

Jib Fowles, Ph.D., is Professor of Media Studies at the University of Houston-Clear Lake. His books include *Mass Advertising as Social Forecast, Why Viewers Watch: A Reappraisal of Television's Effects,* and *Starstruck: Celebrity Performers and the American Public.* His articles have appeared in *The Atlantic, New York Times, TV Guide, Advertising Age,* and many scholarly journals. He is chair of the Mass Communication section of the Popular Culture Association. Through an American Academy of Advertising fellowship, he worked in a New York advertising agency on a major beverage account.

278